You can renew it at
norlink.norfolk.gov.uk
or by telephone: 0344 800 8006
Please have your library card & PIN ready

B

ACY

NORFOLK LIBRARY
AND INFORMATION SERVICE

CRO

Please return / renew by date shown,
it at:

TELLING TALES

Growing up on a farm in the north of Scotland could be both rewarding and challenging. Now, bestselling author Jane Yeadon recounts her childhood before her nursing adventures started, in her own unique and entertaining style. *Telling Tales* recounts how Jane learns about her place in the scheme of things, the hard way. Poignant and touching, this nostalgic account of life on the farm recalls a way of life which was so recent but now is all but forgotten.

TELLING TALES

TELLING TALES

by

Jane Yeadon

Magna Large Print Books
Long Preston, North Yorkshire,
BD23 4ND, England.

British Library Cataloguing in Publication Data.

Yeadon, Jane
    Telling tales.

A catalogue record of this book is
available from the British Library

  ISBN   978-0-7505-4182-4

First published in Great Britain in 2015 by
Black & White Publishing Ltd.

Copyright © Jane Yeadon 2015

Cover illustration © mirrorpix

Published in Large Print 2016 by arrangement with
Black & White Publishing Ltd.

Magna Large Print is an imprint of Library Magna Books Ltd.

Printed and bound in Great Britain by
T.J. (International) Ltd., Cornwall, PL28 8RW

To Liz

ACKNOWLEDGEMENTS

Without the good guidance of Black & White Publishing, the bright comments of my niece Ellie Tipple, my family's tolerance, the help and support of Forres's *for* Words writing group and my agricultural advisor, Brian McDonald, this book could not have been written.

The books *Leaning on a Gate* and *Clap Hands for the Singing Molecatcher* by authors Elizabeth Macpherson and Roderick Grant were delightful keys to helping my recall.

Jane Yeadon

CONTENTS

1

STORMY WEATHER

'Janie! Go awa' inside an' pit on yer coat!'

'No!'

'Jane. Go inside and put on your coat. Now!'

'Do what Dod tells you,' says my sister, smug in a tweed coat, so hairy it makes her look like a small but tidy haystack.

Elizabeth has a two-year advantage over me. As she grows older, she'll start taking bits off her name so that, by the time she's grown up, she'll be happy with the finished product, which is Liz.

Right now, Elizabeth seems rather a large handle for a small six-year-old, although personally I find the name useful for breaking into syllables: a handy emotional register.

'Eee-lizz-a-beth!'

It's wonderful how much rage and passion you can get into one word. But I've done it once too often today. Boredom has turned us into bickering monkeys. We might still be inside in the warmth of our home, but my sister, indifferently kicking the door, shutting us into the lobby, where our exasperated mother had incarcerated us, says, 'This is all your fault. When Mum told us to be quiet, you should have listened to her instead of your own voice.'

I get no further than a retaliatory 'Eee-lizz-a-beth' before Mum yanks the door open, shouting, 'Right! That's it! Outside… Now!'

I must have reached a certain note and perhaps she's feeling edgier than usual. Tomorrow is Monday, the day our widowed mother chooses to be herself, writing newspaper articles about everyday life on an upland Morayshire farm. Since family discord isn't her chosen subject, we're not useful material.

Now, bonded in the adversity of having a mother who's about to forget she is one, we hurry to grab our coats.

'At least Mary's here the morn.' I think of the girl who comes to help on what could only be described as a tricky day. Comparing her to our neglectful mother, I add, *'She's* nice.'

Elizabeth sniffs and says, 'Well, I won't see her. I'll be at school.' She does up her coat buttons with careless ease. Her fingers are nimble and neat. Hopeless for shaping mud pies, which I so adore making. 'Come on. Can you not do these yet?'

'Course I can,' I lie, and, anxious not to be left behind, add, 'But I'm not bothering with a coat. It's not cold.'

'Jane! It's the middle of winter and there's snow on the ground!'

'It's all right. Let's just go.'

With my breath showing as small clouds of vapour, I've pushed past her and gone outside, glad of wellies. Even if they might be on the wrong feet, they're fine for taking the path cut through thick January snow leading from the house to the farm steading. I finish the icicle grabbed off the house eave and open my mouth skyward to catch a falling snowflake. It settles on my tongue first, then tastes sweet and cold and even purer than the icicle. I wonder if I'll remember this when the summer sun pricks my skin and covers it in freckles.

In final protest, we'd slammed shut the house door and now, here we are, watching Dod, the farm grieve, shovelling pitchfork-loads of hay through a hole he's cleverly cut in the steading wall to feed the cattle inside.

Their noses are wet and their pink tongues reach out like fingerless hands. They grab the hay and it disappears. I think that feeding hay into the maw of the wall must be keeping Dod warm because he's not wearing a coat either. Maybe I could get a shot of his pitchfork. It looks like fun and I could always menace my sister with it. I move closer, hoping that Dod and the cattle will appreciate kindly interest.

17

'Put on your coat, Jane.' Second time around the words are clear. Dod, stooped over a loaded fork, stops, whilst Elizabeth starts reversing and I catch another snowflake.

I swallow it and because Dod's maybe deaf, shout, 'No!'

Our ancient duck comes out of nowhere. She doesn't look anything like the ones in picture books. This one is fat and wheezy, wears a different colour of white from the snow, and she's loud and demanding. With startling originality, she's called Duck and must be one of the few creatures on our farm without a proper name. Unmoved by any potential drama, she flounders through the snow towards us. Like the cattle, she considers humans useful only as food providers. As she advances, she readies her flat and predatory bill.

'Come on, Duck,' says Elizabeth, unrecognisably hearty. 'I saw some cold tatties in the kitchen that Mum's left out for you. Let's go and get them now.'

And she's off, Duck quacking disapproval at having to struggle to keep up with her leader.

Dod, meantime, has plunged the fork into the ground and comes towards me.

'I said, for the third and last time, put on your coat!'

I might be feeling the cold seeping

through my thin-soled wellies, with an icy wind searching out vulnerable areas with forensic skill, but it's nothing to how fed up I am of people always telling me what to do.

Swamped with the unfairness of my life I repeat, 'No!'

The word is clear. It rings out with the same defiance as I show in stamping my feet.

In the distance from over the moor that is part of our farm comes the chuff-chuff of the train steaming towards Grantown-on-Spey. Nearer, I hear the busy gurgle of the wee Knockack burn that runs at the bottom of one of our farm fields. But much closer is the odd squelching sound of wellingtons coming fast towards me.

They're Dod's and he's close enough now to aim a careless swipe, which, thanks to my kilt pleats, is painlessly absorbed. But I am outraged. I shake a cold fist and, in the absence of meantime-motherly support, yell, 'I'm telling Mary on you!'

And then the man who will be around our lives for a very long time completes the indignity. He laughs and goes back to feeding the cattle.

2

A SMALL CROFT

Our farm, Tombain, lies halfway between Forres and Grantown-on-Spey. In time, pylons will march on metal legs across moors bringing electricity to Dunphail, the parish of which our croft is part. I'll be ten when power comes to our house, and the smell of paraffin and the hiss of our tilley lamps will give way to a noiseless, reliable light. However, Tombain's name stays and, being Gaelic for 'white hill', is a reminder of the past.

I like the name. It lends the hill farm a history, suggesting that it was a long-ago people with a different language who named it and made a living from it. I wonder who they were.

They've left little mark, other than some cultivated fields flanked by a wine-red moor only useful, my mother believes, for heather and sheep. Maybe it's because, seen from the road, the farm, standing high above the Moray Firth, gets snow early, unlike the green fertile land far below: the Laich of Moray. But at least, shawled by fir trees planted after the war and now growing so

20

dense they can only manage a sigh in the wildest of storms, the farm gets added shelter from the lee side of the Knock of Braemoray.

We think it's big but our mother is dismissive. She says, 'It's just a frumpy wee hill.'

I'm sorry that the charm of its gentle shoulder-like contour is lost to her but when the bonny days come and we grow older Elizabeth and I'll climb it. Afterwards we'll boast, 'From the top you can see the whole of Morayshire, its Firth as well as the Cromarty one, and even beyond that to the Sutherland hills.'

In that matter-of-fact way that Elizabeth imparts knowledge and which is as impressive as it's annoying, she'll add, 'You can even see Morvern, Embo and the Sutors of Cromarty. They often look as blue as the sea between us.'

It'll sound as if a spell's been cast over places whose names enchant me and might say so, only our word-alchemist mother is lost to any magic on this particular day. She'll glance up from scouring clothes in the scullery's white heavy-duty double sink and say, 'I can see that every day if I get a minute to look through the window and it's not misty or snowing.'

It couldn't have been like that when she and our father, beguiled by the views, decided to give up a precarious living writing books and flogging vegetables in Badenoch.

Their *Happy Hawkers* book chronicles these days and I try to connect the young, care-free couple illustrated in the pages with the childless pair in their thirties who came to this tenant farm two years before the war.

When Elizabeth was born four years later, she was something of a surprise. And not only to our parents, who'd been married long enough to imagine they'd never become ones, but to their family doctor as well.

A good bedside manner is hardly needed for appendix removal. It's an operation at which he apparently excelled and for which (this being pre-NHS days) his charging fee was small. Still, his approach to a breech birth bordered on something like callous indifference.

'Expect her to be dead,' he'd said, dealing with the unexpected appearance of a baby coming backwards. Then, subject closed, he sucked on his filthy, smelling pipe whilst watching over an experienced midwife who would eventually manage the miracle of a safe delivery.

Two years later, I took the more conventional route.

Smithy was Tombain's resident land girl. Apparently, my father told her, 'The new baby's got navy-blue eyes.'

Before she joined the land army, Smithy had been a Norland Nanny so, thanks to her fancy training, she probably knew it's a common enough colour for a newly born baby. Still, she was tactful enough not to say so. Anyway, she'd worked long enough on the farm to know that my father wasn't big on being corrected.

With her own first name lost to the additional 'y' on her surname, she'd been curious. 'What are you going to call her?'

'Jane. Betty thinks it's a bit plain but I like it.'

As Elizabeth is our mother's name too, I'll grow up thinking that our wordsmith parents have had lapses in originality. Could they not have thought of Margaret? She's a real princess. I'd love that name and bet if she shared my title she wouldn't suffer the usual introductory reaction.

'Jane, eh? That'll be Plain Jane, and No Nonsense then. Ha ha!'

You think you're so original, I think, amazed at how much fun people can get out of so few words.

But all this will come later. When I'm born, there's little to laugh about. My mother may have found birth easier this time, but six weeks later she was widowed.

When Elizabeth and I are older, and despite the armour of stoicism we've come to recognise in our mother, she is still only able to speak, just once, about this time.

'You know, when I was asked to identify your father after the fatal motorbike accident and saw the body' – she paused for a moment in recall – 'I only looked for a second. Then I said, "That's not Ian."'

'But it must have been!' cried Elizabeth, who remembers only a shadow but holds the memory dear.

'No, it wasn't. It was just a shell. This is where he is.' She tapped her head and we wonder if that's what's made her hair the white we've always known and watch as she tightens her mouth, the lines around it deepening. 'And I was left to bring up you bairns and mind the farm. Anyway there was a war on with no time to grieve and lots of people far worse off than me.' She sighed, then brightening, added, 'But I'm glad to say that at least on Tombain we always had food, grew it for others, and we were never called upon to man any engine of death.'

Widowed, she now had a new role as a she-crofter. Italian prisoners of war were already working on the farm. They must have been a help and, despite losing their youth to a war and living in a land surely alien to them, she said they brought her a little of their home's sunshine. They communicated in pidgin Doric to my mother's ungrammatical Italian whilst Elizabeth, of whom they made a great fuss, learnt a little of both.

And of course, for a time, there was Smithy. Not only was she used to the farm's routines but her classy training also made her well able to care for us.

'Smithy used spit on it to fix it,' Elizabeth says to explain her curly hair when we get older. But I'm not convinced. Although she'll always be Smithy to us, she's now a Munro, having married Beel, who farms over the moor from us. No matter how much I try to copy her shining example of Norland Nanny care, my hair remains straight and hostile to the ribbons which sit so biddable and prettily on my sister's head.

'Why do you think your sister got all the curls?' people sometimes ask.

I have no answer but Elizabeth springs to my defence.

'Well, *she* got a dimple.'

Starting to realise that, confident of right on her side, my sister will face any army single-handed, I'm torn between admiration that she feels strong enough to do so and a fear of landing on the army's side by mistake.

3

MUM GOES TO TOWN

The Italians manage fine when it comes to farming but struggle working the farm's metal-wheeled Fordson.

'We'd be lost without Belldie,' says Mum, tapping the machine's flanks in an encouraging way. The prisoners of war probably have another name for something with a temperament more suitable to a diva troubled by asthma. She only revs into action if nursed and, after coughing and spluttering, clatters in discordance, as if protesting at being driven over the cobbles covering the byre's square.

When she does make it to the fields, an eddying cloud of gulls arrive. They try to outscream the bronchial *whee whee whee* of Belldie. But hers is a steadier noise and easily carried on the wind as she hauls a plough, better than her at obedience, as faithfully it follows, turning furrow after furrow.

Belldie's mechanical challenges are, however, nothing compared to the uncertain temperament of Frankie, the farm's Ayrshire bull. With a ring in his nose, he's handsome –

in a flashy sort of way: looks that are lost on the Italians. Unlike our mother, who is on amiable terms with Frankie and surely tuning into his feminine side, they reckon he's plain dangerous.

'Mio dio! *Guardare quelle corna!* (My God! Look at those horns!)' they cry, blocking their ears to shut out the bull's shrill screams of frustrated testosterone. A new level of aggression comes with the sighting of any possible rival and when, in the absence of any, the men see him gore a wooden tripod used for making haystacks, they take note.

'He's nothing to do at the moment but eat,' Mum declares. 'He's just bored.'

But they're not convinced, nor sure that his barbed-wire field's enclosure's as safe as she says it is. Have they not seen men come to visit the farm only to be trapped in their car by an advancing bull? And have they not heard a petrified bawl? 'Hey, wifie! Come an' tak awa' yer bull!' What, the Italians wonder, will they do if Frankie escapes and she's not around?

On a day she's to go into town, and recognising that male pride versus fear of a bull might stop farm work, she calls her team together. 'Look, boys. We need pink petrol. You know Belldie won't go without it, so I *have* to go to Forres to get it, but don't worry about Frankie. I'll shut him in.' Then, making a point about girl power, she adds, 'And Nell

27

will help me.'

'*Ah si si!* The collie,' they say, sounding relieved, and disappear until La Signora Macpherson assures them that she and her fearless dog have safely incarcerated Frankie in the byre.

'So! Eesa in his preeson?' they ask as she climbs into her old battered saloon Hillman car.

'Och yes, but dinna go near him. He doesn't need *your* company.' She is sanguine as she leaves.

This is a pity because when she comes back there's trouble.

'Eets Frankie! He no like our voices,' the bravest Italian tells her, his eyes wide with horror. 'Come!' He beckons, then slinks behind her as they near the byre. Undaunted and guided by the shrieks of fury coming from Frankie's quarters, Mum makes the distance as if she too is pink petrol-fuelled.

Normally the barn, which you've to go through to reach the rest of the farm steading, is a soothing sort of place. But today it's loud with the sound of apprehension. The cries of an enraged bull disturb the easier tenor of rustling straw stored under a high roof, round which the wind so often speaks. The sparrows who fly in through an open skylight window to gossip amongst the rafters fall silent.

When the bolt of one barn door gets

28

slammed back and the caller yanks it open, not one cat comes to greet the noisy visitor. Instead, they all flatten their ears and squat low. They watch from under the stairs leading to the grain loft as Mum strides past to burst through the other door, which gives on to the steading.

But nobody needs to open Frankie's door to see him. He's missed that. Instead, he's made a hole in the wall and now his head fills the gap. Were it not for his massive shoulders holding him back, he'd be out.

Our mother halts for a second, draws up to her five-foot-three height; tightens the strings of her Fair Isle pixie hat; pulls the belt of her tweed coat with the same force; stamps her sensible brogue shoes and starts.

The words snap out. 'Stop that racket right now, ye orra vratch – ye scabbie brute – ye midden runt...'

As she continues, her voice drowns out Frankie's squeals. He shuts up. This makes the Italians think that if Hitler had been at the end of a similar tirade he might have had second thoughts about going in for them himself. And, even better, they wouldn't be here.

Nevertheless they are drawn to the spectacle.

'Like the Colosseum, no?' they wonder.

The byre might be its poor cousin but the spectacle of man, or in this case Mum, against beast, draws them to watch. Not only that but their vocabulary is stretched by a whole lot of new words. Swapping sly grins, it's clear the Italians understand such terms are for selective use.

'So stick that stupid lolling tongue of yours back in, stop rolling your eyes and tidy yourself up,' finishes my mother. 'And go and do something useful, ye cranky limmer. See what you can do with that garland.'

She points to an old horse harness resembling a dusty ornament and hanging from a peg on the wall. Frankie, as sheepish as it is possible for an Ayrshire bull in his prime to look, lowers his head and backs in. Eyeing the harness, he aims his horns and lumbers towards it.

Mum explains to her audience, 'That's for Frankie to see if he can get it down so he can gore it to death. I *thought* it'd be enough to occupy him whilst I was away.'

She picks up a pitchfork that looks as if it's been cast aside by someone in a hurry and adds, 'But he's in such a state you'd think he'd been tormented.'

There's a scuffling of feet and lack of eye contact with the men before she continues, 'Nobody likes imprisonment. Doubtless you'll know the feeling. Go and block up that hole *now*.' Then she stamps off.

For countless reasons, the Italians would be delighted to know the war will soon be over and they'll be free to return to their original lives. They won't miss Frankie or he them, but our mother will miss her depleted workforce.

Still, there's a new person who comes around and he's not fazed by Frankie, hard work or our mother.

4

GETTING OUT

I miss Elizabeth when she goes to school. She's not here to help lug out a big cardboard box from our clothes cupboard. Apart from our dolls, and my best friend Rabbit, it holds all our toys. Once the box is trailed through to the kitchen, it's always tipped out, which is probably why it's getting so bashed-looking.

Mum would have got it from Mattie. As well as running the local shop, she's Dunphail's postmistress. If she gives us another, with a bit of luck it won't have 'Government Property Toilet Rolls' written on the outside.

Mum often says, 'I wish you'd play in your bedroom,' but once you put two beds and a huge chest of drawers into a limited amount of space there's little room left, Anyway, I

31

don't want to play on my own: not this morning. There're witches riding on the larch trees outside the window. The branches are writhing and swaying as if they want shot of their unwelcome passengers.

'You must see them. There's loads. Look at all those bony knees and evil faces. I bet they're just waiting for a chance to fly in here,' I say to Elizabeth, but she is far more interested in searching under the bed for her garters.

Eventually surfacing, and without even bothering to look, she says, 'Larch looks like that with its old cones on bare branches. Honestly, Jane! You and your imagination.' With a shout of triumph, she brandishes two black elastic circles. 'Look! Found them!' Pinging them over her home-knitted thick grey stockings, she starts to tie her liberty bodice. Now, where's my knickers? I bet you've pinched them.'

Somewhat reluctantly, and pulling them out from under my bed, I throw them. 'Here.'

Catching them, she says, 'You're so annoying. You're always taking my stuff.' She points to a letter embroidered on the pocket. Against the knicker's navy blue, it's a definite pink.

'That says "E".' She taps her chest. 'For me! I sewed it on after Granny showed me how to do chain-stitch and, Jane, take your thumb out of your mouth! That poor Rabbit's going to be bald with you twiddling his fur all the time.'

I ignore her, putting one arm round my doll, Belinda, and clutching Rabbit with the other. Such a fuss about an occasional borrow! She should be far more concerned about the witches, but all she does now is pull on the knickers, the rest of her clothes and look round the bedroom. She wipes her nose on her grey jersey sleeve, picks her doll off the floor and plunks her on top of the chest of drawers. 'There, Bluebell. You sit bonny.'

'I'm telling Mum on you,' she says, by way of a parting shot.

Belinda hasn't a chipped head, unlike Bluebell, who got it after her caring owner clunked her over the doorknob of the bathroom when she'd locked herself in by mistake.

I think about this, getting up, then, putting the dolls together, say, 'There, Belinda. You can sit bonny, too. Have a wee chat and tell her my sister really does love her. She's just got a funny way of showing it.'

Belinda's never very good in the morning. Apart from Bluebell and Rabbit, I'm the only person that she speaks to, and often that's not until after breakfast, so I pat her perfect head and explain that I'm taking Rabbit with me. 'You know he's usually under my pillow through the day? Well, I'm taking him with me. I've a feeling he'll like some company this morning. I'll see you later.' It only seems fair to add, 'And, not to worry you, but mind out for the witches.'

With much huffing and puffing I get the box through to the kitchen, pleased to be near Mum, busy in the scullery.

'What're you doing?' I ask, even if it's perfectly obvious that she's making the daily hens' mash. It's a mess of stuff left over from food scraps and old vegetables. Combined with oatmeal, the cooking mixture might smell quite tasty was it not mixed with the nauseating fumes from the Rural gas stove.

There's no reply, so I put my shoulder to the box and heave, overbalance and fall alongside the newly tipped-out toys. Surely the rattle of things crashing out onto our linoleum floor will get some attention.

Only the smell floats through.

Maybe Rabbit's not so smart-looking as he once was, but if it wasn't for his comforting presence I might be feeling abandoned amongst a collection of jigsaw pieces, crayons, yo-yos and just the body-bit of Dobbin my horse. The other night I dreamt that someone found his head and fitted it back on. They'd even oiled the wheels under his straight white legs. He could've run smoothly, only he'd hitched a lift in a doll's pram.

Elizabeth and I would love one of them. We often imagine wheeling the dolls round the farm. We'd point out things of scenic interest and in the absence of passers-by introduce Bluebell and Belinda to the barn cats. They'd be bound to look on with glimmering eyes: their sign of approval. Then, if cats could talk, and once we'd passed but were still within earshot, they'd murmur amongst themselves, 'Oh! There go the nice little Tombain ladies with their dear little babies. Such a pity about the one with the scar on her face. Wonder how she got it!'

'What's Dod doing, Mum?' I call, aware that pram or no pram, he'll only connect with a pair of hands. I'm not keen on getting mine either wet or dirty and it's begun to rain.

'Snedding neeps.'

She must have heard a sigh because she adds, 'Now, Janie, if he doesn't cut off the tops and put them through the hasher, the calves'll get pains in their pinnies. You wouldn't want that now, would you?'

'No,' I clutch my stomach in sympathy, thinking of their mothers. They wouldn't like it either: Charlotte especially. She was a bit tricky until she was de-horned. Now, if you keep clear of her hind legs and tarry rope tail, she's easy to tie up in her stall to be milked.

It's my favourite job. She's got a coat of

hair as red as mine. It covers her neck in such velvet-like folds that I stroke them. Sometimes, when I think nobody's listening, I whisper in her wooshy ear, 'I know Dod said you'd to be watched when you're being milked, but I think you're a nice wee coo.'

My mind drifts to Old Maudie whose horns aren't apparently a problem but as soon as anyone speaks to her she breathes out like a dragon. Then she sweeps up her head and, just as you think she's going to attack, she tugs out straw from the wooden haiks above her. The securing chain gives quite a rattle but that's not a worry. I still feel useful. Maybe sometime that Elizabeth's not around helping with the milking I'll get a go.

I'm looking forward to that. Neeps, however, are different and, to be honest, Dod's tapner is petrifying. It's like a small, curved sword, used for slicing off turnip-tops. Even if it's biddable in Dod's hands, it's easy to imagine it slipping. Already I see it, arrow flying through the air, sharp, hungry for blood. If it makes contact, Bluebell's scars will be nothing by comparison.

Then there's the neep-hasher! It's like a monster on four metal legs with a ball weight resembling a head at one end of a moveable metal bar. At the other is a handle, whilst a masher-like weight sits in between.

The first time I saw Dod snedding neeps he was whirling the tapner to fill the wire

36

basket he calls a scull. It was a worrying name because it held scalped neeps, identical to our dolls' bald heads.

After Dod finished with the tapner and moved the full basket beside the hasher, I felt it safe enough to ask, 'Can I help?'

'Aye. Jist gie me a minute.' He pulled on the handle, making the weighted end swing up. 'Right, Janie. Ye can throw in your neep noo.'

I hadn't calculated on their weight. Dod made it all look so easy but between needing both hands for carrying, then having to stand on my toes to reach up to the top of the machine, it took a while to tip in my neep. No sooner had it fallen into the sharp-bladed, V-shaped basket below than Dod leant on the handle. Helped by his and the ball's weight, the masher came crashing down.

'That could hiv been ma heid,' I cried, horrified by the squelching sound of a neep being sliced.

Dod has a unique form of encouragement: 'Ach, Janie. Dinna be daft! Just you keep going. Ye'll make a fine shot putter yet.'

'I think I'm too little to help.'

'I'll tell your mam you said that the next time I hear you telling her it's too early for a big girl like you to go to bed.' He pointed to the scull, 'But even a wee quinie can lift neeps.'

Thinking back to this, I think it's probably best to stay inside but, as I check and only see familiar play things, boredom comes calling. It's enough to make you weep, especially when Mum, stirring-spirtle in hand, comes and, taking in the floor covering, of which I'm part, says, 'You'll put these all back. Right now!'

It takes effort to squeeze out a tear and a bleat like the cry of Shadow, our pet lamb. If it was her, she'd get immediate sympathy, but all I get is a sniff and, 'That's a gey dry greet,' before my mother goes back to hen-wife chores.

I could shout that a softie would be crying much more and she'll be sorry when her brave daughter's dead but the last time that was tried she and Elizabeth laughed like grown-ups sharing a superior moment.

I sigh and, righting the box, hoping it'll hold, climb aboard.

5

GRANNY RULES

'Never mind, you've got me,' whispers Rabbit. He's clever and, despite Elizabeth's disapproval, never complains that his vest's getting so worn. He's as reliable as my thumb and though he can sometimes get as chewed-looking as his ears, he doesn't mind. He's so cute at reading minds, I seldom need to say anything as, snuggled together at the bottom of the box, eyes shut, with nothing better to do than feel sorry for ourselves, we remember our last holiday with Granny. She lives in Nairn, half an hour's journey away if our wonky old car can make it.

'*Everybody* needs a break,' Mum says, which is odd because she doesn't go anywhere herself. I miss her and the farm, so it's a comfort having Rabbit, but Granny gets annoyed when she sees us together.

'Sucking your thumb will give you sticking-out teeth. Why can't you be like your sister? Look at her! She's happy enough without having her nose stuck in a smelly old rag all the time.'

She exaggerates. I know Granny really,

really loves my sister and cared for her a lot after our dad was killed, but, fair's fair. I bet Rabbit's heard her and there's the poor animal's feelings to consider. It seems only fair to reply, 'Yes, but Mum says Elizabeth bites her nails and if she's not careful she'll get worms.'

Granny's selective hearing kicks in. She doesn't say anything just hums in a tuneless way and goes off to clatter dishes in her huge kitchen.

That's one good thing about being here. The house might be called Fern Cottage but it's excitingly big, with five massive bedrooms upstairs. On the landing wall, there's a picture of a donkey's head on a dark-blue background. I spend ages looking at it, wondering why it looks so sad. Maybe it's homesick, too.

Unlike Tombain, Fern Cottage has stairs. Jumping off them and sliding down the bannister is great fun and even better than bouncing on Granny's bed – it's in the room above the sitting-room and she only objects when plaster starts to fall off its ceiling.

'Oh, for goodness' sake,' sighs Elizabeth. 'Jane – you're *so* annoying. Go and put Rabbit away. It upsets Granny. It makes her think you don't like coming here.'

'I do really,' I say, thinking about someone who takes us to the circus and Nairn's outside paddling pool. She also writes books and tells gripping tales in which Elizabeth and I are always funny, clever heroines. 'But I hate her Sundays.'

It's a day very like Mum's Mondays. It stretches long and dreary, with a starting point of Granny reading out what she considers inspirational bits from her Bible. We have a very long grace before breakfast, after which we go to church.

'I can't stand the organist,' Granny says, obviously in full Christian spirit and so loudly that he must hear her. That's bad enough but then, as if in competition with the music, she belts out the hymns – flat. It's mortifying.

After the minister harangues the congregation about its sinfulness, he follows with a welcome to visitors to the town. Then he leans over the pulpit and says, 'And now its time for the collection.'

'Aye,' observes Granny as we come out of church, 'his timing never changes.'

Relieved of our sixpences, Elizabeth and I trail after her, both looking forward to the evening, when we'll be on our knees thanking God for a good day. Silently, we'll be praying for a better one tomorrow.

'Mind you...' I scratch Rabbit's ears, 'Not every Sunday's boring. Remember the last one?'

He shudders in my hand.

Granny's got a walnut cabinet so big it's practically up to the sitting-room ceiling.

Half of it's got glass-fronted cupboards that are full of books with small writing and no pictures. Between them and more storage places below are two blue felt-lined drawers holding little of interest other than a pack of cards and a pair of specs, minus an arm. I tried them on, wondering why Granny had kept them.

'Fancy a wee game of Snap, Elizabeth?'

She's just learnt to read, and likes it so much her nose is never out of a book. She did manage to look up for a second but only to say, 'Tch! You look daft. Anyway, I'm reading. Go and play that game of Clock Patience Granny's friends showed us yesterday.'

'You *never* want to play with me,' I complained but she just turned a page, so I sat on the floor close by her. Patience isn't really my thing: it's more fun making a card house. I'd just managed to build up to a second floor when Granny came into the room.

For a second she froze. Then she began, her voice scandalised and sharp, 'Cards? Don't tell me you're playing *cards on the Sabbath?*'

She raced towards the little house, then with the skill of a professional football player kicked it. The cards slipped from under her flying feet, with the Queen of Hearts landing on the floor. She looked startled, as if surprised by an attack.

Granny ground out, 'That's a sin. A real

42

sin. I don't know what your grandfather would have thought – and him a minister. I hate to say this, Jane, but it's a blessing he's dead.'

It was obvious that talking about him had upset her as well. Wanting to make things better, I shook off the specs and held them in front of her. 'Look, Granny!' I smiled, hoping that she'd share in the joke that she'd held onto specs that were broken.

I could have added she must be glad she was wearing a whole pair but she'd crashed a hand over my ear (an OK pastime for a Sunday apparently) and hissed in the other one, 'Ye wee limmer!'

All I could do was listen to what ear-ringing sounds like. Elizabeth, however, threw away her book, erupted from her chair and, as she ran to the door, shouted, 'I'm going to phone and tell Mum to take us home!'

Granny chased after her into the hallway, crying, 'Now, let's not be hasty. I just thought for a minute they were my good specs and she'd broken them. You know I'd be blind without them.' Her voice floated back. 'Anyway your sister's always been tricky: she's just like your father!'

After she stopped Elizabeth from dialling 999, and the dust had more or less settled, she grabbed Rabbit by his ears.

'This thing stinks. It's positively un-hygienic,' she declared and, before I could stop her, she'd popped him into a pan. It was so full of hot soapy water I'm sure she'd have heard him scream if his head hadn't been held under the suds.

Remembering the lowest point of that holiday, I bury my nose in his soft ears and inhale. It took ages to get that poor Persil-smelling Rabbit back to normality. I can't really understand her thinking that she was doing us both a favour. Still, it's maybe time to forgive her.

'She can be scary, Rabbit,' I now whisper, 'but she's brave as well. I don't know how she managed to look so cheerful saying cheerio at the end of our holiday. After we'd gone, she'd have to go back to living all on her own in that big empty house.'

In case he's not feeling so charitable, I say, 'At least we have each other. Woops!' We spill out of the box and I show him how to make a game of filling it. 'It's a game of Aim. You throw the toys in from a distance – the further you're away, the better the sound. For a start, I'll hold onto you so you can watch.'

Eventually, it all becomes so noisy that Rabbit, getting hot in my grasp and a bit sweaty, admits to having a sore head and suggests that he goes back to bed whilst Mum appears, waving a dish cloth.

'Hoy! Instead of making that racket, come and give me a lift out to the henhouse with the mash pot. Mind the handle, though. It's just off the stove and it's hot.'

A larch fence separates the house from the farm, as well as enclosing a space that Mum says she wants to make into a garden. There's only grass there at the moment, so it's not clear why she gets in such a rage when the rascally stirks break in. It's a shame she doesn't read their hoof marks embedded in the ground as luck signs. 'Hoodlums,' she calls them. I tried the word out on Rabbit. He liked it.

I'd supposed Mum could use Tombain's old kitchen garden, even if three gean trees have established a strong foothold in the collapsing stones of the lichened dry-stane dyke surrounding it. It's a few yards away from ours and close to the original house, where Dod and his parents now stay. His dad minds what's left of the garden, so maybe that's why Mum wants to leave it to his care.

Dod calls him the Old Boy but everybody else seems to call him Lala.

'Why's he called that?' Elizabeth and I asked on a day that Mum had time to answer questions.

'Some wee bairn found it easier to say than his real name, William. I think folk may have thought it cute and the name stuck.'

Cute or not, Elizabeth and I are both a bit wary of Lala. If he's in the garden, rather than approaching we'll climb the gean trees and spy on him kneeling at work.

He looks a bit like Granny when she's praying but she hasn't his permanent shake. Nor does she use a walking stick either for balance or poking unwary children. She only uses hers to keep on her hat when the wind blows. And she certainly speaks. Blackbirds caught under the strawberry net in her garden get a right row and, thanks to her sin-searching soul, a clout to help them get the message. I couldn't imagine Lala doing that. He's too busy shaking.

Bent over the tattie pit, he slowly inspects, then pulls and tugs at dockens, which have grown abundantly beside it but now tremble in his grasp.

'I dinna ken fit the Old Boy thinks he's daen, he's only makin' them worse,' says Dod in exasperation. 'He's nay even managing tae get oot the roots.'

This may be true. The docken patch that Lala's working on looks so healthy you'd think it's an actual crop. Mum's idea of her own garden begins to makes sense. She's bound to appreciate the offer of some help.

The other day Dod was creosoting the barn doors. Attracted by its clean smell, I watched him making black swirling patterns with a big paintbrush. When the Knockack burn at the bottom of our fields is in spate, the water pools churn like boiling sugar on its way to becoming toffee. Dod's artwork looked the same. Drawing with a pencil over our sour cream-coloured bedroom wall has its attractions but we're running out of space and this looked far more exciting.

Standing back to admire his handiwork, Dod said, 'Grand! As the monkey said when he painted the piano green.'

'Dod, maybe I could paint our fence that colour too?'

'Aye – fine that, but you'll need to scrape off the lichen and moss first,' he said, which finished any idea of fun, and the conversation.

Now, as Mum and I get to the as-yet-untouched fence, Duck, Shadow and some hens are waiting on the other side. As soon as they see us, they race to the separating gate in a state of greedy excitement.

'They sound like Old Macdonald's Farm,' I say.

Mum laughs and opens the gate. 'But not so musical. Shoo, you lot. You're not getting this here.' She kicks out in a casual way and clears the path from questing beaks.

The hens cluck in an irritated way. They look clumsy with their wings outstretched, as if they're trying to fly from Mum's gumboot, but Duck doesn't bother. She stands apart with her head held high: obviously too grand to be seen with riff-raff.

Mindful of keeping out her hoodlum stirks,

Mum shuts the gate then, pausing for a moment, says in the same kind voice she uses when we're sick, 'You know, Janie, when there's a full moon I'm sure that Duck forgets she's fat and wheezy and dreams of flight.'

'But she aye wakes us up.'

'She doesn't mean to. It's only because she's warning the moon to watch out in case she lands on it.' Mum takes a tattie from her pocket and, handing it to Duck, says, 'Look, it's nice and warm. Just how you like it. Actually, Duck, I'm thinking that if you were a proper mother and didn't leave your eggs to rot in hidden places, you'd be a lot better off.' She wags a finger. 'Think of it, girl, you could settle down and lead a respectable life.'

It's always a one-way conversation with Duck. She fixes a spot in the distance with a cold unblinking stare as she takes the tattie, then swills it down with a drink from an old basin full of water. Her beak makes a clattering racket against the enamel.

'And a wee something for you too, Shadow.' Mum drops a spoonful of mash on the ground. Shadow, forgetting her urge to follow, skids to a halt whilst the hens run after us and into their henhouse, where it's warm and dry.

Even if it's sturdily made, the homebuilt place creaks on stormy days. Mum, who grew up in seaside Hopeman, says it reminds her of a boat listing in the wind but I think of the witches catching a ride on the larches this morning. If I didn't think she'd laugh, I'd tell her that, whatever the weather, the hens are safer to forgo those very branches where they sometimes fly and roost in their henhouse instead.

The old car windscreen makes part of a wall and lets in enough light for us to see to fill the trough. The mash smells almost better than our own breakfast porridge and I haven't had any yet. I'm starving.

Dod's mother, Mrs Bremner, makes something called brose that look likes this – it's got oatmeal in it too. I sneak a look around. Nobody's looking. I poke a finger into the mixture to taste it.

Yum.

6

A HOUSING MATTER

Despite the dished-up mash, the stay-at-home birds remain at post in their nesting boxes. As they look down from their straw-lined thrones, their stares give a very 'clear off' message.

Reading their sign, Mum says, 'Oh, it's

OK, my hennies, we're not going to steal your eggs.' Then she whispers, 'Come on, Janie. We'll do it from outside. It'll be easier. Then all we'll need to do is lift up the nest box lid.'

Duck's gone but Shadow's finished her mash and, hopeful for more, follows as we go to the jutting-out nesting boxes. Their tarred-felt lid is easy to lift and we're able to look down on the hens. They must think we've gone because they've broken into a contented croon.

Mum whispers, 'Your hands are fine and wee, Janie. Slip one in and see if there's any eggs.'

What happened to the 'we' bit I wonder. I've never done this before and am anxious enough without hearing Shadow chewing in that nervous way she has in the absence of food.

'I'm feart I might get pecked,' I try.

'Don't be frightened. They won't notice you. They'll maybe even think your hand's an egg. Anyway, Janie, these hens are Wyan-dotte's and they're lovely and easy-going birds. On you go, now.' Mum's very confi-dent. Then of course, it's not her hand, is it?

I sigh, shut my eyes, slip a hand down the side of a box, then, finding a hen, grope under her. It's a strange feeling: warm, feather-prickly, damp – and belongs to a suddenly still hen. Quickly, my hand moves about and finds something that feels like a stone. Cautiously, I draw it out. It's egg-like but heavier.

'Ach! That's a china one. You'll need to put it back.' Mum explains that it's there to fool the hen into thinking she's already halfway to making a clutch of eggs.

I think it's a bit unfair to the hen but do what I'm told and move on to the next one. This time it must be a real egg because it feels light, slightly damp and as warm as the hen's under-carriage. I draw it out carefully, hoping the hen doesn't notice and that she's laid it so recently she hasn't recovered from the shock. She continues looking ahead whilst I glance down at the egg in my out-stretched hand. It's warm, brown and with a feather stuck to its slightly sticky surface. Perhaps that's her signature, I think, and, more boldly, continue foraging.

Mum, teaching me how to count, says, 'Eleven! You know, I don't think there's any-thing bonnier than a newly laid egg.' She points to the pan, now full of them. 'Look at their shiny bloom. *That* shows you how fresh they are.'

Once we're back in the house, we put the eggs in the larder. It's a room at the far end of our back door porch and handy for the scullery. 'After you've had your breakfast, see if you can find where Duck's been laying her eggs.' Mum shakes her head in exasper-

51

ation. 'I don't for a minute suppose that if you do find any they'll be nearly as fresh as the hens' ones, but I'm sure she's been laying somewhere near. But don't you be going near the stranghole. Remember what happened to Elizabeth?'

How could anybody forget? Mum used to call it the cesspit until Dod called it a stranghole. 'Strranghole?' she says, imitating him and making him laugh. 'Now, that's a better name for somewhere not particularly attractive.'

Unless the wind's in the wrong direction, it's far enough away from the house for its rotten-egg smells to be lost. Apparently it's where the house sewage ends up and I bet I know where Duck's gone.

It's probably as fascinating for her as it was for Elizabeth and me. Last summer, we were drawn by the attraction of its black boggy depths, edged by grass an impossibly bright shade of green. For some reason, there was a wooden board across it.

Nodding at it and looking thoughtful, Elizabeth said, 'The teacher's been reading us a book on pirates. I loved it. It was so exciting, especially the bit about how they made their enemies walk the plank.' She gazed faraway, plainly enjoying the memory, then took my arm. Her nudge bordered on a shove. 'On you go, thou beastly varlet!'

I wasn't sure what a varlet was but, knowing the meaning of enemy, broke free.

'No! You go first.'

'Ha! Softie!' she scoffed. 'Look! It's easy-peasy.'

Confidently she strode onto the plank, and just as confidently, it tilted her straight into the marshy depths.

'Help!' Her scream interrupted the clear silver voice of a lark pouring out its song high up in a bright sky and the sound of the wind sighing in the nearby larch trees.

It was a terrifying sight. Instead of my nice, clean, bossy big sister balancing on a board, something horrible lay sprawled over the muddy stinking bog. She'd transformed into a smelly black monster. When it got on its knees, crawling and spewing out joined-up swear words, fear rooted me to the spot.

'Dinna just stand there. Give me a hand and help me out,' the black something shouted.

A juniper bush grows near the stranghole. When we first came to it, I'd been picking berries from it, pleased by their clean, cool pine smell. The bush is often planted near homes and is said to ward off evil.

Plainly untrue, I thought, throwing away the berries and readying for flight; only the monster's voice was familiar. After a little consideration, taking care not to fall in beside it, and with my heart chased from my mouth, I stuttered, 'Ssay please ffirst.'

Even if the reply was anything but polite, I relented and helped fish out what was, after all, Elizabeth.

Trying to comfort my wet, filthy and miserable sister, made a pleasant change. I said, 'You'll be fine but we'll need to get you back to the house and Mum. Come on.'

Hearing squelching noises combined with sniffing, our mother looked up from the book she was reading whilst turning the handle of the butter churn in the scullery. It's a really boring job, and one I suspect could soon be mine.

'For the love of Mike, you poor darling!'

At the sight of a book being thrown down, the churn stopping and the anguish in our mother's voice, all bravery went. Elizabeth burst into tears: a rare event.

'Och, ma wee lamb!' cried Mum, grabbing a cake of the red soap used for dirt-ingrained clothes and steering her now bawling daughter towards the bathroom. 'Come on, lovie, you'll need to have a bath. Dettol in it as well.'

'I just hope there's plenty hot water.'

Her voice, losing its thread of despair, now extended. 'And if you've nothing better to do, Janie, you could take over the churn.'

It may have been during last year's summer, but the stranghole memory remains fresh as I set off on another egg search.

'Shadow, if that dratted Duck's gone guddling for worms there, she's welcome to them, but you never know, she maybe decided, for once, to use her own place and laid her eggs there. Let's go and have a look.'

Our cute and cuddly lamb's disappeared. She was given as a present last year when her mother died and her owner hadn't time to look after an orphan. Elizabeth and I loved bottle-feeding and caring for her, but now she's grown and so's her appetite. She doesn't look for a bottle any more. She's happier hanging about the neep shed, waiting for a chance to burst in and gobble turnips as if she's been starved for a fortnight. She also hankers after the calf nuts and treacle kept in the barn.

Meanwhile, as she can't get either, she's nothing better to do than follow me. Responding to my question, she stops chewing and squints down her nose. It makes her look snooty. Mum says it's because Shadow's tribe of Cheviot sheep all have long noses.

'Like the Romans,' she says. Wondering who they are, I stop for a moment.

'Well, Shadow, we might not know who your grandparents are but, I can tell you, your straight white legs are just like Dobbin's wooden ones and they're so thin it's a wonder they're able to carry that muckle body of yours. Mind you, it's just as well you've such a thick coat. Remember the bees?'

Shadow flicks an ear. She must be listening.

Last year, one of Mum's friends living in the Laich of Moray asked if she'd keep his bees so they could make heather-honey. They came in autumn, their hives, cute-looking little houses, were parked beside Duck's quarters. Nosy Shadow was curious about the new tenants, so she was lucky that when she upturned a hive, her fleece was thick enough to make her immune to the bees' rage. The only beehive left now is the one she destroyed, but there's a sharp edge left, handy for her to sort the itch her troublesome fleece gives her.

'No wonder Duck doesn't want tae stay here any mair,' I scold her. 'All that bees bizzin' about the place and she didn't have your coat to protect her from them either.'

Duck's house may once have been an old two-door sideboard, but as she doesn't seem to be using it much, if at all, it's been a good place to play stables with Belinda and Dobbin. There's room because the shelves have been taken out. Branches from the sheltering nearby firs have made a resin-smelling bed. Wire mesh has replaced the wood of one of the doors to allow in light and air. Once we're inside, and the other door's closed, we can see out and settle down to watch the world go by, as horses do, according to my picture books.

Duck doesn't seem to mind.

'I can never get a hold of her, especially at night when sensible people are thinking of going to bed,' says Mum.

'And that's when she keeps us awake,' I remind her.

'Well, I know some wee quinies who've also got a job going to bed,' comes the un-satisfactory answer.

Sometimes, my playmates and I change from playing stables to making nests, think-ing that Duck might like that, although we're not sure we'd want to be too near that beak of hers. Now, if it wasn't for the gentle shush-ing of the fir trees, and Shadow munching the grass, this would be a silent place. It's certainly quieter than when she decided to investigate the bees. I crawl in and, leaving the door open, stretch out on the cushioning branches, trying to imagine where Duck may have laid her eggs.

'Gettaway, Shadow. You smell!' I shout, as she sticks her woolly head in.

She reverses, looking offended. I shut the door and try to settle down again but now feel bad about shouting at the poor beast and start to wonder where she's gone.

It's not long before it's obvious. She hasn't gone anywhere and neither has her itch. Realising that the wrecked beehive's not as handy as the duck-house sides, she puts her shoulder to one and starts to shove. As it rocks under the weight of her labours, I'm trapped and tumbled about.

Now hearing Duck's mocking laugh coming from a safe distance, it's obvious why it's not only the bees that keep her away from here.

7

A TRAINING SESSION

Spring should be well on its way but winter's returned, sending a wind with icicles in its breath to bother the barn's roof slates. They rattle in protest but, heedless, it blasts beneath one door, making a chilly tunnel through to the opposite one leading to the steading. It's the same route Mum took on her way to sorting out Frankie but I'm staying here. I'm keeping away from the draught on the stairs leading up to the grain loft.

It's full of calf-feed sacks. As I sit dreaming of the future, a whiff of linseed escapes through the bags' hessian. It wafts past with the same odd pungency of the sawdust at the circus where Granny once took us.

Looking round, everything suddenly becomes so crystal clear that it merits jumping up and dusting my hands on my kilt. It's a piece of luck that we've got this barn. Why didn't I think of it before? It's got loads of space: ideal for practising. What could be more exciting than life in a circus?

When I grow up, I'll join one.

As a starting point: something simple. Remembering the ease of the trapeze artists flying through the air, I check the rafters. They'll be perfect for swinging on, and if I jump high enough, easy to reach from the top of the stairs. The barn's stone floor might have its drawbacks and even from this vantage point does seem far down below. Still, it's mostly covered in a high pile of loose straw. It's not quite a safety net but it'll do.

Occasionally on a dark night at home shooting stars rain silver showers on our dimmed moor with the same magical ease that the circus artists gave to their act. As they flew, twirled and pirouetted from one trapeze bat to another, the sequins on their scanty satin costumes sparkled in glittering arcs under the spotlight. Who could imagine so many of these bright discs could be fitted onto so little a space? One day I'll get to wear one of those costumes, then, starburst-like, will fly through the air to the rapturous applause of a huge audience.

It's an inspiring dream. Of course everybody has to start in a simple way but the experience of being brought up on a farm with a wild bull should guarantee quick promotion in the circus world. Look at Frankie! Have I not managed to survive living alongside this awesome animal?

As if mind-reading, he lets out a high-pitched shriek. It cuts through the barn's thick walls with as vicious a sound as that of logs being sliced on our circular saw. The combination of the roar of the tractor that drives the belt and wood being cut makes such an endless racket that I should be grateful that Frankie's cry is brief.

Still, I shout, 'Awa' an' bile yer heid, Frankie. I ken you're mad cos you're shut in, but it's for your own good. Instead of making that horrible racket you should be glad you're inside. It's miserable outside. Just listen to that wind!'

I've never been close enough to stare back into our bull's red-hot eyes but they appear too often in my nightmares. Today, however, he's not grazing in some field you might have thought was empty and so get a fright to see him there. We're safe enough because Dod's properly fixed the hole in the wall that Frankie made.

Still I remember the warning. 'Dinna go near that beast. Nay animal likes to be shut in, especially Frankie. He's right enough outside but, to tell you the truth, when he's penned in and I'm feeding him I feel the better o' having a pitchfork wi' me ... just in case. Of course, your mother,' his voice softens as he continues, '*she* says that all he needs to keep him in order's a good row, but that's your mother.' He shakes his head in admiration. 'Aye, she's a bit of a control merchant, right enough.'

A pitchfork together with Mum's method of managing Frankie seems a good combination. It would probably work on caged circus animals too. I remember the penned-in lions. They sounded like lots of trapped bulls on a bad-weather day but I also recall them slinking into the ring, looking more sad than angry.

And it did seem a bit daft getting them to sit on seats far too small for them. The trainer's free use of a whip to help them get the idea meant they did as they were told but it looked cruel to me. It was probably just as well that Granny had nodded off at this point in the show and that Mum wasn't there. What's the betting she'd have been shouting advice at the trainer? I nearly did it myself but, just as I opened my mouth, Elizabeth shut me up with one of her dark looks and an elbow jab.

The black stallion was far happier. For his performance, he held his plumed head high as he galloped round and round the ring, his coat gleaming, tail streaming and mane flowing. It was easy to see that he was proud carrying his bareback rider. She didn't need a whip. Instead, before standing up to wave to us, she whispered to him, gentling his neck. The sound of his hooves thumping on the sawdust added so much excitement that we all got to our feet to cheer at the end of the performance. Perhaps the horse enjoyed it too. He bowed his head right down to the ground, as his rider acknowledged the applause.

'And *I've* got a horse too! I've got you,' I call to Dobbin, patiently waiting at the bottom of the stairs. His head's back on. It surfaced in Duck's house under the fir branches. I had forgotten it was left there. Dobbin looked so much better when returned to his other half. He was also long-suffering when I tried to fix it on for good.

'I'm afraid bits of wood's not the answer,' I'd to tell him, 'but I'm sure if I get some Copydex glue that'll do the trick. Let's have another go tomorrow. Mum says it sorts everything out. Only I need to get it from her first. She says it needs to be rationed out. The last time I had it, it went everywhere.'

I hadn't reckoned on Dod's joinery skills.

'When you were in bed last night, I nailed your horse's head back on.' He sounded so pleased it didn't seem right to say that it would have been nice to have helped. Dobbin's my horse so it would have proved to him that he's got a caring owner. I'd have had a shot of the good stuff in Dod's toolbox as well.

The vet medicine cupboard hasn't the same attraction. From where I sit on the stairs, it's easy to look down on what was an old wardrobe. Dod didn't manage to fix the door, which is always open, but he did fit the shelves that hold Cow Drench, boxes of M&B tablets and huge tins of ointment for soothing cows' cracked teats. There's also black rubber ones and they're for putting on feeding bottles for orphan lambs. I wonder if Shadow remembers that. She certainly knows how to drink out of a pail. If you're carrying one, she'll butt you to get at it.

And she's persistent. The battering sound coming from the other side of the barn door announces that she's trying to force her way in.

'Stay outside,' I shout. 'You only followed me so you could sneak inside to steal the cattle feed.' As her pathetic bleats continue, I harden my heart. 'Look! I'm only here to practise for the circus an' I know you wouldn't want to be part of it. Whoever heard of a performing sheep?'

There's other more suitable cast members. Nell the collie, meanwhile, out helping Dod with some cattle work, might do but it's doubtful. As soon as she saw a collection of anything, she'd herd it into a corner. She's not beyond giving the odd ankle nip either and I suspect she wouldn't worry about sinking her teeth into somewhere even sorer. You should see her biting the Fergie tractor's wheels.

All in all, beginning to be aware there's limited choice, I say, 'Right, Dobbin. It's going to be you and me, and now that your wheels and head are together I'll come down and get on your back and we'll round up the barn cats. They'll be great and they're bonny as well.' I raise my voice for Shadow's benefit. 'They're clever and not half as greedy as some animals I could mention.'

Cats might not be quite the same as lions, but you have to start somewhere and there's quite a few of them around now. A horrible insect used to scuttle about the barn walls. They were tempting for those natural hunters to catch and eat. Unfortunately, they were also deadly poisonous. Mum was at her wits' end trying to keep cats but never succeeded until she got Pansy, our tortoiseshell tabby.

She was the runt in a litter of healthy kittens but the only one to survive. Since then she's boosted the numbers of insect-immune cats to a very healthy count. Actually, now that I look properly at her, rather too healthy. She could have more kittens and any minute now.

She comes to watch and starts to groom her ears as I fiddle with a stick and a length of Glesga Jock. It's a funny name for thick twine, which looks more like a lion's tail of the same colour. Normally, it's used for tying onto weights to keep corn stacks in place, so I suppose that's why it needs to be so strong. It feels harsh in my hands and difficult to knot but at last I manage to make something that looks like a whip.

For a moment, Pansy stops to consult her cleaning-paw and looks thoughtful as I say, 'Hey, Pansy! It looks as if you need to be excused from today's training but you'd better not let Dod see you.' I stroke her head. 'You know he disna want any more kittlins.'

What I don't tell her is that she'd probably be a useless performer: she's too independent to be trainable. As well as that, she's got a wonky leg from trying to pull herself out of a snare. If Dod hadn't rescued her and carried her home, she'd have had to settle for a three-legged future.

At the time, he'd said, 'She's a proud wee catty, and doesn't usually take you on, but what a fuss she made of me. Ye'd have thought I'd rescued her fae a blazing inferno.'

These days, however, he's fallen out of favour, but I haven't. She purrs and watches as I experimentally flick the whip.

'I'll no' be using it for hitting anything, Pansy. It's a lure. Maybe you won't, but I bet the other cats will chase it.' Imagining them running after Dobbin and me in a circle exactly like a circus ring is beginning to get me excited, but just as I'm preparing for action, Pansy starts.

'Miaow!' It's such a loud cry, nobody could ignore it. Her tail's straight up as she pads towards the barn door leading to the steading. Then she stops and looks back.

'Prrh!' It's the encouraging noise she uses when coaxing her young to follow her and it's a very clear message.

I use my strict voice. 'Look, Pansy,' I say, 'it's freezing out there and can't you see I'm busy? I'm on my way to become an animal trainer and, you might not know this, but it's a fiddly business getting things for a training session. I should've known you'd want to do something different.' I nod at the other cats. 'They've come to see what's going on. Look at them. They're just happy to watch.'

'Miaow!' She comes back, looks at the rope in disgust. 'Miaow.' Her call grows more insistent. As she heads back to the door again, she looks over her shoulder as if to say, 'For goodness' sake. Just follow me. Can you not take instruction?'

I sigh and throw down my labours. 'Well, Pansy, if you freeze to death or drown, don't blame me.'

When I open the barn door, she slips through, but before I can shut it, she runs on a little way, turns, then calls to me in the most wheedling of tones.

Between Shadow crying to be let inside and Pansy caterwauling to be allowed outside, it's becoming apparent that Shadow's the brighter of the two, especially when I get a clue as to what this is all about.

Pansy might not want to be in the barn but she still wants to be inside. Tail still up, she mixes her calls with purrs, glancing up at me with the same encouraging look that Mum gives when I can't down thick, lumpy porridge.

Mesmerised, I watch from the door whilst she trots back and fore to the last place on earth anybody would want to go. Then, horrified and making the other cats scatter, I squeal, 'No, Pansy! You must be mad. You canna go there. That's Frankie's pen.'

8

CAT AND BULL STORY

Pansy's given up on any idea of human help. She shoots out a last and withering look, then flattens her bulging body to the ground, just managing to squeeze under the door of Frankie's pen. As she disappears it must be clear, even to her, that she's about to use the last of her nine lives. All that'll be left of our supposed-to-be-clever cat will be guts and gore. I'm terrified, and how will Mum and Dod take the loss of our beloved animal?

I wish Rabbit was here. He'd tell me what to do. Alone, I listen. Tears fall. There's neither a bull roaring nor a cat yowling, only the sound of Shadow's bleat and the wind sobbing round the steading buildings – competition to tears.

A good bawl can help in a crisis. It's a matter of timing. If Mum's not too busy and it isn't a Monday and we've good enough reason, both Elizabeth and I'll get kind words and a cuddle. Later I'll sneak into the 'best' room only used for listening to Saturday night's wireless programme and Dod singing and playing his melodeon.

There's a wind-up gramophone that sits on a table just big enough to hold it. We've only got one record, which Mum tells us is Hungarian folk music. If nobody's around to mock, I'll dance to it and afterwards feel ready for anything. But things will never be the same after today. I'll never dance again or forget allowing Pansy to go to her death.

A new wave of grief takes over as, imagining her tossed into a corner of a wild bull's stall, I cry out to the bitter searching wind, 'Oh, me my ma mo!'

It's what somebody beyond sorrow says in

a wireless programme called *The Mac-Flannels,* then, careless of the fact that there's no audience, I go on, 'Och, what a miss that cattie'll be. She's survived so much and was braver than any old lion and here's me wi' nay even the courage to get back what's left of her.'

Thinking about this but eventually running out of steam, I consider the next move. It's scary but Pansy deserves a decent funeral. I'm going to have to recover her body.

'Stay there,' I instruct Dobbin, then, grabbing Dod's 'just in case' pitchfork and holding it like a spear, I take a deep breath and run.

My feet slide over the cobbles whilst the wind plucks at my clothes like the cold fingers of a spiteful witch. It's a good thing that I cut my fringe the other day. It might be squint now but at least it improves vision.

Unfortunately Frankie's pen, in the furthermost building, is approaching faster than feels comfortable. By the time I reach it, my heart's pounding and drumming a distress message in my ears. I blow out my cheeks, square my shoulders, take a deep breath, hold it, then duck down to peep in the gap under the door. It shows huge cloven feet. Clear as anything comes his low menacing breath. Then he moves. With visions of him blasting through the door, I'm ready to flee, but then hear a small spitting sound.

'Pansy?'

Silence.

Louder this time, 'Puss, puss!'

Frankie bellows and I toss away the fork. It clatters on the yard's cobbled stones as I fly over them and back to the barn. Hoping that what I've heard is Pansy in fighting form rather than her dying breath, all idea of bravery is sacrificed. I grab Dobbin and make for home.

'Your horsie keepin' his heid?' asks Dod, who, too, is heading homeward.

It seems an odd thing to say but, upset as I am, I manage a stout, 'Aye, min!'

Dod seems to be amused. I can't think why. It's what he says to folk when they first come around the place. Mind you, if they saw him with his clothes and face all white they might actually believe he was a ghost. If he hadn't spoken, I might have thought that too, and that Pansy had sent him as a messenger from the dead.

'Your mam'll be wondering where I am. Wid ye tell her that as soon as I get cleaned up I'll be round for the milk pail.' He slaps at his overalls, making a small cloud of powder. 'Lime's evil stuff if you dinna wash it off.'

I should have remembered that he'd been spreading it in the fields. The wind blowing the white stuff everywhere must have made him feel he was working in a snowstorm.

When Elizabeth and I saw lime first, it was after a lorry-load was delivered. We were curious about something that, when dumped on the field where it was to be spread, looked like a solitary snowdrift.

'We get it to sweeten the ground,' Mum explained. 'We were so busy in the war years coaxing food from the soil, there wasn't time to put much back. Now we're trying to get it in better shape and lime helps.'

'Did you have to pay for it?' asked my sister, who is doing sums at school and likes to show she can now count money as well.

'I get help from something called a Marginal Aid Production Grant. You've no idea how much it's helped us crofters to grow things other than oats.'

Keen to be part of what looked like a grown up conversation, I tried, 'Neeps?'

'Them too, but barley's mostly what I'm thinking of. But yes, and it certainly sorted out neep roots.' She made a fork-like gesture with her fingers. 'That's no good for growth. One's enough.'

I begin to think that it's good to be treated the same as Elizabeth but know that Dod only ever asks her to help, if she's around. He calls her the halflin, which I thought was a nice name until Mum said, 'Geordie! She's not a boy.'

By way of making a point, she must be

giving Dod his other nickname, but he just laughed. 'Ach! She's far better than a fully grown loon.'

'Well, remember she's maybe tired after school, and until she learns to ride a bike she's got to walk two and a half miles there and back. That's a long day.'

'I'm not too tired that I can't help with the milking,' Elizabeth protested.

'Prayvat! Prayvat!'

It sounds like the start of a song. Actually it's the call that an ex-German prisoner of war made when he used to help Mum on the farm and he wanted her cattle to come to him. We understand that it rings across our glen. It certainly sounds a lot nicer than the regular four o'clock blast that shatters any afternoon peace and comes in the other direction from the Nairn Quarry sixteen miles away.

Maudie and Charlotte, used to their signal for feeding and milking time, appear from the close-by fields when Dod and Elizabeth, tilley lamp in hand, repeat the cry.

I usually love it in the byre but tonight, waiting with the scoured milk pails, it's too worrying thinking about Pansy to appreciate the lamp's soothing hiss or its beam lighting up the thick clay-biggened byre walls. When everybody arrives, there's a rustle from the cows' bedding straw as they step over it. It's as soft as the clink of their neck chains when I hook them in place: but I'm listening for another noise.

'Frankie's quiet tonight,' says Dod. 'Maybe he's full up with all that hay I tossed in to him earlier.'

There's no mention of Pansy, so Frankie must have killed and eaten her. The horrible pig!

'Right, Lizzie,' continues Dod, 'You do Maudie and I'll milk Charlotte.'

The cows are in stalls, separated by a wooden partition. It's low enough for the cows to see each other but higher at the tying-up stances at the top. It's to stop them snitching feed from each other's trough and haik.

Dod sees me watching and, perhaps misinterpreting my miserable look, leans down and, pulling on Charlotte's teats in my direction, sprays me with warm milk. 'Hey, Janie, come and have a shot.'

For a moment, Pansy's forgotten. The milking stool's a fine height for me. Elizabeth's one is higher, so I see her resting her head against Maudie's flank. She looks cosy cuddled up to her cow and knows by instinct where to put her hands to grasp the teats. From where I am, only Charlotte's undercarriage is visible but it does put the targets within easy reach.

They feel like warm carrots newly out of

the ground. I squeeze one. Nothing happens. Charlotte stops eating and flicks an ear. I try again and at last manage to squeeze a thin spray of milk against the pail. Silently, it dribbles down the side of the pail, making nothing like the regular thin sighing song that my sister's brisk milking makes against hers.

'Well, Catties – at this rate, you'll maybe hiv tae wait until morning for your coggie to be filled,' says Dod.

If he hadn't spoken to them, I'd still have known the cats had arrived by the sound of their purring. Out of the corner of my eye I see all but one watching. She's a little out-side the velvet circle and busily washing her face.

'Pansy!' My heart lifts and in my excite-ment tug so hard on a teat that Charlotte shifts, rattles her chain and glances round with a reproachful look.

'Ca' canny! You'll pull it off. Here, let me,' says Dod and, as he takes over, adds, 'By the look of that dratted cat, she's had her kit-tens. Go and see if you can find them.'

Pansy lifts her head and gives me a long look before going back to her toiletries. The byre noises are almost as friendly as those in the barn and certainly more hospitable than where I'm sure the kittens are.

'It's ower dark,' I protest, rather pleased to be telling the truth. Just as Dod tuts, further argument is stopped by a sudden violent

74

movement. A short vicious-sounding clang follows. It bounces round the byre walls and is so loud it must reach up to the rafters.

9

HAVING THE LAST WORD

Maudie's kicked the pail and probably Elizabeth too. She topples backwards off her stool and all the cats scatter except for Pansy. She soars to the top of the separating partition. Between her thin figure and flying ability, she's just shown there's no kittens aboard, whilst Elizabeth's proving she's dumber than she looks.

Honestly! If you were almost drowned in milk and knocked over with a cow's hoof flying past your ear, wouldn't you expect some kind of instant reward? Lots of sympathy with the promise of a free hand into the rationed-sweetie jar, at the very least. But does my silly sister grab this heaven-sent opportunity?

No. She does not. She hasn't even cried. Despite being covered in dubs, straw and a gift from Maudie's tarry tail, her face is pale but her voice is matter-of-fact.

'Ach, I'm fine.' She gets up, wipes her

brow with the back of her hand, then shakes her head as if to clear it. 'Maudie didn't kick me – she only shifted her foot against the pail. But look at all that spilt milk, Dod! What a waste.' She chews a fingernail and would have picked up the pail if Dod hadn't got there first.

'That bloomin' Maudie's a besom and it's no use crying ower spilt milk, darling.' He looks as if he's had a much bigger fright. Maybe it's because he's called her darling. Dod's usually too strong to show any soft side. Now, to my surprise, and by her expression, *hers*, he puts an arm round her and says, 'I'll come back to finish the milking after we get you to the house. Come on.'

'Are ye sure?'

'Aye, aye! Come on. Janie – you carry the tilley.'

As if nothing's happened, Maudie and Charlotte go back to eating. The sound of their chains chinking and contented chewing restores the byre to its original peace. Pansy jumps down to join the rest of the cats, reassembling round the spilt milk. They pull their tails, cosy and muff-like round their feet, unworried about the closeness to Maudie's hooves or that the sound of them lapping her milk might disturb her. I strain my ears but not even the faintest mew comes from Frankie's stall. Praying that Pansy's still got a family to return to, I hurry to join mine.

The pool of light the tilley sends out is as soothing as the normal atmosphere in the byre. Usually, the walk back to the house in its encircling light allows us to appreciate seeing other lamps being lit in the homes of our glen. They send back their beams to ours as if in friendly recognition whilst, in the far distance, and out across the Firths, Tarbat Ness Lighthouse blinks its mercy message.

Tonight's different. Nobody lingers. Shadow must be sleeping in some sheltered corner, and even if the Merry Dancers were staging their Northern Lights Show in the sky they wouldn't stop us from hurrying into the house.

Mum's face goes as white as her hair whilst Dod explains our early return. 'And Lizzie's fine but that damn Maudie! I should never have let the quinie milk her.' He looks stricken.

So, for a moment, does Mum. Then she takes a huge deep breath, sighs, bites her lip and visibly drops her shoulders before she says, 'Well, it's a blessing you're all alright. As for you, Eliza darling, we'll get you out of those clothes and into the bath. The water's fine and hot.'

I look at Elizabeth who, under sympathy, has begun to look shaky. At least she's been spared caster oil, one of Mum's specialities. Instead, she pops in another. 'And it'll be an early night for the pair of you. You too, Janie, you'll have had a scare as well.'

I could try the *it's not fair* card, but sometimes you know when it'll be a loser.

Maudie's tarry tail and temper might be the villain of the piece, but Dod's the hero.

'You heard him. He called me darling.'

Tucked up in bed, Elizabeth says it in a voice so full of wonder it demands profound and silent respect.

'But d'you think you'll get to milk again?' I eventually ask, hoping that she might now forget about her accident and suddenly become aware of its hazards, and discuss whether she sees a future in milking. There's no reply. I'm dying to tell her about Pansy, as well as entertaining her with my *Cow-Pat Sagas*. Surprisingly, she's either fallen asleep or she's pretending to be.

I snuggle under the bedclothes, supposing that it's a bit of a bonus that she's forgotten our nightly competition. It's called *Having the Last Word*. Pleased to share with Rabbit, proof of winning this round, I whisper into his ear, 'Listen, Rabbit, you can hear me saying this, even if she can't. "Goodnight, Elizabeth."'

10

RED-LETTER DAY

Maudie's calf Fanny Annie's back with her mother.

'I think it's bound to put a strain on maternal instincts,' says Mum. 'She's a greedy wee calfie and more than delighted to swap drinking from a pail to taking it direct from source. She wasn't long in finding out that if she butted her ma's udder, it encouraged her to let down more milk.'

'Serves her right,' I say.

Mum agrees. 'As well as that, it'll save us a lot of scuttering about. Really, it's not like the war years when the workers at the timber camps were relying on us to provide eggs and milk. Charlotte's got plenty for us and Dod's folk as well. He'll manage her himself, so you won't need to do it any longer, Liza.'

Elizabeth takes this in her stride. 'Uh huh, but Dod says he's going to learn me tae drive the new tractor an' that wee Fergies are easy and then,' she adds, rubbing her knuckles on her jersey as if polishing them, 'I'll be up with the Big Boys at school.'

This obviously pleases her as much as her

79

reading. She's so good at it she can even read the *Red Letter* magazine without having to run her finger under its small print.

Dod's mum gets it every week. We call her Mrs Bremner and never wonder why we should be formal with someone who welcomes us into her house when we call her husband, who ignores us, Lala.

'He maybe canna cos he shakes so much,' suggests Elizabeth. 'That'd make anybody grumpy; weary, as well. The only time I see him happy is when Nell's around and, even then, he's got a funny way of showing it. D'you see him put his hand on her head? He keeps it there so long it begins to annoy her! That makes her start to chew his nivs.'

Consulting her own fist, she screws up her face. 'It must be sore, but he disna seem tae mind. And I'm beginning to think that bad weather suits them. It's a good excuse to be inside in front of Mrs Bremner's bonny fire that she's always got on. I bet Lala's pleased he disna need tae go oot tae the tattie-pit or saw logs in the stick shed and as often as not Dod doesn't need Nell.' Elizabeth rolls her eyes. 'Anyway, I heard Dod complain to Mum that she'll only do what Mum tells her.'

The old Tombain house is a but-and-ben, with a small bathroom added. Given its ice-box temperature, and that there is only a working cold tap on the bath, it's unlikely the Bremners ever jump into it willingly. It's probably the same when they go to bed, which is in the ben bit. The mattress covered in ticking-type material looks as un-giving as the iron bed it barely covers. In the dim of this quiet little room, with its still and cold atmosphere, the brass knobs at each end of the headboard's metal bars shine to reflect a loving attention. I wonder how Mrs Bremner manages to get her hair, with its straight parting, pulled into such a neat-looking bun because there's neither a mirror here, the bathroom nor the kitchen.

But at least it's a warm place with an open fire heating the kitchen range alongside it. Mrs Bremner keeps it gleaming with something Dod calls 'elbow grease'. A matching big black kettle sits on top of the range, sending out puffs of steam like a constant smoker.

Light filters through two small half-netted windows. If Mrs Bremner's at the sink and Lala's sitting by the fire, they'll see our house from one. The other looks out onto the moor but its view's slightly blocked by a big plant with blue-green leaves on the windowsill.

Once, I picked off a leaf and squished it, surprised by how much green liquid came out of it. I thought no one was looking, but Lala was. To my surprise, he winked.

A horsehair sofa's in front of the window and it's where Elizabeth and I sit, usually after we've had our tea and delivered the daily milk. However, it's Saturday today and Mrs Bremner's asked us to come early.

She looks round from the sink. 'Ah! The milkmaid quinies. You'll hae left the milk in the porch? Grand! It's fine and cold there. I'll be using it for makin' bannocks for the mill day on Monday. There'll be plenty folk tae feed.'

She's obviously part of the team, as she squints out the window and says, 'Ed's always so busy with folk needing his thresh-ing machine, I hope he can fit us in and bring a bonny day with him.' She wrings out a cloth with red swollen hands, dumps it on the wooden draining-board, then comes to the table. 'Aye – there's a lot of work making food and your mam's hands'll be full enough.' She shakes her head, sighs, then brightens. 'See and help yourselves to a couple of Butter Ba sweeties.'

They're in the top drawer of a huge chest of drawers which, as you come into the room, is on the left-hand side. There's a low bed jammed in behind it, which must be where Dod sleeps. As we stand on tiptoe to pull out the drawer, then reach in, I hear the constant dripping sound of the tap into the white sink and wonder if it disturbs him at night. Maybe that's why he so often stays late at our house.

Alongside the Butter Ba sweetie bag, there's a packet of poppy seeds with a picture of a flower on it. It's old and faded and unimaginably beautiful. I've never seen it growing anywhere other than on the packet. I often wonder what it's doing here. Maybe Mrs Bremner keeps it to look at to cheer herself up. It would help after emptying Lala's disgusting spit bowl down the toilet. But she's always so busy, perhaps she hardly notices despatching the slimy contents.

'Do you ever stop working, Mrs Bremner?' asks Elizabeth.

'Many's a time, and at night I've that.' She nods at the *Red Letter* lying on the sofa.

'Can I read it?'

'Of course and when you get bigger you can learn to knit and do it at the same time with this.' Mrs Bremner pats the leather belt she always wears. It's got a pouch-like affair in the front with holes to stick in knitting needles, 'It's handy too if you're on the go, but you'll need to remember to wear something with a pocket for holding the wool.'

'So, did you do Dod's bed's blanket?' I ask.

'Uh huh. Squares knitted in plain-stitch are fine and easy,' she says and goes back to the sink to finish off her washing.

She chuckles when I say, 'My! But you're right hardy.'

Whilst sucking her Butter Ba, Elizabeth loses herself in the *Red Letter*. It specialises in murder stories and must be exciting because

83

I hear her nibbling her nails. I'm dying to go to school so I can learn to read too. Meantime I've nothing to do other than look up at the high mantelpiece, where a fancy wooden clock surrounded by curly bits ticks its solemn message. The people in the nearby black plastic-framed photographs are more interesting.

There's two, both showing a mixed age group. Both pose in front of a tall, immaculately clipped hedge and all the young men wear sporting caps, so flat and large they remind me of huge pancakes. In one photograph, the three blokes at the back look more relaxed than the one at the front. He's got his hand round a collie cuddled close to him. The other seven stare out from the front, with Mrs Bremner and Lala in the middle.

The two girls wear dark frocks, brightened with long beads, whilst the men and the elder boy, who I think may be Dod, wear ties that look as if they're strangling them. Tie-wearing days are yet to come to the two other young boys, tucked in close to Lala and Mrs Bremner.

'Mrs Bremner, I'm thinking you're not the only hard worker. The chappies in that photo must've used a ton of elbow grease to get their boots that shiny,' I say.

I quite often mention the photographs to Mrs Bremner and she'll often come and glance up at them and smile, but I get nowhere when I add, 'Maybe that's why some of them look so serious.'

At least, there's something cheerful about the false teeth grinning out from the thick tumbler sitting between the photographs. I spit out my Butter Ba onto my hand to consult it. Yes! False-teeth gums are the same colour. I bet they belong to Lala and are the reason for Mrs Bremner mashing his tatties. I might have my own teeth but I'm envious because he gets such a lot of butter and tomato ketchup added to his plate as well.

The other picture shows a less formal and tie-free group gathered round a wooden sign on the ground saying 'Drumin'.

Lala and Mrs Bremner aren't in this one, and neither are two of the young men nor one of the children – the one with the curly hair. There's a new face, though. It's a young man, fag in mouth, and he's holding a melodeon.

'That looks like the one that Dod plays, but isn't that him?' I point to a serious-faced boy standing a little outwith the group. His hand's on the collie's head whilst it looks away, as if searching for someone else.

'Aye,' Mrs Bremner turns round. 'That's Dod, right enough.'

'And what about the ones that are in the first photo – were they not around?' I ask, but Mrs Bremner, her face clouding over,

85

ignores this. She checks her bun, then points to the sign. It's got a horse's head drawn at one end of the name, with an upside down horseshoe speared with a whip on the other.

'That's over in Glenlivet. We farmed there.' She nods at the window behind us. 'It's no so far if ye walked ower the moor there, but you'd need your wellies and ye'd hae tae cross the railway line, an' of course there's the kelpies.' I'm dying to ask about them but it's as if we've lost her in recall. She sounds sad and as if she'll never see Glenlivet again. 'If ye went by the road, it'd be a lang, lang time afore ye'd reach it.'

She dries her fingers, carefully, one by one as if they're painful, whilst Lala, looking straight ahead, cuts a twist of black Bogie Roll tobacco in his palm. His long fingers push the cut tobacco into his pipe, then he takes a long white spill from a jar beside his chair. His bones creak as he bends over to light it at the fire and we wait until he disappears in a plume of smoke.

I'm determined that in the absence of kelpie and a photographic conversation there should be a musical one instead. 'Well, Dod's melodeon's very like the one in the picture an' he's a right bonny singer *and* he plays the fiddle, though I've never heard him.'

Mrs Bremner looks surprised, so I explain, 'Well, when I asked Mum where he was the day, she said he was fiddling out in the field. I add reflectively, 'I'm sure that's what she said, though it did seem a funny place for doing that.'

I think of the nights when Dod comes to our house. He makes them special, especially after he gives up singing and playing the melodeon and chases Mum round the table. We love it when she laughs. 'Maybe he's practising for tonight and he's going to give us a surprise.'

Elizabeth glances up. 'It's not a real fiddle. It's something he uses to sow seed.'

'Aye, the only thing Dod'll get oot o' it's oats,' laughs Mrs Bremner, and even Lala lets a flicker cross his still face. Usually, the only thing that he allows over it is his cutthroat razor.

It's a morning chore so we don't often see him doing it, but when we do even Elizabeth, so often lost in the *Red Letter* blood-and-guts tales, is drawn from its pages to watch the bigger drama of Lala shaving.

In silent patience, he waits until Mrs Bremner takes a leather strap off a hook beside the fire and places it over the oiled cover on the cleared kitchen table. Lala, despite his tremor, sharpens the razor, sliding it back and fore over the strip as if spreading butter.

Mrs Bremner tips hot water from the kettle into an enamel mug and puts it beside Lala, alongside a shaving brush and soap stick. She loads the brush, making it foam, then she soaps his face. For a moment, he looks like Santa Claus, then slowly, and with great care, he raises the razor with a trembling hand whilst we girls hold our breath.

I've to stick my thumb in my mouth and wish Rabbit was here.

11

KILLER ON THE LOOSE

'I'm goin' oot tae the hens,' Mrs Bremner announces.

They're penned so close to the house you can hear them in its wee wooden porch. It doesn't have a door but there's a bench on one side and it's a great place to sit, shelter and watch if there's curtains of rain. As they sweep over the fields and moor, they come, like callers, to beat on the corrugated-iron roof. Depending on the weather's severity, the variety of sound is amazing, but it always makes a perfect drumming accompaniment to the hens' chat.

Today, however, Mrs Bremner has no sooner gone than clucking sounds break into the house. They speak of agitation. As if unaware, Lala draws the cut-throat very slowly down one cheek. Then he tracks the blade down the other side. As the noise level outside increases, he shakily manages the razor back into the shaving mug.

The fire crackles and sparks with the larch logs I've seen him sawing on the wooden sawhorse outside the stick shed. I'm getting so warm it's uncomfortable and I wonder if Lala's stubble feels as rough to his palm as the horse-hair sofa does to my bum. At least the old man's spared the discomfort of up-holstering-buttons. I move off one, then freeze, terrified this might have distracted the razor now scraping under his chin.

Undeterred, he continues in a practised rhythm, moving on to his chin and finally over his upper lip. There's not a spot of blood and we breathe again: drama avoided. But a few seconds after, there's more to come. The outside noise of hens in distress has moved into a terrible commotion.

'Wonder what she's going to do with that one,' says Elizabeth. She sucks her bottom lip as we peek round the pot plant to see Mrs Bremner walk past the window with a hen under her arm. Its beak is wide open, squawking its distress.

Suddenly both heads disappear, as the car-rier bends down. All we can now see is her back bobbing, as if she's stamping on some-thing, whilst at the same time her shoulders move as if she's also pulling something. Then there's silence.

'Think we'll be going now, Lala,' says Elizabeth, jumping off the sofa. 'Dod'll be looking for us. He said we could go with him to the station and shop. Come on, Jane, he's got to pick up provisions for Monday.'

But I'm glued to the sight through the window.

'Look! The hen's escaped.' Surprised that Mrs Bremner's not chasing after something heedlessly running about, I'm shocked when it drops, twitches a little, then lies completely still.

I see an axe raised and close my eyes, sorry on opening them to see Mrs Bremner. She's back in the house, swinging a headless bird by its feet. They're dripping blood on hers and, worse than that, she's looking pleased.

'This'll mak' a fine droppie hen broth for the millie. Ma flour brush wis getting bald so I'll get some feathers for it too.' She means those tied with an elastic band that she keeps in a jam jar on top of the range. 'Noo, tell your mam I can guarantee her soup as well as scones for Monday.'

'What took ye? I thought you were only delivering the milk.' Dod urges us towards the car.

Elizabeth and I exchange glances, but before I can ask if he knows his mother's an axe murderer she says, 'Sorry. Ye must hae got the sowing done early. We thought you'd be much longer at it.'

Dod nods. 'I ran oot o' seed.' He shakes his head, blows out his cheeks, then continues, 'Next year, if I can get your mither tae buy a machine instead o' that fiddle, it'll be a lot quicker, easier and give a better spread. Now, hop in, quines. The one at the back'll hae tae stand. I've taken oot the seat tae mak' room for when we get the millie rations and calf-feed sacks. We're only goin' three miles doon the road, so the back-seat driver winna hae a long stand.'

I'm not sure what this means. Dod crinkled his eyes when he said it. Hopefully it's a joke, so I don't really mind when Elizabeth takes the front passenger seat. I see better standing and can annoy her, breathing down the back of her neck, and don't have to shove for space. As we wait for Dod to get back into the car after it fails to start, we listen, fascinated by the number of curses needed to get it going with the outside help of a cranking handle.

Tombain's got two farm roads leading onto the main Forres to Grantown one. Our original has shrunk into a track and winds its mossy way through an avenue of spruce and larch. Halfway down it, Dod's fashioned a huge sack into a hammock and has slung it between two trees. It's a bit high to reach and, once there, a bit nerve-racking because it's a long way to fall, and that might explain why we don't use it as much as I think he'd like.

'We'll use it mair when the bonny days come,' we promise him.

That's when the wild flowers appear, garlanding the way with their scents and colours. We'll try to capture their beauty, picking some to press between the pages of heavy books.

Flattened, they never look the same and we're disappointed until Mum says, 'Ach, it's probably best to learn their names and leave them where they are. Then they'll come again next year. I think you'll find it's like meeting dear old friends who'll lift your heart with their loveliness. And maybe, too, you'll find that that path makes an ordinary walk special. As for the other one, now, that's quite different.' She grimaces. 'It's far too exposed and it certainly doesn't have any charm, even though it's the one most folk use. You wouldn't know we'd a front door the way it drives rough-shod up its brae in a flourish of granite chips and spent cinders, then spills travellers out at our back door.' She goes on, 'Not only that but if the bloomin' road was more sheltered the last winter wouldn't have left it with such a damaged surface.'

Actually, it's fine that we're on this one. It's too early for flowers and the car's too wide for a narrow track. Anyway, it's a lot more exciting driving along a road that's full of ruts and pot-holes. As we're carried in judders, leaps, stops and starts, Dod jerks the steering wheel this way and that, shouting, 'Hang on!' Elizabeth grips the sides of her seat whilst I grab its back, trying to keep balance. It's a bit disappointing when we hit the smooth surface of the main road.

It takes us past Tomdow. It's our other farm and means Black Hill. When our parents first came here, they took it over because it was too small to support a separate living. But they didn't need its cottage. Empty, by the roadside, it looks more unloved and lonely than an orphan.

'Ghostie nay at hame the day,' I say as we drive past it.

'There's nay sic things as ghosties,' states Elizabeth.

'There is so. I peeked in one of the windaes an' saw a quinie.' I blurt it out.

I hadn't told anybody about the afternoon when, bored at home, Belinda and I went exploring round the cottage and its old, neglected garden. Attracted by the sight of a splash of yellow hiding under a red currant bush, Belinda had murmured, 'I wonder, would that be gold?'

On closer examination I said, 'Sorry to disappoint you, but that's daffies. Granny grows them. Of course you mightn't know that, seeing as there's none at Tombain, but you

93

smell them. That'll tell you. It's a fine big clump. Maybe we'll pick one or two to take home with us.'

The flowers grew so healthily I wondered if there was somebody in the house who was caring for them. Yet the windows were blank and, at the front, too high to see into. However, there was one at the back and I managed, standing on my toes, to peep into the dusty interior.

Belinda had been left beside the daffodils, so she never saw the small, sad face looking back. I turned away, all thought of picking a couple of daffodils gone, and just remembering to grab my doll before racing home. I hadn't felt like speaking about it until now.

'Are you sure it wasn't yourself you saw? There's still a mirror advertising Guinness hanging on the wall. It's huge and left over from the days the house was an inn. Your mam says it was a bit of a den,' says Dod. He looks back at me and smiles: 'Mebbe it was a thirsty ghost wanting a wee dram?'

'Ghosts don't drink,' says my sister firmly.

'I did see someone,' I persist. 'An she gave me an affa fleg.'

Whilst Elizabeth and I settle down to an argument about frights and ghosts, Dod puts the foot down and before we know it we've turned into the short road leading to the station.

'Right, you quines. You can both jist bide

here.' Dod parks the car and gets out. 'I've parked on a slope so it'll be easier if I need a push to get started.' He adds, 'An' by the time I get back I hope ye've feenished yer argument.' He slams the door, giving us the chance to have an argument about something different.

'Bloomin' ghost! It's all your fault we're stuck here.' Elizabeth crosses over to the driver's seat and tries out the steering wheel. 'Now we're going to miss seeing the train coming in. It's due any minute and we'll see nothing with them in the way.' She means a wall of green laurel bushes that come between where we're parked and the railway line.

I'm disappointed too. The station, part of the lonely strath that makes up our parish, is its busiest place, and when a train arrives it brings an even more excited bustle. At home, the plume of smoke and sound of an engine puffing over our moor carries a little magic and suggests that there might be another world beyond the one I know. Still, it's nothing to the actual sight of a huge fire-breathing dragon racing down the line so powerfully; it's difficult and a little frightening to think that it'll stop to take anybody anywhere.

When it does, it's to the accompaniment of much sighing, creaking and squealing of brakes. The huge metal wheels make a grinding sound, as if reluctant to halt. It's fascinating to watch the passengers, who sit as comfortably in their little room-like carriages as if they were at home, but with an ever-changing view. Stopped for a little while here, they'll probably spot startled blackbirds flying out from the rhododendron bushes lining one side of the track and, if they're quick, catch Jo, the stationmaster, on the other, swapping something with the engine driver.

One day when Mum and I'd been at the station, I'd wondered at the quick, skilled exchange of something fixed to a loop-shaped handle. She'd explained, 'That's a key-token. It's proof to the driver that his train's allowed on the line. He'll be looking for that at every station so he'll have had plenty practice. If he's heading up to Grantown, he'll do the same at the Dava station.'

It's four miles up the track towards Grantown. I wonder if either name sounds as impressive as the 'Dun-phail!' Bert, the station clerk, porter and signalman, shouts. He stretches the name to make sure everybody's clear as to their whereabouts.

'I bet you Dod's sitting in the office, catching up with all the news,' girns Elizabeth, beginning to move restlessly. 'And when the train comes in, and as soon as Jo goes out, Dod'll be off the high stool into Jo's chair and toasting his feet by the fire.'

'It's not fair,' I agree, thinking of a cosy

den-like place where there are shiny levers, ticking instruments, weighing machines and smelly paraffin lamps hung on hooks. There are waiting rooms opposite, reached by a footbridge across the railway line, but nobody uses them. It's much nicer and far more interesting in the main office, where there's a lot of local chat and people arrive to buy their tickets or wait for passengers coming off the train.

'But maybe it's a bit early for folk,' I say. I'm lost in thought and annoyance in case the place is thronged with people and we're missing the excitement of wondering who they all are and what's their story, when something strange happens.

'Hey, Elizabeth! The bushes are moving.'

She's bent down to look at the foot pedals – practising for her tractor-driving skills perhaps. When she looks up, she freezes for a second, then shouts, 'It's nay the bushes, ye gowk, it's us.'

It's awful, but the car, like us, must've got bored of waiting and, having a driver at its wheel, has opted to go. It's amazing how this old machine can gather speed without the petrol Mum keeps moaning she needs coupons to get. And it's terrifyingly noiseless too. Leaves catch its sides as if saying their last goodbye whilst, gaping out the front window, I see the main road coming closer and closer.

In the distance we can hear the train's whistle – the signal that it will arrive any time now. But the sound of a tractor on the main road is more immediate. As we head towards it, I brace myself. Trying to remember the rest of the prayer Granny taught us, but pretty sure it didn't mention cars, I settle for, 'Dear Lord!'

12

A JOURNEY ACCOMPLISHED

Prayers suspended. Speech ready for meeting the angels. Station road stretching fast behind us. In front: certain death. We're seconds away from soaring onto the road when Elizabeth, in a super-human effort, shoots up to stand on the driver's seat.

'The handbrake canna be working. Hold tight,' she mutters, yanking the steering wheel hard to one side.

I'll say this for my sister. She's got a cool head. Just before we run out of laurel bushes, she's aimed for them. The car ploughs into their green growth. Leaves slap at the windscreen, thin branches snap and crack as, slowing down and clearing a space, we crunch to a leafy halt. Birds scatter out, scolding whilst the train shrieks its arrival.

Elizabeth crosses over to the passenger's seat. As she sits down, she bites her nails. 'I bet Dod's not going to be pleased,' she says.

When he does come back, we're as surprised as he is because after his initial reaction, he's amused. 'I didna expect tae find you pair sitting in the car as if it wis quite normal tae be parked in the middle o' bushes,' he says.

After Elizabeth's explanation, he says, 'I don't know what your mither will say to the scratches or the odd dent, but I hiv been telling her for ages there's something wrong with the handbrake. Still, what can ye expect of a 1938 saloon?' He clears his throat, which is usually a sign he's a lot more to add, but, catching Elizabeth's worried look, gives her a kindly poke instead. 'Lizzie, what ye did wis quick thinking. You're a smart wee quinie. Now all we need to do is get the car oot o' here.'

Once back on course, with the collected sacks loaded in beside me, he says, 'But I'll mebbe need tae give ye a few lessons afore I let you near the Fergie.'

Just along from the station, and on the main road, is the shop and post office. They're run by Mattie, who lives in the house adjoining the long, low building. As we stop outside it, Dod says, 'Come on, quines. I dinna wint ye havin' any mair crashes.'

We scramble out of the car, taking a moment to admire Mattie's fenced-off garden.

'She must be a right good gardener.' Elizabeth, looking approvingly at the neat lines of vegetables and fruit bushes, points to some huge leaves on red legs. 'She's even got rhubarb. My favourite – that and custard – especially Mrs Bremner's kind. Ye ken this, Dod? She puts a wee droppie salt in hers. It tastes even better than Mum's.'

I can't believe my sister! Not only is she comparing our mother's cooking to someone else, but I've never seen her killing anything – and certainly not a hen. I got a right row once for squashing a fly with the net curtain covering one of our windows. But Dod's grinning, so I don't want to dishearten him.

'Aye – she's a grand cook,' he says.

Lest a car's arrival, slamming doors and our chat's gone unnoticed, a bell rings to tell Mattie that she's got customers. There's a room at one end of the shop where posties are sorting out mail whilst the shop bit has a wide wooden well-scrubbed counter.

Close up, the counter's too high for me to see over, so I stay beside the narrow entrance door. From there, it's easy to see the shelves of jars of multi-coloured sweeties, with jelly babies gazing out as if dying to be set free. There's also pandrops, Dod's favourite mint-flavoured sweets. On show too, is a mixture of goods, from bottles of Camp coffee to bleach, shoe polish tins to laces – their leathery straps look like Pansy with a mouse, its tail hanging from her mouth.

Mattie is small, round, smart and cheerful; her hands, neat and busy. Her free use of 'uh-huh' fascinates us. 'You'll be in for Mrs Macpherson's messages, uh huh, uh huh,' she says, and in a cheery way adds, 'A good thing she phoned down the order, otherwise I'd still be trying to make out her hand-writing, uh huh.' She clucks. 'And her a writer!'

She consults a list written in a clear hand, presumably hers, then fishes in her sleeve for a small hanky edged with lace. She deli-cately dabs her nose with it, then consults Dod gravely. 'It's unusual having a millie at this time of year.'

'Aye – we're running oot o' seedcorn an' straw. I canna get enough but wi' a bit of luck the weather'll hold, then I'll get the spring sow finished.'

'Uh huh. I'm not surprised that farmers always moan about the weather, it's that changeable, and feeding all the workers on a millie day must be a right nightmare.' She rubs the counter with her index finger, thoughtfully. 'At least I've got everything Mrs Macpherson's asked for. Uh huh, uh huh. I've even managed to get her some bully beef.' She glances down at the floor. 'Hoy,

101

Charlie, could you give me a hand with this box?'

I recognise Charlie. He delivers our papers and post every afternoon; the lady in the Big House, known as Glenernie, and near to us, gets hers delivered first thing in the morning.

Mum says in an annoyed way, 'We've to remember our place and that Charlie works to a higher calling.'

He's got a round, red cheerful face made for smiling. It lights up the shop as he takes over from Mattie.

'Let me do it. Here you go!' He heaves a boxful of groceries up onto the counter. It's so full that tins stick out over the top. Pictures of pink meat on one might be an effort to brighten each side, but their shapes are far more interesting. They've got corners: perfect for playing hoosies and entertaining that fussy doll Belinda.

Standing at the shop door with nothing else to do, I think about her. Over time, she's made it plain that she's only ready to chat once breakfast's over. Then, if we're alone, she's plenty to say. She used to speak in a babyish voice but lately she's changed it to a posh, high-pitched one, like Granny's friend Eva. She's so grand she perches her pinkie when she's holding her teacup. Surprisingly, this is guaranteed to make Granny wink at us.

Being more polite and having tried the gracious nod that Eva sometimes gives, I do it now, whilst remembering Belinda's words, One day when we were playing at the big hole we use for dumping old tins, she said, 'Unless one squashes these round ones into a V-shape, one can't get a decent spout and I do like milk to be nicely poured into my tea. It saves the use of a saucer.'

I must remember to nab these square tins before they get thrown into the dump. A Mr Toad lives at the bottom of it. He stares so much you'd think all the old tins were his. I get quite nervous climbing down into his home to get them, and when scrambling out feel as if his eyes are stabbing into my back.

Returning to the present, I see Mattie pushing the box towards Dod. 'Between the weather, catering for the helpers and rationing constrictions, it must be a right fash, but Mrs Macpherson's got good friends and neighbours and they've already been to me and bought stuff from their coupons for her.' She nods approvingly. 'You'll know yourself, Dod. We used to call it the Love Darg.' She eyes him keenly and he gets a sudden attack of coughing.

"What's that?' Elizabeth enquires.

'Work done for love,' says Mattie, with a mischievous glint. Then she elaborates. 'It's when everybody helped each other, which we still do as much as we can in Dunphail.

Now, Dod, you'll have her book?'

'Right! That's it up to date, uh huh uh huh,' she says, showing that normal service is resumed. She hands the marked book back, but Dod lingers. 'A quarter of pandrops, some Butter Bas an' a sweetie for the bairns,' he says and hands over another book.

'That's my folks' one,' he says. 'The old lady told me to get some. She thocht the quines needed a treat.'

On the way back to the car, I notice someone with white hair in Mattie's garden. She's dressed all in black. The railway line is just across from the post office. Drawn by the sound of the train's clickety-clack as it passes, I take my eye off her but, on looking again, she's gone.

I could ask who she is, but bet Elizabeth and Dod'll say there's nobody there. I get into the car, deciding to keep this ghost a secret.

Last year, a steam-driven road-roller, preparing for major road works the next day, was parked overnight near the stackyard at Tomdow. Had it not been for the huge roller at the front, it could have been mistaken for an escaped train engine.

It had *Cock of the North* engraved on a brass plate on its side. 'Just so it won't get lost,' Mum had joked, then continued, 'And you certainly wouldn't want to lose the person who polished that plate. I've never seen brighter brass.'

When the roller went, it left a wide flattened area on the road verge and it's where Dod now parks the car.

'I'll need tae store this here,' he says, lifting out a sack. He crosses the road to get to the Tomdow steading. It's a few yards down from the cottage and guarded by an ash tree. The elm tree opposite looks down on the stacks waiting for the mill.

With a row of them on each side, the stackyard's like a small street, the resident foraging birds its shopping people. Belinda and I often come here but since seeing the little girl we avoid passing her house. Instead, we cut through the field below Tombain. It's probably quicker now that it's been harvested, but the left-over stubble would scratch your legs if you're not wearing stockings or wellies.

My mind goes back to our last visit.

'You're lucky I carry you,' I told Belinda.

'I know,' she said, 'but never mind, dear. When we get there, we can rest and enjoy the yard's sheltering magic.'

Once we were sitting, backs against a stack, and I tilted her face skyward, she mused, 'One likes it here. It is rather jolly. One feels one's surrounded by fat people in tweed jackets, there to protect us. So comforting! And you know, my dear, it's not in the least bit lonely with the birds singing all around. I don't think they've even noticed us.'

'Some of them's corn buntings,' I told her. 'Dod's good at recognising birds. He told us their names. They're a bit like sparrows and seem to get on all right with them, too. Now, ssh, Belinda. Just listen to that bonny chorus. I think the straw's joining in – just hear the wind rustling it.'

That's not the case today. As soon as they heard the sound of a car door shutting, a cloud of birds flew up above the stacks and headed for the elm tree. As they flocked onto its branches, they made the tree look as if it was singing a song of chatter and complaint.

There's a bit of that going on in the car as well, but not as musical.

'I'm starving. Just as well we got these,' says Elizabeth, biting a head off her jelly baby. Her eyes sparkle as she waves the body in the direction of the Tomdow cottage. 'Of course, you'll be wanting to give yours to your ghostie.'

'No,' I say coldly, '*You* said ghosties don't drink, so I dinna suppose they eat sweeties either.'

She says she doesn't believe in witches or ghosts, but when Dod comes back to the car and we drive past the cottage, she snatches a glance at it before turning her head to look straight ahead.

13

MILL WORKERS

'What are you doing?' I'm grumpy because it's so early.

'Looking out the window,' says Elizabeth. 'And hurray! It looks as if it's going to be a grand day for the millie. That'll please Mum. I heard her blethering to Mary and Smithy. They're already here to help. I love it when they come.' She sounds excited as she puts on dungarees and a thick jersey.

'Suppose this means that you're not going to school?'

'Uh huh!' My conscientious sister is definite. 'I'm going to be helping Mum. If you dinna want tae be a nuisance, you should bide in your bed. Otherwise, you'll get in the road.'

Honestly! She's so bossy! The minute she's gone, I say to Rabbit, 'I already knew that she wisna going to school cos I heard Mum having a conversation on the phone wi' the teacher and she talks to her in a different voice. Maybe it's because she was once one herself. Sometimes Elizabeth speaks the same when she comes hame fae school. Says she gets a row if she disna talk proper in the classroom.'

Rabbit looks as if he's fallen asleep but I keep going with Mum's side of the conversation. 'The thing is, Miss Milne, threshing mill days are always so busy and, now that the prisoners of war have gone back home, it's hard finding casual labour. Elizabeth's as good as any adult. I'd find her help really useful.'

Mum must've been pleased with the reply because, when she put down the phone, she'd a big smile, then passed on some message to Elizabeth about her being clever enough to miss a few days at school without the building falling down.

I'm not looking for witches in the trees today, and much as Rabbit's company might be a temptation to stay put, I whisper to him, 'I'm going to get up now. That bloomin' Elizabeth thinks she's so smart, but I'll show her who's really clever and helpful in this house.'

I roll out of bed and carry on speaking. 'I won't take out the toy box today and that's just for starters.'

Belinda wants to get up too, but I pat her head and speak to her a lot more nicely than my sister does to me. 'No, dear. You'll just get in the road. Anyway I'm takin' Dobbin. He's handy for carrying things.'

In the kitchen, I'm ready to tell Mum that

Dobbin's in the barn and as soon as he's taken back to the house, she'll have two extra helpers, but she's with Smithy and Mary in the scullery. There's so much merriment coming from there, they don't hear me arriving. Only Elizabeth does.

She's sitting at the kitchen table, intent on spooning tea leaves into a square of muslin. If I was speaking to her, I'd ask what's she's doing but stick out my tongue instead. Actually, my words are dying to fill the silence but just as they're about to spill out, Mary appears.

She's like a beam of sunshine, with her ready smile, easy way and light tread. A dimple shows as she pats my shoulder. 'Hello, Sleepyhead.'

She looks at the tea, heaped in a neat pile, and nods. 'Och, Elizabeth! That's the very dab. What a grand wee worker you are. You've such neat fingers.' She hands over a piece of string. 'Now, use this to tie it up into a wee baggie and leave a length for pulling it out of the kettle. It'll be handy once the water's boiled and the bag's been long enough in it to make the brew a right colour.'

'So, what colour do you want, Mary?' Elizabeth asks.

'Tar. The millie boys like a good strong cup of tea. Now, quines,' she says, wagging a soapy finger, 'we must all help your mam today and in every way we can.'

109

'Ready, willing and able,' I say, shooting a dirty look at my sister.

Mum's laughter mixes with the sound of plate, pan-clatter, chat and cup-chink. It's good to hear her happy, especially when it's going to be such a busy day. I peep into the scullery.

'Hi, Janie,' says Smithy, waving a hand with a dishcloth in it, 'How's your catties?'

Whilst Pansy visits us occasionally, and only when she's fed up of bossing the barn cats and the brose that Mum makes for them, Smithy's got four who all live in the house. They'd be white, only they've toasted themselves so close to the peat fire they're more a singed-brown colour. Sure she can keep a secret, I'm thinking to tell Smithy about Pansy and her young when Mum says, 'Pansy's had her kittens, but we don't know where she's hidden them.'

'If I know that cat, she'll produce them when they're old enough to look after themselves,' laughs Smithy. 'I never knew a cuter cat. Now, will I butter the bread?'

I almost blurted out about Frankie, but Mum puts in, 'Elizabeth could help you with that, Smithy. You'll find the sliced pan in Mattie's box. And maybe, Mary, you could give Janie a hand taking out the hens' mash. I'm hearing them complaining they haven't been fed.'

My stomach rumbles. *Never mind the hens,*

110

I think. The pan on the stove's bigger than the normal one and the smell coming from it's a lot better too.

'Is that for them?' I ask.

Mum chuckles. 'No! That's Mrs Bremner's hen broth and it's for the millie folk, and I hope to God it's all eaten, otherwise you'll be having it for breakfast, dinner and tea for the next year. No, the hens' mash's at the back door.'

I'm hungry and there's still been no mention of breakfast. Wondering what Granny would make of the God mention, and just in case he obliges and there's nothing left to eat, I'm about to sneak a little of the hens' mash before they get any when Mary catches me.

'You poor wee lamb,' she exclaims. 'I'd forgotten you haven't had any food. Look, as soon as we get the hens sorted, I'll get you something to keep you going.'

The larder's a small, cool room with high shelves and on one of them there's a tray of newly baked queen cakes.

Mary winks. 'Ssh! I know your mam's been busy baking these. They're to be for the afternoon cuppie, but I don't think the millie men will miss one.' Dropping one into my cupped hands, she adds, 'And we'll get you some puffed wheat as well. That should give you enough energy to help Elizabeth carry the cups' basket to the mill. The workers've been on the go since early. They'll be looking for their tea.'

The cake's so good, I'd love another, but Mary's right about the puffed wheat. A plateful's revived me, even to the extent of going back to speaking to my sister.

'Look, Elizabeth,' I say. 'I winna be a minute. I'll just go 'n' get Dobbin. He'll be the very dab for carrying that.' I mean the basket she's holding. It's big. Mum bought it from a tinker who came to the door the other day. She came back laughing after some intense haggling.

'That tink told me that the last time he visited I wasn't nearly so grippy and I'd aged an awful lot since his last visit.'

Meanwhile, Elizabeth's impatience spills out. 'Ach, Jane! Dinna be daft. Dobbin's wheels will only work on a smooth surface. He'll get stuck anywhere else.'

'In that case, why don't we go in the car?'

'There's no room. Mum, Smithy and Mary will be in it with all the other stuff, whilst you and me should cut through the field.' She shoves the basket towards me. 'Jist take a half. Come on!'

The cups are heavy and we stop in the middle of the field for a rest. My garters feel tight, so I roll them down to my ankles; my stockings closely follow. The heart-breaking cry of a curlew rises above the distant roar of the millie at work.

'That's a terrible sad sound. Reminds me

of someone lost in the mist in the moor.'

Elizabeth sighs and puts her hands on her hips. 'Jane! It's not likely to be today – not with this wind blowing about our ears.' She glares at me. 'Anyway, when were you ever lost in the moor?'

'Oh, it'd be easy enough. The mist can creep up on you without anybody noticing. Happens anywhere. At sea, too.' I clasp my hands and aim for a devout look. 'Remember that terrible drowning accident somewhere near Nairn? It was that terrible Granny wouldn't even talk about it. We'd to listen at the door to hear her speaking to her neighbours about it.'

My sister sniffs as she bends down to the basket. 'I know and it was awful but it's a fine day today so don't you go spoiling it with tales of gloom and doom. Take your side and let's go. They'll all be waiting for us.'

She's right. Dod's already helping to take out a big, steaming kettle.

'I tied that bow,' says Elizabeth. She means the neat one tied to its handle. 'I hope the tea comes out the right colour.'

As soon as Mum and company are ready, they shout above the din of the mill and the tractor whose belt is driving it. 'Come on, folkies. It's fly time!' It comes in a chorus.

The quiet corn yard's gone. It's been replaced by something like a circus, with an army of hands attending the needs of the

113

huge red monster that is the threshing mill. The tractor roars as if furious at being tethered to the mill by a belt, whilst the mill makes a whining noise as if complaining about being hungry.

There's a slight figure at work on the top of it. The wind catching on her patterned head-square makes it flap like a flag. She's wearing dungarees, gumboots and something that looks like a glove in the hand holding something sharp. A man on top of a stack spears a sheaf with a pitchfork and swings it to her. She bends over it, and with effortless ease slices the binding twine, then feeds the loosened sheaf into the mouth of the mill.

The sound changes to a groan as it gets to work, then the threshed grain drops into a sack whilst the straw, as gold as the day it was cut, lands on a waiting cart.

Ed, the mill owner, wears blue overalls and a red spotted hanky knotted so tightly round his neck it's amazing he's able to breathe. He switches off the tractor, then shouts, 'Right, boys! Time fur oor fly!'

After all the machine racket, it's so quiet, I point to the woman in the headsquare and whisper to Mary, 'I thought it wis just mannies that wis helping.'

She smiles. 'No, there's us for a start, Janie, and that's Kate. No millie would be the same without her. She's the best louser in Dunphail.'

114

'Aye – she fair knows how to use that knife,' admires Elizabeth, who's obviously lost her school voice. 'An' daen that at the top o' the mill disna look very safe tae me.'

Whilst we hand out the cups, the mill hands gather round in neighbourly chat. It mingles with that of chirping sparrows and corn buntings. They haven't been scared off by the machine's racket and as they hop about our feet searching for dropped crumbs they sound as if they're discussing local matters as well. Maybe they're wondering where they'll find shelter once the stacks have gone. Already minus two, the yard feels different.

'You're fair cracking on,' says Mum as she pours out the tea, Remembering Mary's description of it, I'm curious to see its colour, but the rich brown liquid's nothing like the colour of tar. It's a bit confusing when Ed takes a long sigh after the first swallow and says, 'That's a grand cup of tea. I like it black.'

Kate's last to join the group. She jumps down in such an easy way I wonder if, with her confidence with heights, she's ever thought about a circus career.

'Aye, Kate, we were hashin' ye a bittie,' says one man, as she bites into a bannock. She laughs, showing white teeth in a windburnt face. 'Ho! Ye'll nivvir dae that. I can easy keep up wi' ony bloke. Nay bother.' She turns to Mum. 'Yer gey hardy yersell. Hiv ye still that coorse bull?' Her eyes are a sharp blue.

'Yes, but don't worry. He's shut in.' Mum looks thoughtful. 'Dod and I were just saying how he's usually bawling his head off – bored, I think, and needing to be outside, though Dod thinks it's just ill nature.' She sounds doubtful, 'Mind you, he's been strangely quiet lately. I hope he's not sickening for something.'

'Aye weel, after the millie's over we'll get him outside,' says Dod, 'Once he gets fresh grass he'll be good as new, and, you're right, Betsy, he'll be the better o' bein' outside.'

I didn't know that was another of my mother's names, and neither apparently did some of the millie workers. I see Ed and Kate exchanging glances.

Dod continues, 'He's been that quiet lately I hivna felt I wis takin' ma life in ma hands putting in his hay, tho' I still widna be sure of goin' intae his pen.'

I'd agree with him, though for different reasons. Having seen Pansy popping into the pen, her teats bulging with milk, and coming out with them flat, it looks as if things are going to be all right for her and the kittens.

Chat turns to the weather and everybody's in agreement that it's a grand day for the millie when Ed suddenly darts to the side of the mill and lifts a handily placed huge stick. His scream breaks the harmony.

116

'Jesus, a rat!'

Something bigger than a mouse, sleek and grey with a long tail, slides out of a stack. It's bent on escape. The hind legs are bigger than the front, giving it a hunched appearance as it moves, but that doesn't stop it speeding towards the field we've just come through. Ed follows in hot pursuit, stick raised.

As he brings it down onto the ground in a great whack, I cover my ears and look away.

14

WORK SHARE

'Did ye get him, Ed?' asks Dod.

'Naw,' Ed says, spitting into the ground as a mark of frustration. 'Mind you, I hivna seen many the day. Ye should have seen the swarm we had at a mill last week – we were nivvir done killen them.' He bangs the stick on the grounds as if in recall, and maybe even disappointment at the lack of our rats, then goes on, 'Aye, Mrs Macpherson, I'm thinkin' yer catties must be workin' overtime.'

'If we didn't have Pansy and her squad, we'd have the same problem,' Mum says, busy collecting in the empty cups.

I've been trailing after her. Keen to contribute to the conversation, I say, 'Aye, the barn catties are good in the barn, but we need plenty others, so it's nay all doon tae Pansy, even if she is affa clever.'

For some reason, this seems to amuse everybody. They return to work, repeating the words, whilst Elizabeth and I get a lift on the cart carrying a load of straw back to Tombain.

Soon, Ed's brother Bob will buy a baler to accompany the mill. It will package the straw into easily stored rectangles. The 'stray soo' that Dod's about to build will be the same shape but making it with loose straw is a harder task. Covering it with green canvas tarpaulin and securing it with Glesga Jock will remain a chore for every kind of stack and for some time.

It's a challenge getting to the top of the load. The straw, as if trying to stop us from climbing, is slippery, but we persevere, then like conquering heroes arrive. We crash down, and for a moment I lie back and look up at the sky, stretch my hands and waggle my fingers.

'What're you doing?' Elizabeth asks.

'Nothing.' I'm not letting on that I'm waving to a passing cloud. It changes shape so it's maybe waving back, but the straw's jabbing into my neck so I sit up. As we're gently bumped over the field by the tractor pulling

118

us homeward, the ground seems almost as far away as the cloud. I wonder if the homeless rat's found a safe place to hide.

'I bet next year it'll be me driving and not Dod,' says Elizabeth.

I'd be quite happy to be on this cart forever. I bet Belinda would like it, too. I can hear her say, 'What fun! This is like being driven in an open carriage and one can see all around. It's so much nicer than a car, and look! Don't the workers seem small from here?'

As the mill re-starts, Kate gets back to her work place. She's bending, slicing with that evil-looking blade, then straightening her back to shout something. It must be funny because the sound of laughter comes to us, carried on the wind.

Just over the march fence dividing Tombain from our Woodside Farm neighbours, there's two pine trees. They break the moor's line. I used to think they were an old bowed couple until I got fed up of waiting for them to move. Now it's comforting just to see them bent towards each other. Perhaps they're tree spirits in permanent green, talking about our doings and, like kindly sentries, keeping an eye on us.

'You'd think that we'd at least have been given a bannock for helping. I'm starving,' I complain, but Elizabeth's in one of yon dreams that's maybe taking her out and about on a Fergie and she's silent until we

119

get home. Just as Dod stops to let us off at the house and I say, 'I bet we'll hae tae help wash the dishes before we get anything tae eat,' my sister slides down to the ground and shoots into the house.

'I'm going to the toilet!' she shouts, slamming the door behind her.

That's *such* an old trick!

'I'm telling on you,' I call but too late. I expect we won't see her until the dishes are done.

Mum's back with Mary and Smithy, and I hear them in the scullery.

'I hope it doesn't rain before I get home,' Smithy says. 'I've left my washing out. You're lucky, Betty. You've got your pulley.'

Mum agrees. 'Mind you, Smithy, I know you've got a washing line but I've never known clothes to smell so sweet as the ones you bleach over the gorse bushes.'

Smithy laughs. 'You'd better not let Beel hear you say that. We've too many of the bloomin' things. They look bonny in bloom, right enough, but they spread like the devil and no beast will touch them.'

Elizabeth reckons adults change the subject when we're around, although I figure we're not missing much with the present conversation. When I grow up, I'm *never* going to speak about washing or prickly old gorse.

Everybody's so engrossed in chat I manage to sneak past without being handed a dishcloth, then, racing through the house to the toilet, rattle on its door.

'Go away,' Elizabeth shouts.

I listen closely, then sure to have heard a page turned, cry, 'You've got a book!'

'I have not.'

'Liar!'

Hunger and rage spur me into action. She's asking to be spied on. The bathroom window's got frosted glass halfway up and it's already too high to see into, but I know where there's a ladder.

'You *have* got a magazine!' I knock on the window and shout in triumph, 'I'm going to tell Mum you've pinched one of Mrs Bremner's *Red Letters* and you're reading it instead of helping.'

That should do the trick. Mum's not usually fussy what Elizabeth reads but she is about what she calls rubbishy magazines. I don't know why. Mrs Bremner reads this one. Actually, I was a bit worried that all those murder stories might have inspired her to start killing hens until Elizabeth reassured me.

'Dinna be daft, Jane. A'body kens ye hae tae kill hens if ye wint tae mak hen broth an' Mrs Bremner's a grand cook – ye ken yersell.'

So that's all right then. I can go back to lik-

121

ing someone who, apart from how she deals with hens, is kind, caring and sings a little under her breath as Lala slurps his soup. When his shaky hand crumbles his oatcakes on the oilcloth, she sweeps them up with one hand, then into the waiting palm of her other, then shakes them into his soup.

'Waste not, want not,' she says with just a whisper of a sigh.

At the thought of food, my stomach rumbles too much to ignore. Its message is clear. *For goodness' sake, surely nobody's going to miss a wee bit out of a cake.*

Even if the scullery door's open, Smithy, Mary and Mum are so busy working, they don't see me nipping into the larder with a pail.

Up-ended, it makes for a handy step, putting the tray of cakes within easy reach.

Go on, urges my rumbling stomach and watering mouth. They force my hand to reach out to take a golden brown cake, and put it to my lips.

The sweet light taste might be heaven but the bite's too big to go unnoticed. It makes the cake look odd beside the others. It's such an obvious difference that the simplest thing to do is to get the others to match. I set to work.

'Where's Jane? She should be here to help with the dishes.' Elizabeth's voice is worryingly near. I'll have to hurry, jam in a few more bites – I'm beginning not to be too fussed about their size. The cakes on the wire tray are starting to look as if they've been attacked by something horrible. There's crumbs everywhere. Panic! Stomach lurches. Maybe I should hide the cakes. Maybe Mum will have forgotten she's made them. Maybe the millie rat could get the blame. Maybe, thinking fast now, it's time to disappear.

'Jane! Where are you?' The call gets nearer.

15

FERRET AFFAIRS

'I'm nay weel!'

But clutching my stomach and rolling my eyes is pointless.

'Nay wonder, ye wee limmer, you've ruined my cakes!' Mum had cried. She was as cross as the time I'd to confess that the reason the oil lamp wicks had disappeared was because, encouraged by Belinda, we'd both been curious to see what happened when the metal winders operating them were turned, turned and turned again. It'd been a surprise when, without exception, each wick disappeared into their lamp base. Apart from the tilley lamp often needed for outside chores, the oil lamps are our main light source.

Mum had raged, 'Don't even think of blaming that bloomin' doll! No, Jane, you're responsible for me having to guddle about, fishing the wicks out of the paraffin. Then it'll be a right fiddle getting them back onto the feeder-rollers and these'll stink all day.'

She'd held her hands up in despair. Now she was wagging a finger. 'So, seeing as you're sick, you'd maybe be the better of a drop of caster-oil.'

'Oh, no, Mum! I'm not that ill.'

'In that case, you'd better just go to bed and, Jane, *stay* there. At least you'll be out of the road.'

Now I know how Belinda feels. Cross, because she'd been told the same thing, and possibly remembering being blamed for the lamps episode, she's not speaking to me. She gazes up at the ceiling with such a silly smile I push her out of bed.

'And *stay* there.'

Only Rabbit lends a sympathetic ear when I weep into it: 'If it wasn't for you, I'd have no friends.' My tears soak his vest as I go on, 'Anyway, I heard Smithy tell Mum that nobody would see any bite marks if she clarted on enough raspberry jam. Honestly! There was such a fuss about nothing ... really.'

'You're right,' he soothes. 'Ach! Why don't

you have a wee sleep? Then you'll be fine. Look, let's hum a wee tune first.'

I wish folk could hear Rabbit. He's got such a fine voice; it's a pity he's too shy to be heard in public. He mightn't know the words, but once he hears a song he can hold the tune. I used to only have a few – mostly hymns, thanks to Granny – but lately I've been learning loads of cheerier numbers from Dod.

'Afore I came here, I used tae spend time with the farm workers in their bothies,' he'd told Elizabeth and me. 'They weren't great places to stay in. In fact, some o' the workers thought the cattle had better accommodation, but after we'd finished work we used tae gather together an' have a song or two. That fair cheered us up, an' of course a musical instrument helped. When he heard I wis comin' ower tae Tombain wi' ma fowks, the melodeon player gave his tae me.' Dod twinkled, as he eyed us both. 'He thocht ah might be lonely!'

'Is that the mannie in the photograph on the mantlepiece?' I'd asked.

He'd nodded and before there was a chance to ask if the two missing brothers sang too, he'd burst into 'The Muckin' o' Geordie's Byre'.

It's a funny song, so that's the one that Rabbit and I settle on, both falling asleep after the second verse.

We're wakened by a noise.

125

Apart from another rattle on the door, the house is silent.

'That's somebody at the door, Rabbit, and there's nobody here to answer it. They must all be back at the millie.' Getting out of bed, I explain, 'We dinna get many visitors and, even if I've been told to stay put, it'd be a shame to have someone call and get nay answer.'

'Is your mum in?'

I stare at the caller, astonished that the tousled brown haystack thatching his head is actually hair. He stares back. Maybe he's nervous or dumb. Continuing to say nothing, he shifts from one stout rubber boot to the other. He's got a wooden box with holes in it. It's slung over his shoulder and rustles as he checks it. Suddenly, Granny's lectures about staring come to mind. 'It's very rude. Think of saying something polite instead,' she'd advised.

'Ye winna need a hat wi' all that hair you've got,' I say, then because he looks as if he might rush away, I try for a friendly note. 'Mum's at the millie. Ah'm surprised yer nay helpin, but mebbe you're not interested in being part of the Love Darg.'

His hair flies as he shakes his head in a disbelieving sort of way. Then he bursts out, 'I'm too busy for that. No. What I'm here's for is your ferret.'

126

Now it's my turn to be struck dumb, and in the absence of further conversation I think about something that lives in a smelly hut near our stick shed. Mum's soft about most animals but doesn't really care for Troity, who's got pink eyes, a snaky way of moving and a habit of turning his head quickly as if ready to bite, even if it's the hand that's bringing him food. Elizabeth or I take out his brose and milk in its enamel bowl on mornings that Dod's too busy to do it.

I wonder what this stranger would think if he knew that Dod sings 'Troity-Troity'.

It's to tease Mum but she doesn't take it too well. 'Och, Geordie!' she says and shudders.

She said the same but in a different way the time that he and Elizabeth came back from a ferreting expedition chattering with excitement.

'Troity put up a fox in a rabbit hole,' said Dod. 'We got sicca a shock I never got the chance to shoot it. It wis a good job Lizzie wis there otherwise I might have missed catching Troity when he came oot o' after the fox.' He beams. 'But you managed to catch him in time, didn't you, Lizzie?'

Every so often I have to admire her, and it's at times like these I'm delighted that she helps Dod the most. She doesn't seem too worried about guns going off or foxes bolting but the thought of them bringing home

127

dead animals makes me scream inside.

'Janie's ower soft,' Dod told Mum the one time he took me on a shooting expedition. 'After the first shot, she dropped like a stone. I'd a terrible job convincing her the gun wis pointing in the opposite direction an' that she wisna covered in bullet holes. One things for sure, she's nay coming wi' me again.'

Returning to the present, I eye the visitor. With his plus-fours and brown jacket, he's dressed a bit like the toffs who come once a year to shoot grouse on our moor. But he's not as confident. With his big feet, hair and downcast eyes, he might be a grown-up and able to look after himself but giving a little friendly advice will at least break the silence.

'Oor ferret's nay tae be trusted, ye ken. I canna think why ye'd want him. Ye'd maybe be better o' gettin' ane for yersell. I'm sure you'd get a nicer ones than ours.'

'I've one already,' he says, checking the bag as if reassuring himself it's still there.

I'm astonished and ask why would he want another.

After a sudden bout of coughing, he mops his brow with the back of a brown enormous hand but ignores the question. Instead he taps the box. 'It's to carry him,' he says. 'I've put straw in so he'll be safe and comfy enough.'

It's a fact that animals come and go on our farm. There's Shadow, for a start.

'Why did she go?' Elizabeth had asked.

Mum clicked her teeth, then said, 'The dratted animal was so greedy, she saw me with the milk pail and butted me, and she's now so big she sent me flying. We put her back to the people who gave us her in the first place.'

Then there's Pansy's kittens. There's a good chance they'll disappear too. I'm sure that clever cat's still got them, and maybe even Frankie likes their company, but I worry what'll happen to them if Dod lets him out, then finds his lodgers.

The ferret's a bit different. I'm not too bothered about him going, and doubt if Mum'll care when she hears he's gone in a box belonging to a man with lots of hair. Dod might be cross, though, and it's a bit scary when he is. I rack my brain and come up with something simple.

I'll disappear from this encounter. Pretend it never happened. Easy!

Squaring up to the man and trying for my best English, I say, 'Look here, I'll show you where our ferret lives, but if he bites you, dinna say I didna warn ye. Anyways, I'm rather busy, so I'll just leave you to it, shall I?'

'Aye, that'll be OK,' he says and I go back to bed, pretending to be asleep when everybody returns.

I clutch Rabbit on hearing Mum call my name, then say, 'It's a wonder she's not

129

awake, but I see the ferret's gone. Campbell must've called and, getting no one in, just taken him.'

I've an odd feeling that, asking Mum why we don't have the ferret any longer, will mean she'll put on her teacher's voice, look strict and use big words that only Elizabeth will understand. Later, and when we're in bed, I ask her instead.

She says, 'Why's the ferret's gone? Ach, Jane, that's a daft question. He's off to be a husband.'

Thinking about his smelly presence, I say, 'I didn't know animals got married. Poor Mrs Ferret!' and Elizabeth laughs in a way that's as good as having the last word.

16

A PRACTICE RUN

It's easier to get out of bed when Elizabeth's around in the school summer holidays. She's usually in better tune and we don't fight so much, especially when we can get outside. One morning when the sun's stirred us early and she's not being important helping Dod, she says, 'Hey, Jane, let's go! I've found a great place for us to do acrobatics. There's a couple of birches near the burn, perfect and a lot safer than barn rafters. Come on, I'll show you.'

It's true. She means young trees, growing back to back, on a mossy stretch dotted with green grass-shoots. The lowest branches are the same few feet above the ground and grow straight and parallel to each other.

'They're that close, they'll make a handy ledge,' approves my sister.

Our kilts have been packed away for the summer and we're in dungarees. They save us wearing tight garters that make your legs scream. They also protect us from skinning our knees and barked shins and are perfect for the present activity.

With the branches offering an easy hand-hold, Elizabeth catches one. 'Look!' She starts to swing. 'See? You can get a good rhythm going too.' Her speed's increasing, making the green birch leaves above her rustle, as if complaining at disturbance. Any minute now, I think, my sister's going to take off.

She doesn't but manages to make such a good leap away from the trees I'd have applauded it if it had been anybody else. Instead, I say, 'Huh! I can do better than that.'

'Oh, really? Well, try this, Smartie-pants.'

She spits on her hands, rubs them on her dungarees, then approaches. Pulling herself up so that she's leaning over the branches, she bends over them and keeps going until the only thing to hold her from falling are her feet. Dangling upside down, her fingers brush the mossy turf below. As if to prove her versatility, she pulls a grass-shoot and tucks it into her dungaree pocket before collapsing onto the ground.

'I'd have done a backward summersault, but you were far too near me,' she says.

'Liar! I'll show you how to do that. Stand back.'

It mightn't be that simple but I don't have to worry about falling – really falling – and the upside-down world is not without its fascinations. From the nearby Knockack burn comes a constant chuckle. I consider it gentle applause, whilst the sky makes its blue canvas an offer of artistic freedom to passing clouds.

'Hey! Look!' Elizabeth bends down to whisper. 'There's a heron.' She points to the burn, then clicks her teeth as I right my position. 'Och, blast! Could you not have made a quieter landing? I bet it's been in the water for ages and now you've gone an' disturbed it.'

We stop breathing as the grey bird lumbers into flight. It's astonishing that something so large can manage it. It looks spooky with its wings tipped in black, beak like a dagger and short witch-like cackling call.

'That sounded like a warning,' I say. 'It

doesn't want us here.'

She scowls. 'That's the kind of thing that Granny would say. Honestly, it's all drama with you two.' For all that, she shrugs, then says, 'Anyway, it's time we went home. Bags me tell Mum about the heron.'

We race back, and breathlessly tumble into the house, anxious to be the first to impart startling facts about birdlife, until we see something even more amazing. Mum's swapped her dungarees for a mustard-coloured suit. She's even got on the brown felt hat with a feather that she wears for church, and powder and lipstick.

'It's a Cairngorm,' she tells us when we finger the bright stone set in its silver clasp and pinned to her jacket. If we're going to Grantown and it's a clear day, we can see the mountains of the stone's origins in the far distance. Today, we've got a bit of them here. This one shines as if sunning itself on the tweed material.

We'd forgotten that today's the day of the Highland Show. For the past week, Mum's been trying to persuade Dod that they should grab the chance of some free time to go to it, since the tatties, neeps and oats have all been planted.

'It'll be the first one since the war *and* it's going to be in Inverness.' She'd taken his arm and shaken it. 'Inverness! I never thought I'd see the day they'd have it somewhere only

133

forty miles away! I'm sure the car will manage that, and if not we'll take the tractor. At least that'd save on white petrol.'

He must have thought that she was serious. 'Dinna be daft! The car'll be fine but whit aboot the hoeing and Roma?'

'The neeps won't care and it isn't Roma's first calf. Anyway, she's not due until next week. Look, Geordie, the show's not going to wait for us. Forbye that, it'll give us a chance to see old friends and what's going on in the world. I was beginning to think there wasn't one beyond Dunphail. And we'll have fun.'

Her eyes had sparkled and she'd said the last word as if it was unusual. When she'd put her head to one side, Elizabeth and I knew it wouldn't take much more to convince Dod. She'd clinched it with, 'We'll see the latest in new implements.'

He'd almost sounded enthusiastic. 'Ach weel,' he'd said, and to celebrate he'd offered us all a pandrop.

'Are we coming too?' Elizabeth had asked.

'No. Mary's coming to look after you through the day. We'll be back in time for the milking.'

My sister had folded her arms, pouted, then cried, 'But I could dae that. I'm seven now, you know, and Maudie's feeding her own calf and Charlotte's used tae me.'

But Mum said no, and when she said it like that we didn't argue. Anyway, we were

134

delighted about Mary. She lets us do pretty much what we like but we hate to see her worried so we wouldn't tell her that Elizabeth had recently fallen into the big water butt at the byre. She'd managed to get out without help, but despite Dod's follow-up demonstration of the breaststroke on our kitchen floor Mum wasn't convinced it would work in water.

'Now, you're not to go near any, without an adult around. Look what happened to poor Corrie.'

'What?' We'd pounced on the name.

'Drowned.' She'd said it in such a matter-of-fact way it seemed silly to have asked. 'He was Dod's nephew, but dinna speak about him to either Dod or his folk. It'll only upset them.'

'That must be the wee one wi' the curly hair. He's only in one of the photos on the Bremners' mantlepiece Elizabeth had whispered. 'We'd better not ask about the other missing ones, maybe they drowned as well. Anyway the Knockack burn's that small I'm sure Mary winna mind us going down to it. It's only wee but perfect for damming. I love it when the water rushes out when we let it go!'

I had nodded. Elizabeth's birch tree branches were a new attraction, but in the past we'd played at the burn without anybody ever stopping us. We'd fallen in loads of times without drowning. The water always makes a happy gurgling noise as it runs over stones and under rough banks overgrown with heather, but once dammed, the noise peters out, lost to the moorland birds and distant cattle cries. When we release it, the sound of running water is so joyful, you'd think the burn was grateful for its returned freedom.

Returning to the present, Elizabeth says, 'Maybe Mary'll give us a shot of her bike as well. Mum's manny one's hopeless. I can't get my leg over the cross bar and if I try going under it, it dunts ma head.' She bites her lip and shakes her head. 'Oh! I'm dying to learn how to ride a bike. Then I'd maybe get ane o' ma own. It'd save me walking all that way to and back fae school.'

So now, Show Day's here and, as far as we know, Mum and Dod haven't mentioned water to Mary. They've been too busy dealing with all the needs that running a farm demands.

'I so wish we could turn it off at the mains,' says Mum before they leave, then, turning at the car door, she brightens. 'But we'll meet other farmers with the same predicament. They'll all be at the show and we'll love every minute of it.'

Now that they've gone, I'm disappointed not to have asked if they'll buy a birthday present there. In two days I'll be five and, as

136

Dobbin's getting too small, I'd really like a horse.

Mistaking my look, Mary says, 'They'll be back before you know it.'

She arrives, as always, by bike. It's got a bell that shines like a silver beacon and she lets us ring it as soon as she appears. She lives with her mum and dad at the Glebe, which is a small croft beside the church and manse and is overlooked by a railway viaduct. Its huge arches show grey against the lush green of the wide valley it spans. Far below, a twisting road leads to farms on the other side of the railway line from us and the Divie river. It's got such deep pools and is so fast-flowing there's no danger either Elizabeth or I would go near it, never mind trying to dam it. Anyway, Mary's mum and dad have told us there's kelpies in it.

I still don't know what a kelpie is but it doesn't sound very friendly.

The Glebe's two miles, mostly downhill, from us. Coming the other way, of course, is not so easy.

'We don't know how you're not out of puff. At the end of that great long pull, there's the Tomdow brae and our own road's just as bad a slog,' says Elizabeth, watching Mary prop her bike against a side of our larch plank-built garage. In an absent-minded way, she polishes the bike's bell with her coat sleeve.

137

'Ach! You get used to it. It's better than walking anyway.'

'So, Mary,' hope fills Elizabeth's voice, 'could I get a shottie please.' She rings the bell as if to plead her cause.

Mary rubs her hands, re-secures the crimson beret on the bike seat and takes off her headsquare.

'Of course you can. Jeepers! It's a fair old walk to school. It'd be great to get you on wheels. Once you get the hang of cycling, it's easy and you'll love it, but don't you do anything until I'm good and ready. I'll need to hold onto you to begin with, but I've some chores to do for your mam. After I've done them, I'm all yours.'

An old horse cart's been abandoned near our back door. Even if it's been mouldering under a big larch tree since time began, there's still enough of it left for Elizabeth and me to climb in. We play in unusual harmony, probably because going together to one end makes it tip down to make a satisfactory clatter. Then, when we run to the other end, it does the same thing.

'See-Saw, Marjorie Daw,' we sing, running to and fro, faster and faster and to an ever-increasing racket. A short time after, either Dod or Mum will come along and shout to us to stop – they can't stand the bloody racket, and Duck won't shut her competitive voice unless we do.

As yet she's not around and we only stop when Mary, with her gentle smile, returns. We climb out and troop after her as she takes the bike and pats the seat. 'Right, Elizabeth, let's see how we go.'

Were the bike not such a highly polished black, it might have more of the importance and glamour of a gold chariot. Still, it holds the promise of freedom and adventure, and I'm envious of Elizabeth as, wiping her nose on the back of her hand, she adjusts her dungarees, then climbs onto the seat.

Duck registers rage in a loud sudden arrival. Mum must have forgotten to feed her.

'Don't mind her, Elizabeth. Just concentrate,' urges Mary.

Elizabeth slides off the seat. 'It's a bit too high. I'll be better off standing on the pedals,' she says. As she does so, after reaching up and grasping the handlebars, her knuckles show white.

'Right as usual,' says Mary with a wee grin. 'Now, look ahead.'

'Yes – look ahead,' I repeat.

'What would you know, Jane? Just shut up,' snaps Elizabeth, making Mary laugh, as, with her staggering support, both set off on a zig-zag course.

Certain that unless Duck's fed she'll go on the attack, I find her some bread and milk. By the time she's fed, Elizabeth's gaining confidence, whilst Mary's completely breathless. She blows out her cheeks, then Kirby-grips her brown hair back into its tidy waves.

'My! But you're a quick learner, Elizabeth. You were going at such a lick, I nearly had to let you go and just look at me!' She wipes her brow. 'I'm fair done it. Look, quinies, I'm going to have to go inside and have a cup of tea before I can do any more.'

Left to our own devices we remove the beret, tie a hanky over the bell, then turn the bike upside down.

'Mind out!' says Elizabeth as she cranks the pedals. There's something exciting about the way the back wheel spokes spin into a blur.

'I bet you don't know how to stop it,' says my sister. She doesn't wait for an answer. 'See? Watch this.' She presses her foot on a lever at the handlebar. 'Brakes are important.'

I'm unclear about the lecture and why she's using her foot. Anyway, why would anybody ever want to go slow? When I learn to ride a bike, I'm not ever, ever going to bother with brakes.

Tutorial over, Elizabeth is on another track. She's looking at the bike in a considering way. Suddenly, she rights it.

'Here, hold it steady.'

'But ... Mary...'

The set of her jaw means that it's no use arguing, so I straddle the front wheel to stàbilise the bike. Elizabeth grips its handle-bars, saying, 'Good thing it's a lady's bike. No bar to swing my leg over. Look!'

Already she's in control, with a leg on either side of the bike and feet planted on the ground. Using a lever-type movement of her foot, she kicks up the furthest-away pedal.

'Hold it steady,' she shouts, but it's hard work holding onto something that plainly wants to escape, especially now that its rider's got her full weight on one of its pedals. She stands up on it. Unless she wants her other leg to be left behind, it has to follow. It lands on the other pedal. I can't hold on any longer. I've just enough time to tug the hanky off the bell and ring it when she shouts, 'Let go!'

As if I could stop her!

'Look straight ahead,' I cry, determined to be part of her success and waving the beret as if it's a starting flag. But she's off and cyc-ling, albeit in a wobbling fashion, down our farm road. Birds wheel above her, their cries mingling with hers in a chorus of jubilation, but, watching her, head down and certainly not looking ahead, I get a sudden pang.

With this key to freedom, my sister may well want to explore a world beyond us and the farm.

17

A WALK ON THE WILD SIDE

It's impossible to think anyone would want to leave home but, waiting for Elizabeth, I've had an inspiration. It's a sure way to beat her newfound mobility and, what's more, it's even more exciting than cycling.

Flying's the thing.

Floating will be the first challenge but should be easy enough with a parachute. Recently, I saw a picture of a happy-looking bear in a comic and he was drifting down to earth holding an umbrella. Mum got one the other day. She's so proud of something that nearly matches her suit, I was surprised she didn't take it with her, but I'm in luck. It's been left in the porch and she didn't say not to use it. I distinctly remember her saying, 'The weather forecast's so good for the day, I'll not be needing this.'

Granny once told us it was bad luck to open an umbrella inside. Mindful of the warning, I take it outside and press the opening button. As the umbrella unfurls, an unexpected gust catches it and I nearly topple over. It doesn't feel that safe but some-

142

thing as strong as this has to be perfect! Quickly I fold it away, tuck it under my arm, then, grateful for the knee-protecting dungarees, scramble up onto the garage roof.

It feels risky crawling towards the highest point of the sloping roof and takes even more courage to peep over the side. A small world away, our hens, in their intent and matter-of-fact way, scratch about the place, whilst Duck strikes out for the byre. She's her usual dirty-white colour. She could do with a bath, and she's heading for the water butt, but if I know her, she'll only want to cool her feet in it. Today's hot enough. Even the tar in the felt covering the garage is melting. Black marks streak my dungarees and the umbrella as well. Heck!

Mary is still inside, but I can see my sister heading back up the road. Carefully, I stand up, unfurl the umbrella, close my eyes and jump.

'Honestly, Jane. You could've broken your bloomin' neck,' says Elizabeth, who's got off the bike and swapped her breathless look of triumphant return for one of shock. 'And look at the umbrella – it's been turned right inside out. It'll never work properly again. Mum'll be furious. She got it as a present and's awful proud of it – well, she was.'

'Don't tell Mary,' I say, from a bed of nettles. Then, unsure whether to turn, die or be lifted out, settle for, 'Gie's a hand up. Ouch!'

After placing the bike to one side with the care of an attentive mother, Elizabeth grabs some docken leaves and throws them in my direction. 'It would have been worse if you hadn't been wearing dungarees, but try these.'

'No bloomin use!' I throw them away, but forget stinging hands and ankles when Mary comes and doesn't go mad. Instead, she inspects everybody and everything, nods, then replaces the beret on the bike seat. She takes the umbrella, looks at it for a second, straightens the bent ribs, then magically clicks it back into shape. 'There now! It's a pity the tar's probably there to stay. Otherwise, it's as good as new, but, Janie, you're a wee terror.' She dimples. 'I never know what you'll be up to next.'

I might be feeling loads better but this is so unfair, especially as all that Elizabeth gets are approving words. 'And you're a wonder. Fancy you learning to ride a bike, and by yourself too. Thank goodness you were here to help Janie when she fell off the roof.'

She could easily have fallen too, I might have said, and even if she didn't, all she did was rage and hand over some useless old docken leaves. However, it's best to say nothing because there's an outbreak of sunshine and she's grinning and pointing to the basket

144

Mary's prepared.

In it there's a thermos flask, some cups, sandwiches and a small pair of plum-coloured opera glasses. Mum says they're a legacy from the days when she was a flapper. Wondering if she's tried flying too, I don't get the connection. Still, the glasses come in handy. I often use them to see if there's anything happening on the main road, and if it's worth investigation.

'Look, quines, it's such a bonny day, I thought we'd have a picnic,' beams Mary. 'I promised your mum and Dod we'd check to see if Roma's all right. She's not supposed to be due till next week, but apparently she's crossed the Knockack burn and gone out to the hill away from the herd. We'll go by the wood. It'll be fine and cool, then once we're on the hill' – she flourishes the glasses – 'these'll help find her.'

A track cuts through the plantation at the back of our house. It's sheltered and lovely in its quietness, and if we wanted to visit our neighbours at Culfearn and go by foot, we'd follow it, then, when it comes out at the main Forres to Grantown road, we'd cross it to go down the farm one.

However, the path that we're taking today branches off to head up to our moor with the plantations now on one side, whilst older, taller pine trees flank the other.

Elizabeth gazes up at them. 'It's a wonder

145

these trees weren't cut down for the war effort,' she says.

Mary nods and changes the basket to her other hand. 'Uh huh. It was lucky that peace came before it was their turn. They'd have been chopped up at the sawmill that was here.'

Heaps of sawdust are all that remain of a place that once must have been busy and noisy. I wonder if the workforce got used to the racket of the sawmill. I think about the tractor's fan-driven circular one at home. It's not big, but before Dod starts it he takes off the saw's home-made wooden cover and something like the huge mouth of a hungry monster appears. It's got grinning jagged teeth, and when powered into action, they spin into a cruel cutting blur. There's a horrendous shriek as they bite through what's to become our firewood. Elizabeth and I've to help stack it in the woodshed. We can't hear anything for ages after, so I think it must've been horrible working somewhere that the noise was constant.

Now, in kinder and softer voice, the trees sigh; their tops sway a little. They allow the filtering sun to glance over Mary as she muses, 'Tombain wouldn't have been half as sheltered without those big fellas.' She points to the ground. 'But mind you don't trip over these roots.'

She means the ones that have surfaced and

146

meander over the path as if, like us, they're out for a dander. They, however, are leaving their tracks like maps: handy for beetles and wee beasties. I imagine them tuning in to Earth's heart and wonder if a human can share in that world.

I fall back far enough, so neither Mary nor Elizabeth can see me. I kneel down, then put an ear to the ground. I listen hard. Hidden birds sing in trees that whisper back forest news that only they can understand. At length, disappointed to be so excluded, I give up and run to catch up with my companions.

The clean resin-like smell of pinewood escorts us to a big grey gate. When we climb over it, we're onto the moor and the heavy coconut-like scent of gorse takes over. Their bushes make brilliant golden splodges in the moor's more muted colours. A sentry bird with a pink waistcoat is impossibly perched on the spiky top of the highest gorse bush. I don't know what it is but it makes a funny sound like a clock being wound.

'That's a stonechat,' says Elizabeth, squinting her eyes against the sun.

'How d'you know?' I wonder.

'Dod telt me,' she says, smug. 'We were out checking the cows one night that you were in bed.'

I'm jealous. How did she manage that? Ordinarily, by the time a bonny summer day fades out, the farm world drowses into sleep as well. There might be a whisper of magic and mystery in the air, but by that time we're both usually in bed and Mum's shouting, 'Go to sleep, quines. It's half-past nine.'

Mary jumps in before an argument starts.

'Well, whatever that bird is, it's doing a good look-out job. Actually, I think it's a bit like Roma. Your mum says she's got a suspicious nature too *and* a taste for the wide open spaces.' She scans the moor with the binoculars, before handing them to Elizabeth. 'See if you can find her. The trouble is there's so much here the same colour as that dratted beast and the heather's so high, it'll be difficult enough seeing her, never mind a calf.'

Milkwort grows in sharp-blue scattered patches. They remind me of the little flowers that sprig the black of Mrs Bremner's best cross-over pinny. She only wears it for the doctor's very occasional visit to Lala. After the last one, Mum had to start giving him monthly injections for something called pernicious anaemia.

I know what that is. It means Lala's getting more tomato ketchup than mince.

I heard Dod more or less say so, and he look worried about who'd be able to give him an injection until Mum said, 'Jabs are easy enough to do. I learnt how to when my father got diabetes. Your mother's got plenty

148

on *her* plate without having to stick needles of vitamin twelve into her husband.'

'Let's look and see if we can find any unusual flowers so we can tell Mum,' says Elizabeth.

'Like those?' asks Mary, pointing to a spray of small sunshine-yellow flowers growing in the shelter and clefts of a heap of boulders piled carelessly beside the fence separating the moor from a cultivated field.

Elizabeth launches off. 'These ones are called Tormentil and they're nay that rare. We see them a lot on the moor, but ye'd wonder at anything managing to grow in the crooks and crannies o' those stones. They must've been here a long time for the flowers to get a foothold.' She looks around the moor. 'There's no other one stone heaps, so I wonder whit this one's doing here.'

'I think that they'll have come from that field. It's obviously been cleared and improved. Look how green it is compared to where we're standing.' Mary shows a rare moment of irritation as she jumps on the soft peaty ground, making it squelch and her sensible black shoes turn muddy brown.

'That's cos Dod's been cultivating and spreading lime on it,' my farmer-sister observes.

'Aye, and before his time there'd have been folk trying to wring a living out of here. Hard work in hard times! I sometimes think of them and wonder how they managed to shift such huge stones and did they think it worth it,' Mary observes.

'I bet they'd have been pleased they'd made something a bit like a throne,' says Elizabeth. She hands the binoculars to Mary. 'I can't see Roma anywhere. Maybe you'll see better than me.'

She scrambles up to the top of the pile, throws her arms wide, then, flinging her voice skyward and jumping up and down, shouts, 'I'm king of the castle!'

As if in challenge, with a sound, surprisingly loud, throaty and brave in the vastness of the moor's empty space, a cuckoo calls. With the rounded shoulders of the Knock rising closely behind us, I imagine that if anybody's at its top, they'll hear it.

'I'll bet that's the same bird we keep hearing in the mornings and at night. I don't like cuckoos – they're bloomin' parasites. 'P-a-r-a-s-i-t-e-s.' Elizabeth repeats the word as if spelling it out. Unlike pernicious, I'm not sure what the word means, but by the tone of her voice it's not a compliment.

Umbrellas having recently been proved useless, she jumps down, arms outstretched instead. She lands well. *She's so annoying.*

In the spirit of competition, I say, 'A cuckoo's much cheerier than a lapwing. It sounds as if its heart's been broken.'

'Ach, Jane!' Elizabeth begins, but Mary

stops her.

'I think it's time for our picnic,' she says. 'You'll both be hungry. Come on, you two!' She sits with her back resting against a boulder and pats the ground beside her. 'It's such a bonny day, we should enjoy the sun whilst it's shining.'

A bee goes by, sounding so full of purpose it's easy to understand why they're called busy. The tea is sweet and hot and I wonder if Mary'll make us eat our crusts. They're almost black, tough and spoil the rest of the nicely doughy high-pan-sliced bread. It's thickly spread with the butter we churn from Charlotte's cream and the jam Mum makes from the wild raspberries that we picked last year.

I take the binoculars, check the moor stretching before us and spot the viaduct. Beyond the railway line are the hills and fields of distant farms. Before, they'd been edging the fringe of the moor in faraway patchwork but now look so close as to be almost reachable. There's one in particular.

'Mary,' I say, pointing, 'would that be the Lurg where Smithy and Beel stay?'

'Good for you, Janie. Well spotted, and of course not so far from the Glebe really.'

'Mm,' I say, taking the compliment in my stride, 'But see that dip in the hill nearer us. Is that where Boganey is?'

While Mary peers in the direction in which

151

I'm pointing the binoculars, I continue, 'Mum often speaks about a Mrs Macdonald who lives there. She says she's got a horse.' I stop for a moment, savouring the thought. 'It's a beautiful white stallion and she rides it alongside the railway line right up to Grantown.'

Elizabeth clicks her teeth. 'No, she does not. Honestly, Jane, you and your imagination!'

Mary looks down at her with a wee grin as Elizabeth delivers her umpteenth lecture of the day. 'She...' she indicates me with a sideways head-nod, 'obviously doesn't know this, but I bet you do, Mary. Mrs Macdonald's got a collie and it's so clever, it swims the burn that runs between Boganey and the railway line. It saves her mistress getting her feet wet and collects the messages the engine driver puts out for her.'

'Honestly, Elizabeth,' I laugh. 'Who's talking about imagination now? He'd have to slow down the train for that. He'd be sure to get the sack for doing that.'

She shoots back. 'It's a fact. Mr Macdonald was a railway worker but he died. Mrs Macdonald's getting on a bittie and she's no so fit to go shopping now. The railway folk are helping her, just like that dog.'

'It's a horse. Look, I'll prove it to you. It'll not take long to get there.'

I put down the binoculars and suddenly

everywhere looks so far away again; it's not much of a disappointment when Mary says, 'Well, if we wanted to see Mrs Macdonald, we'd have to come at it by the other side. We'd need to go by road, up under the railway viaduct and even after we'd reached the end of the tarred surface, there's a couple of miles of rough track to go, then cross the railway line and,' she draws breath, 'at the end of it all there's that burn to ford.'

'Mebbe not today but some other one we could go straight over from here,' states Elizabeth. 'That'd be much shorter.'

Mary's horrified. 'No, you could not! The Kettle-holes are between us. And folk say you only know where they are when you fall into them.'

'Kettle-holes? That's a funny name.'

'Aye, deep pools of water where kelpies live and the Knockack burn starts.'

Now's the time to ask.

'Kelpies?' I wonder.

'Aye, water horses, and I wouldn't be surprised if they live further down the Knockack as well.' Mary must see us exchanging glances because she warms to her theme. 'I know I certainly wouldn't want to go there myself. And they're especially fond of pulling little children deep, deep, down, down into the water so we never see them again.' She drops her voice as if frightened a stray kelpie might hear her, but lifts it to continue. 'Still, I'm here to look after you and I think we're safe enough today. Let's see if Roma's risking anything more dangerous than having a wee calfie.'

Elizabeth's sure there's no kelpies in the Knockack. 'There's not enough water,' she whispers as, leaving Mary behind, we run down the moor's slight slope towards it. I hear it gurgling as if chuckling at not being interfered with by people of damming intentions. I stop for a moment to check a grey stone. Its surface and colour resemble a toad's back, with something like a mustard-coloured stain splattered over it.

In its shelter, a mauve-coloured flower stands up from a bed of emerald-green grass. 'Look, Lizabeth, a wild orchid, and it's a sweet-smelling one,' I say, wondering if kelpies aren't as big as Mary suggests. If they're small, they might think orchids are little pink Christmas trees, for they have that shape.

But as usual I'm talking to myself. Elizabeth's raced ahead. She's slipped off her shoes and sits on the burn bank, dangling her feet in the water. There's some grass rushes near her. She pulls a few, then holding three in her mouth starts to plait the free ends.

Then it's either a very big horned kelpie that comes snorting towards her or it's Roma, and just a few yards away from the weaver lies a new calf.

18

ROMA RULES

'Hello Roma, I see you found a nice bed of rushes tae hide your calfie.'

I'm several yards away but Elizabeth's voice, though soft, carries. In her neat fingers, the plaited rush holds its shape. She waves it before the cow. 'Look, something to put on your horns and if you wait a wee minutie I'll make you another one to match it.' She stoops down and plucks a yellow flower that's been growing at the waterside. 'And, look! Mimulus! Bees love it.'

Somehow or another I don't think that Roma's all that interested in a botany lecture. She drops her head, rolls her eyes, paws the ground and breathes so deeply it looks as if she's about to charge, but my sister seems unconcerned. She stays put and picks some more rushes, then starts plaiting them as if having a cow with lowered head, advancing, is something to expect from the quietness of rural life.

Mary's running towards us, shouting and waving the basket, but all that does is frighten the calf. It gives a small cry. Roma lumbers forward and stations herself between Elizabeth and the calf. She noses it. As if being told to get up, it does and staggers towards its mother's udder.

For a moment, she lets it suck, then, with a gentle chivvying call, she moves away from the rushes, across the burn, then waits, attention completely focused on the calf. It stares at the moving water, lifts its head and gives a bewildered cry.

'On you go, calfie,' says Elizabeth, making a shooing gesture. 'The water winna hurt ye.'

For a moment, the calf hesitates. Roma calls again. The calf sniffs the water, then slowly stumbles through it. No mother could give a loved child a better reception as it climbs up the bank and to her. Maybe she's working on the ration book principal because she allows her calf only a thimbleful of milk before turning towards the moor. Head outstretched as if trying to catch up with the dairy lorry, the calf totters after her.

A breathless Mary arrives, wiping her brow. 'Phew!' she says. 'That's a relief, and your mum and Dod'll be pleased that Roma's calved, and would you look at the pair of them now! I'm thinking they're taking the old drove road.'

She means the faint tracks just visible in the heather. They lead in the direction of Boganey.

Elizabeth jumps up, throwing the plaited

rush into the burn. As her frail craft sails off, she dusts down her dungarees and laughs. 'Maybe Roma fancies seeing a bit of the world.'

I'm curious about the drove road.

'Roma would find it easier to follow if it was springtime, says Mary. 'According to your mum, the tracks are really clear then.'

'So, was it for taking you to the other farms?' Elizabeth asks.

'It'd be handy for that, but these were the days before there were proper roads. If animals were to be sold, men called drovers would drive them on foot to the Falkirk Tryst. It was a big market in the south of Scotland. You know,' Mary marvelled, 'for most drovers, it was such a long way away, they'd to stop the night in places called stances. The men wore plaids but sometimes they weren't warm enough so they slept with their animals. Can you imagine that!'

I can. I think it might have been nice, but maybe not with Roma.

'If she's heading south, she'll have to get past the Kettle-holes first,' muses Elizabeth, but Roma's stopped to lick her calf. With an enthusiasm similar to Mary scouring our scullery floor, the cow's great tongue massages the wet body, transferring enough energy to allow the calf eventually to escape and search for, and this time get, better rations.

'Ah! She's not heading for the bright lights after all,' says Mary, as, once the calf's had its fill, Roma, keeping a watchful eye on us, heads back towards the burn then further down it. There, instead of the rough banks overgrown with heather, she'll find birch trees overhanging the murmuring water, whispering an offer of shade and shelter. She might even stop near our acrobat trees; it's such a lovely spot.

Mum often speaks about a school that was once not far from it and built on a knoll. Now all that's left are its stones, which litter the grass of what may have been a turfy playground. Dunphail's present school is a grim-looking building with high windows and it's halfway along the road between the Glebe and the shop. We'd been fascinated that somewhere nearer us but so far from anywhere else was also a school but couldn't really imagine what it was like.

'Who'd have gone to it?' we'd asked.

'Girls, and over thirty of them attended. I found some records not long ago and they said *the teacher was paid on her own adventure.*' Mum'd given a grim laugh. 'I doubt if it was a paying spec. 120 years ago. I've done my sums and worked out that she'd have been lucky if she got £8 for the year.'

'What would she have taught?' Elizabeth wondered.

'Spinning probably. It would have been

important then. Seemingly the women of the parish were notable for their skill in this.'

The scattered remains of old crofts can be seen all around us. They may once have been the homes of the pupils but, try as I might, I can't imagine the moor holding anything but the song of the wind and the cry of its birds.

'Time to go home,' says Mary. 'Let's take a shortcut. We can go up through the field.'

'No!' we chorus. 'Frankie's in that one.'

'I know that, sillies! I meant the field next to him, but' – she turns to Elizabeth and says with a twinkle – 'I'm pleased to hear that at least you're frightened of something.'

My sister shrugs. 'Uh huh, and I think mebbe Dod is too. In fact, to tell you the truth, Mary, I'm sure that Mum and Pansy's the only ones who aren't. I've even seen Pansy out in that park he's in and hunting close by him.'

I'm dying to tell them about the kittens. I bet they're not frightened of our bull either. They're certainly not scared of me. As soon as Frankie was moved outside, Belinda and I met Pansy taking four fair-sized kittens through the field leading to the Tomdow. I tried to pick up one of her young but stopped when, with its eyes blazing, it arched its back, fluffed up to twice its size, spat and swiped the air with its claws.

'Such language!' tutted Belinda. 'Leave it

159

alone. It's a common little thing.'

'You wait till I'm a lion tamer, ye wee vratch!' I called, watching as it scampered after Pansy, now purposefully heading towards the Tomdow's steading.

'Maybe she's giving them a lesson on rat-catching,' I'd mused to Belinda. 'I don't think I'd ever be brave enough to do that.'

Still, I've enough courage as we walk home, going up the field next to Frankie's one. Taking Mary's hand in case she's scared, I shout loud enough for him to lift his head and look in our direction, 'Bloomin' P-A R-A-S-I-T-E!'

19

TO MARKET TO MARKET

Mum throws opens our bedroom door. She sounds harassed. 'Would you two sleepy-heads wake up? I canna believe you're still asleep. Did you not hear the float arriving and the stirks bawling? They were making sure we knew they'd no intention of going anywhere, least of all somewhere on wheels. Och! I canna wait to see the back of those meddlesome brutes.' She takes a breath, then powers on, 'Come on! You'll need to

160

get up, and now!'

I'm too sleepy to ask why, but Elizabeth's already tumbled out of bed and asked the question.

'We're *all* going to Inverness. The stirks are being sold at the Wool Fair there, and as you two are needing shoes, we'll get them in town.'

Elizabeth sounds puzzled. 'Wool Fair's a funny name.'

'Aye, it's kept its name from the days when people only sold sheep, and for their fleeces especially. Now all kinds of animals are sold – even horses, though I don't imagine we'll be buying any of them.' She's wearing a skirt, jersey and, unusually for her, a headsquare. It makes her look and sound business-like and strict. 'Now, Janie, pit on something sensible an get oot o' that bed!'

I'm in a bad mood. It was too much to hope that Mum and Dod would actually come back with a horse after the Highland Show. Instead, they brought home a beautiful birthday frock. Even if it's the only one I've got, chances to show it off are rare, but it'll spoil in the rain. I look out the window and consider having to wear something more suitable. The ruched bathing suit perhaps.

After our day on the moor with Mary, the sun packed up. Grey skies took its place, bringing rain that's been falling ever since. The only person who seems happy is Duck.

161

Her shouts sound almost tuneful whilst she turns well-oiled cartwheels in the deep puddles that are everywhere. It's terrible weather for hay-making. Maybe a day in Inverness won't be as dismal as the sight of flattened grass in our fields.

'It's bad enough cutting the stuff, but just as difficult getting it dry,' says Dod in tones of despair. At this rate, it'll never make it to be stored inside.'

The other day he ran out of wet weather wear and resorted to wearing a corn bag cornerwise over his head, the rest draped over his shoulder. Today, however, he's smart in a dark suit with a waistcoat, white shirt, tie and hat. Whilst we're waiting for him to fit in the car's back seat for us, Mum, looking pointedly at his head, says, 'That Fedora suits you better. Yon sack made you look like a grimy member of the Ku Klux Klan.'

It almost sounded like a joke. Relieved that Mum's beginning to sound less stressed, Elizabeth and I try out the back seat for bounce and spring, whilst Dod gets into the driver's seat. He looks in the car's cracked mirror and adjusts the hat brim so that it slants. 'Ye think so? Ma mither said she thought I looked like a gangster, tho' I dinna ken how she wid know.' He closes his eyes and turns the ignition key whilst Mum holds up crossed fingers. The car starts without fuss. I look at my own fingers. I must try that. It might be a good way to get a horse.

Elizabeth leans forward so that she's practically sitting between Mum and Dod. 'Are we goin' by Glenferness?'

'Aye, you quines like the switchbacks and it'll be quicker today, even if we've tae gae through the ford, just past Dulcie Bridge. There's times the railway gates on the Inverness–Nairn road are closed long before the train goes through. Ye can get a right hold-up and I bet the road'll be busy enough with ither floats going to the mart.'

Mum puts in, 'And that's the way our stirks will be going. Much as they've been a bloomin' nuisance, I hope they get there in one bit.'

Shortly after, we could apply her remark to our own journey.

'For goodness' sake, Eliza, sit back or you'll go through the windscreen. And, Geordie, would you mind the exhaust!' she says as we fly over the first switchback bump. The car back seat is low but, thanks to the springs, and despite hanging onto the back of the seats in front, we soar towards the roof.

Dod merely says, 'Aye weel, Janie, when you go to school at least ye'll be able tae count tae seven. Are ye counting? Six more bumps an after that there's the ford. Plenty excitement, eh?' He slides Mum a mischievous grin. 'Haud tight, Betsy.'

The windscreen looks as if it's crying. In the brief moment that the wiper manages to clear it, we glimpse a sodden landscape, where tree branches bow low, laden with rain-soaked leaves. Crop fields, like frozen sea waves, lie victim to the weather's tempers. Mum tightens her head square whilst, with a shush of water, the car hits puddle after puddle.

Quiet falls inside; outside, making up for it. Then Mum says, 'Um, not sure about this.' We follow her gaze and see something like a river crossing the road. 'That's surely not the ford?'

But already we've hit and are in it. On my side there's an expanse of water, running fast against the car as it tries to plough through. The engine falters. The windscreen steams up. We start to drift. As water begins to well up through the car's floor, I wonder if Dod's swimming lessons might be put to the test.

Mum, however, is not about to keep her opinion to herself. 'Dod! At this rate, and if we don't drown first, we'll sail into Nairn, no matter how much you'd like to miss going that way.'

This morning, before we left, I looked out of our scullery window and couldn't understand what a huge brown twisting snake wearing a scarf the colour of old lace was doing at the bottom of one of our fields. It turned out to be the Knockack burn, but so

164

heightened and transformed it was easy to imagine that not only a serpent lived there but also that there'd be room for half-a-dozen kelpies as well.

I'm sure there's enough water in the ford for a few here too, but Dod's unfazed. Then the engine dies. Quickly he turns the ignition key. Rain beats down on the car roof. Time stands still. Then, just as I'm thinking how different is the soothing sound of a downfall on the Bremner's porch, the car reclaims its voice.

As if the tortured noise of a revved and labouring engine's normal, Dod raises his voice but says in an easy way, 'Full throttle!'

The car jolts forward. The wiper groans and gives up. The canon-propelled water spray blinds visibility. We shoot through the rest of the ford and must be back on the road because the tyres have grip, and suddenly we're racing along an even surface as if chased by a dozen kelpics.

'What's that smell?' asks Elizabeth, wrinkling her nose and looking green. I feel sick, too.

'Och, a wee bit of hot metal,' Dod says. 'It'll be after us bein' in the water an' I suppose the brakes'll be affected as well. It's easy to sort – they jist need a wee pump.'

We watch as his foot goes from gentle pressure to stamp. When nothing happens, Mum mutters, 'I just have to hope that they work before we go down that brae.'

If we were going in the other direction, it wouldn't be a problem, but we're now approaching a gentle slope with a sharp drop beyond. The car's gathering speed. Mindful of the slowing effect of the laurel bushes at the station, I'm surprised that Elizabeth doesn't recommend driving into the rain-soaked trees bordering the road. They lean forward, as if waiting to see the arrival of somebody special, but we're now going so fast that even if we wanted to we've neither time nor inclination to wave. Instead, we flash past them. All eyes are fixed on a sharp and fast-approaching bend. Whilst Dod repeatedly pumps his foot over the brake pedal, changes gear and makes a distressed engine sound even more troubled, I clutch Elizabeth's hand.

At the same time, Mum reaches for the handbrake. But we know about that, don't we?

With perfect timing, we've been sick. As we flew down the hill, we managed to hold back until we reached the sharp bend at the end of the slope. Then the brakes finally worked. As the car screamed to a halt, we leapt out. We did it in unison, as well as throwing up. After, as we turned our faces to a now lessening rain and Elizabeth said, 'Oh, that feels lovely but I do wish we were in Inverness,' I continued the unusual harmony and agreed.

Now, Mum's promise that 'we're nearly there' does finally come true and we arrive in Inverness with Dod, blithe and confident despite the stink of burning rubber filling the car. 'That's jist the brakes getting back into working order,' he explains.

There's a rattle of something troubling the car's undercarriage, accompanied by the occasional bang, so loud it sounds like gunshot. 'And that's the exhaust,' he continues. 'But there's plenty garages here. I'll drop ye all off at the mart, then I'll tak the car to Macrae and Dicks. They're that quick and reliable, I bet it'll be ready after the mart.' He glances at Mum and pats her hand. 'I'm sure it won't be too expensive. It sounds worse than it really is.'

She sighs, checks her watch and nods. 'Let's hope so. I could have done without the drama but at least we've made it, and doubtless the whole of Inverness will have heard us coming.' She turns to look at us. 'Poor pets. You're still looking pretty peely-wally.'

Lining one side of the road leading into town are wooden pens. They're a permanent feature, except that today they hold the disturbed occupants from the floats that men are busily unloading.

We drive past them until we're practically at the town centre.

'This is as near as I can get you and I'll see

167

you here later.' Dod drives off in a caco-phony of noise.

The mart's not far from the station and I wonder if the cattle would prefer to have come by rail. We're certainly delighted to be out of the car. Sucking recovery-pandrops, we watch as cattle lots, seemingly dazed and muddled by their surroundings and the distressed calls of other livestock, are herded through the mart's back entrance. There's so many, that recognising any of ours, seems impossible. Once inside the mart, there's the same doubt. The place is huge and full of ruddy-faced, farmer-looking people not apparently doing anything but gazing as if transfixed by the sight of cattle circling the auction ring.

Whilst Mum scans the place, Elizabeth whispers, 'For goodness' sake, Jane, dinna pit yer hand up in case ye buy any beasts. It'd be easy enough. Imagine what it'd be like if we'd to take our own ones home. Mum wid be furious.'

Mum's aware of the danger. After she gets a programme, and scans it, she checks her watch, then, turning her back on the auction-eer, says, 'It's not going to be long before it's the stirks' turn. You two should go on up to the top. I'll stay at ground level, and don't for the love of Mike do anything daft.'

There's several tiers of wooden planks sur-rounding the ring. When we reach the top one, we sit on our hands, look straight ahead: terrified to move.

'This place minds me on a circus,' I eventually whisper. Elizabeth, summoning up enough courage, casts her eyes heavenwards.

The auction ring's enclosed with bars, handy for those wanting to put their feet on the lower rung whilst resting their arms on the top one. That way they get a closer look at the animals prodded round the ring by men in dust-coloured coats wielding large sticks. The mart smells like a well-run byre. Round and round, the cattle are driven. The place is loud with their confused cries and the voices of men skilled at conversing over large fields. Still, the auctioneer, sitting at a raised desk, is clearly audible as he barks out the bids in a torrent of words and figures. He connects these with frequent whoops. They're quite fun, but after he bangs a wooden stick to mark a completed sale, there's a short respectful silence and we have to recognise that market is a very serious business.

'I dinna understand this. Naebody seems tae be bidding but that's a new lot coming in noo,' I try to say it without my lips moving.

Since, mercifully, we haven't bought anything ourselves, Elizabeth's growing in confidence. She risks, 'I wis wondering that too, but I've spotted some of the mannies round the ring. They must be the ones bidding but the auctioneer'd need eagle eyes to see them. Look!' she points, then looks at her hand accusingly, before snatching it back. 'There's one – he's winking and another one's scratching his head and, see yon manny wi' the black cap? His eyes are rolling that much you'd think he was taking a fit.'

She's probably right about bidders being near the auctioneer. Still, I mustn't blink or blow my nose in case she's wrong. A drip forms at the end of it. It's really annoying. Before it falls I catch it with my tongue.

'Yuck, Jane!'

'Ssh! Look, there's Mum. She's joined the auctioneer.'

She's one of the few women here. I've always thought she was big but seeing her amongst the auction team I realise that she's small really. I might not have recognised our stirks were they not so nosily going up close to the spectators, then kicking up their heels and joining in a race round the ring, as if proving that they don't need any old prodding stick. Mum, looking anxious, stands beside the auctioneer.

'Fine beasts, bred on the hill and owned by Mrs Macpherson. Lively boys too,' he says it approvingly.

Once again, I'm flummoxed as to who's bidding. It's impossible keeping up with

170

what the auctioneer's saying, but when his stick bangs down I see from her smile that things have gone well.

20

DRESSED FOR THE OCCASION

The rain's given way to a watery-looking sun and Inverness High Street looks as if it's celebrating its appearance. Gaelic voices mix with broad Scots and English spoken in an accent that brings the sound of a pibroch to mind. There's colour, if faded, in the ancient tartans of darned shawls worn by women with brown faces carrying baskets of home-made wooden pegs, whilst country people, most recognisable in their rugged features and heavy tweed clothes, jostle for space amongst townsfolk in clothes meant for a softer lifestyle.

'Dod's more like them,' Elizabeth points out. Then, as someone brushes past her, leaving a faint, pleasant smoky air in his wake, she adds, 'And his clothes don't smell of peat.'

'It's probably because we don't burn them. The peat-moss we've got isn't good enough for cutting them, and you're right, Dod *is* a

171

snappy dresser,' says Mum. 'He's so seldom away from the farm, he makes a special occasion of it when he gets the chance. He'll be going back to the mart to see what trade's like and I bet the folkies there will be teasing him.'

'Won't he mind that?' I ask.

'No, he's used to it.' She laughs. 'He says folk are just jealous!'

Even if Inverness is exploding with hill folk who might not be watching where they're going, there's little risk of accidents. When the crowds occasionally spill onto the street, the few cars that crawl along it aren't likely to cause any either. And certainly no driver seems to mind if the one in front stops for a chat with someone they've recognised in the crowds.

'I never thought that driving along a street would be such a social occasion,' says Mum. 'But come on, bairns. Let's get your shoes, find Dod and then we'll get home: I've had enough of crowds and excitement.'

Dod takes the main Inverness to Nairn road home and I'm happy: not only because it's straight but also because I'm nursing a box with bright red leather shoes in it. They've even bars, so it'll save always having to ask someone to tie my laces.

When Elizabeth does it, she says, 'It's high time you learn to do this yourself.' Then she

172

ties them so tightly my feet must think they're being strangled.

I shake the box and the shoes inside it rattle: proof they're not a dream. These new shoes are the nicest ones in the whole wide world. It's unbelievable that they're mine. And they fit properly! The shoe shop's shiny, wooden X-ray machine proved it. I'd only to stand on its step, put the newly shod feet into the slot there, then, peering through one of the viewing holes at the top, see toe-bones. Against a bright green background, they showed black.

'Wriggle your toes,' instructed the shop assistant, looking through the other hole.

'Perfect. Look, they're not touching the shoe. You can see its outline.' She stood aside to let Mum have a peek. 'See? There's plenty room for growth.'

And this clinched it.

Elizabeth gets shoes too, but they're plain brown in hard, ungiving leather. When she protests, Mum says, 'You need them for school. Janie'll get your old ones, but she always gets your cast-offs. It's not good to always be getting things second best. Anyway, Liza, you're getting a bike.'

I feel a bit sorry for Elizabeth. She sighs, frowns, nibbles her nails and looks longingly at my shoes, but not enough for me to admit that I don't really mind getting either her clothes or shoes – it saves breaking them in.

But, ah! These red shoes are perfect for instant wear, even if Mum says they're to be kept for 'best.'

The car sounds marginally better, though the odd rattle can interrupt Mum's chatter about the stirks' sale. 'Well, here's hoping that bloke who bought them hasn't got a garden, and if he has it's stirk-proof. Honestly, until the auctioneer banged down his stick I wasn't sure if there was anybody bidding. The way farming mannies bid's extraordinary, and, you know this, quines' – she turns in her seat so that we feel included in her story – 'that's how they must think it's done at all sales. The other day, Smithy told me, she'd fancied buying a rather pretty dinner set at a local roup. Beel insisted on going with her. Said she'd be the better of a husband being around, especially one with his special bidding technique. Many a bargain he'd got using it.'

I don't think Dod's all that interested. He's too busy commiserating about the lot of the poor farmers who farm the land alongside the road and whose crops are ankle deep in water: but Mum's determined to finish her story. 'Beel couldn't believe the women at the sale could be so loud or rude. According to Smithy, contempt filling his rugged features, then, come the dinner set's turn for auction, Beel prepared the weapons of his extensive armoury.

174

'He pulled his cap over one eye, pretended he was measuring the middle distance with the knob of his stick, but by the time he'd waved the leg of his horn-rimmed specs, the dinner set was knocked down to a cheery wifie who was waving a flamboyant umbrella and bellowing louder than anybody else.'

As if defending the way farmers bid, and disapproving of our laughter, Dod sounds cool. 'Weel, ye widna get any tinks at something like that so I doubt if she came fae those clootie hooses. There wouldn't be much demand for china there.'

We drive past a group of dwellings made up of bits and pieces of cloth draped over hoops. They're built so low to the ground, and covered in such faded cloth, they merge into the scenery. If it wasn't for the smoke coming from an outside fire, you wouldn't know anybody lived there.

Elizabeth's startled. 'Do folk actually bide there?'

'Yes, tinkers, and I don't suppose the Inverness folkies much like having them so close to their town,' says Mum. 'Oh well! I suppose I should remember places like this when I complain about Tombain's draughty corners, but tinks don't like to be tied down to any place so when the sun shines and the mood take them they'll be off, and taking their houses with them.'

From the way she speaks, I get the feeling that on a bonny day she might like to be a tink herself. Did she and our father not go gadding about the countryside selling vegetables from the back of a car? We don't mention this. We think Dod might not like it.

He says, 'Well, even if the rain's stopped and the sun does come out, they'll no go far fae here the day.'

Perhaps telling us that neither might we, the car backfires.

'I thought the exhaust was sorted,' muses Mum whilst Dod gives her a brief lecture on the thrifty measures taken by the car mechanics, who've managed to re-secure it but not sort it completely.

'But I doot it's hardly worth it. A new one's the answer,' he says.

Mum, who's always happy to let Dod be the driver, looks out the window. 'Car mechanics are beyond me,' she sighs.

Still, despite having to wait for a train to go over the Gollanfield level crossing and the crossing-keeper to come and re-open the barricading gates, we do make progress.

There will be a time when 'something must be done!' becomes the cry after a succession of tragic accidents at this crossing. Nowadays, the crossing-keeper, heavy gates, automatic level-crossing barriers and lights have gone. In their place is a wide road. It's built over the railway line, which has so little importance to motorists now it's irrelevant whether or not there's a train running on the track below.

However, the road leading from Nairn to Grantown, and which we now take, remains remarkably unchanged to this day. No fast driver will appreciate its winding way through green sheltered valleys, neat upland farms and woods where lichen flourishes as much as the trees on which it grows.

'We'll not go by Glenferness, we'll take the Relugas way instead. It's that bit closer,' says Dod, as the distant prospect of the Knock appears. We turn off, as if away from it, and onto an even quieter, narrower road. Not far along it is a whitewashed cottage.

'That hoose is right close to the road but if it was any further back from it, it'd fall into the River Findhorn and would you listen to that racket. It must be in spate,' says Elizabeth.

It's true. The threatening roar of a huge body of water surging almost parallel to the road reaches into the car, even if the windows are closed.

'It's when ye canna hear it that ye need tae worry,' says Dod. 'That's how ye ken it's burst its banks.'

Elizabeth says, 'I'll tell Derek that when I go back to school. He says you hear it in that house all the time. His grandfather stays there. He often tells us funny stories about him at school. He calls him Ginga. Mebbe it's the same way that Lala got his name.'

'Is that the Derek Grant who kicked the teacher's milk pail down the schoolie brae?' I ask, knowing that story but liking it so much I want to hear it again. (Derek will in the future swap footballing skills for writing. *Clap Hands for the Singing Molecatcher* is his enchanting recall of his own years growing up in Dunphail.)

But here, Elizabeth's the storyteller. 'Uh huh. Mary's folk supply the schoolhouse with milk every day, and Derek takes it up in a lidded pail to her. One day after school he was returning it and found that it was easy and better fun to kick than carry it.' She looks sad. 'He got a right belting for that.'

'Did they have to get a new milk pail?' Mum asks.

Elizabeth folds her arms, pouts and kicks the back of her seat. 'No. So it couldn't have been that badly damaged.'

The sound of the river gets even closer as we cross the Divie Bridge, a few miles down from the Dulsie one. There's only a brief glimpse of the Findhorn's seething cauldron of black water and brown spume before we start to climb. We continue, up and up, then through the tiny village of Relugas, where crammed-together houses lean, looking as if, domino-like, they might all topple down

178

the slope.

'Might be something to be said for clootie hooses built on the level,' Elizabeth remarks.

At the continued challenge, the car begins to labour.

'If we don't make it, you quines'll have to go oot an' give me push up the hill,' says Dod, so we sit forward, willing the car onwards. The smell of a distressed engine fills the interior, whilst children who've been out playing on the road point to the back of the car and, scattering, shout, 'Fire!'

'Limmers, but I ken fine they're jist up tae mischief!' chuckles Dod, glancing in the mirror. Still I think he's pleased that it's only black smoke coming from the car when, that long climb finally accomplished, we drive past Relugas House. It's made in an attractively pinkish-coloured stone and far grander than a clootie hoose, but it's also sensibly built on flat ground. And now, wheeling past Tillyglen's, whose farmer's shouts can often be heard echoing across our glen, the Knock once more makes it appearance. With Tombain tucked under it, it's very close.

'Nearly home,' says Mum.

'They're very nice, my dear,' says Belinda when I show her the new shoes and tell her about the tinks and how lucky she is to live in a house and built on level ground.

'I don't know about Rabbit,' she whispers,

179

'but I shan't in the least mind living in a caravan when we join the circus. Anyway, most of the time we'll be in a huge tent. Such fun! Now, look, why don't you try tightrope walking. You've never done it before and it'll be another useful skill. It's jolly nice outside now and I could come with you and watch.'

I've done my chores. The hens have been fed, their eggs collected and Duck's angry shouts silenced with her special mash. Elizabeth's helping Dod with the milking and Mum's busy making the tea. It's a good half-hour until then, so there's time for a bit of circus practice.

'Great idea, Belinda. I could get dressed up for it, too.' I squeeze past the toy box in the wardrobe to get my frock. It's sea green in colour, and made in a material that's so soft and shiny that when I go to put it on it slips over my head like water. I give a twirl and the dress floats out. I can't tie the sash at the back, so tuck it into the pockets at the side.

'Now, that is smart,' says Belinda when I put on the shoes. There's not a mirror, so I have to take her word. For a moment, I consider staying inside, putting on the Hungarian folk music record and trying out some balletic moves, but Mum'll hear. Going by past experience, she'll laugh and I hate that. No, it's best to go outside, where I can practise at the back of the house: out of sight.

All dressed up's made me feel too excited to even speak to Rabbit, but I'll tell him about everything when we get back.

The fence posts have pointed tops but they're broader than the high wire the circus performer used, so they should make the first try easy enough. Remembering the importance of a balancing stick, I cast around for something appropriate.

'Look, Belinda, somebody's left a rake and hoe lying against the fence. They'll be the very dab. Now, you sit there, and you'll get a good view.'

Popped on top of a strainer post, she doesn't look that safe, so I add, 'Don't bother clapping, you might fall off.'

She doesn't answer, probably because she's already looking a bit squint. I'd right her, only getting on top of the fence demands concentration. The rake and hoe do help, even if they are a bit short, but once I've reached my goal, they give a sort of balance.

A late sun shines on my back and a gentle wind ruffles the dress. I'm ready! I steady myself, then inch forward and make it past the first post, but as I try for the next one the sash slips out of one pocket. It's a distraction. I clasp my balancing poles, realising belatedly they'd be of more help if their length matched. The fence posts are still a bit wet. It's not good news because my

181

shoes with their leather soles don't have the grip of rubber ones. Midges start to gather in a cloud above my head. It's useless trying to shake them away. They're after blood and persist. Suddenly, without warning, Belinda tumbles off the post. There's a sickening crack as she hits her head on a stone.

Diverted, I wobble, then, stifling a cry, overbalance. I'd have fallen with the same horrible-sounding repercussion as poor Belinda had the frock hem not caught on a pointed fence-post top. At least it slows descent. However, accompanying it, comes the ominous sound of tearing material.

21

A WEDDING!

It's all a matter of being helpful, and the waitress could do with some advice.

I lean over the table to say, 'If we're haen soup at hame, we usually keep oor plate for the next course. It fair saves on the washing.'

She nods and winks. 'Don't you worry. This is a hotel, so you'll be getting a clean plate for your meat one.'

Very occasionally, we've had afternoon tea

at Austin's Tea Rooms in Elgin. There, the waitresses wear the same kind of black uniform with crisp white aprons and cuffs. As we didn't have to take a turn at the sink there, I suppose the rule's the same here. Still, these present surroundings feel even less comfortable than the tea room, with its hushed chat, shining silver teapots, water jugs, spotless white tablecloths and carefully folded napkins.

The one that I've got's so big that despite being tucked in at the neck of my blue velvet dress it still reaches below my knees. It feels like a tent and is so well starched I can hardly move. Elizabeth's similarly trapped, although she seems more bothered about finding a hair in her soup.

'You're always finding one of them,' I tell her. 'You're so bloomin' fussy!'

She lifts her chin up, freeing it from the napkin's hold. 'I am not, and would you stop fidgeting?'

The sun shining through the hotel's dining-room window makes the Moray Firth it overlooks sparkle. It highlights an entombed feeling the napkin obviously shares as it slips from anchorage then shoots onto the floor. As I bend down to get it back, I'm struck by how dull in comparison to the view of the firth is the sea of dark-coloured clothes glimpsed from under the table.

It's laid out in a U-shape and might make

183

me play a guessing game of when and from where the waitress's feet might appear, but I can't stay down too long. Surfacing, I appreciate that from here, at least, the guests' outfits, perked up with button-hole flowers, make for a jollier sight. And a lot of effort's gone into setting the table. There's enough laid out glassware and cutlery to start an ironmonger's shop. Mum's not around to tell us which to use. I watch carefully.

She and Dod are sitting at the top of the table and get served first. He's looking particularly smart with a spray of white heather in his suit button hole, whilst Mum's lovely in her navy blue frock, and hat and suede high heels all in matching colour. They're so occupied talking and laughing with each other that we might be near them but it feels as if they're miles away. They both look very happy.

It's funny getting a different plate for each course and I might be wondering why I'm in a fancy hotel in Nairn, worrying about food spilling over another new frock, if I hadn't overheard Granny's recent conversation with Mum.

'Look here, Betty, you can't have one of your bairns at your wedding, wearing a frock repaired with Copydex.'

'Well, Mother, actually it was only torn at the hem and I was that proud of mending it, you'd have to look very closely to spot it.

184

Besides, Janie wouldna mind.' Mum sounded exasperated. 'Anyway, God knows what she might get up to at a wedding. I couldn't stand it if she spoilt another frock.'

But Granny was determined. 'For a start, and by way of example to the girls, you should stop taking the Lord's name in vain. Then, and with a bit of grace, start to accept help instead. My books are selling well and I'm happy to pay for both the lassies to wear something decent, especially as we're having a meal at the Golf View Hotel. I know the head housekeeper there. She'll make sure everything's right.'

'I hate fuss,' Mum tried, but Granny was unstoppable.

'Well, you've had your own way about keeping the actual ceremony private and it's going to be done by a minister this time around, but it's not every bairn who gets a chance to go to a wedding meal, even if it is their mother's one.' Granny took a breath. 'And at least *her* mother'll be present at *this* one.'

Mum's voice rises. 'We're surely not going over all that again, Mother! You know as well as I do that, apart from all the expense of a flash affair, neither Ian nor I wanted a lot of ceremony and we certainly didn't ever think there was anything wrong with a registry office wedding.'

'Especially when your father was a minister

and we knew nothing about it until the deed was done. It was the talk of Hopeman for ages and, for all I know, still is.' I think this must have really annoyed Granny because she's just a wee note off shouting.

But Mum's not bothered. 'Och well, as you say yourself, the bairns can aye say they were there when their mother got married. That should stop the tongues wagging about her last wedding. Anyway, the fact that I'm marrying someone who came to work on the farm and is nine years younger than me's probably giving folk plenty to speak about already.'

Whenever I ask Mum her age, and for many years after, she'll say she's forty-eight. That's odd because Elizabeth says she's sure that's not true and Mum's joking. Sometimes it's hard to tell with grown-ups, but this time I'm pretty sure of my facts.

'Did you know that Mum and Dod are getting married, Elizabeth?' I asked one day that we were playing on the see-saw cart.

'Course. I told you a'ready, but I dinna expect you were listenin'.' She spat out something green, then stuck out her tongue, squinting down to have a look at it.

'What're ye eatin?'

'Sooraks. Mum sometimes calls them sorrel. They're fine but ye widna want tae eat a hale panful.'

'Ye'll get a sair belly.' It's the best I could

come up with. However, inspiration came later.

'Your tongue's still green. I bet it'll stay that colour for the wedding.'

So, here we are, and we're actually at its celebratory meal, and sadly Elizabeth's tongue's no longer green and of course Mum's getting a better deal than poor old Mrs Ferret and Dod looks great and our mother beautiful. Still, I can't imagine *ever* wanting to wear any of the stuff that she's got on, unlike what Granny has stored at her house. Now, it *is* beautiful. We're going to be staying with her and as soon as we go back to Fern Cottage she's promised that we'll get a shot of it.

The meal drags on. It's followed by sherry in tiny glasses for the ladies, and not much bigger ones for the men's whisky and well-diluted Kia-Ora orange juice for us. We all raise them after something called toasts. When Dod and Mum, together, cut a cake very like the type displayed in the Ashers' window, there's much applause. Considering how easily Dod cuts kindling sticks, I find this astonishing. Then, at last, covered in confetti, they leave the hotel, hurry into the car and drive off to something called a honeymoon.

'I hope that exhaust holds,' says someone, not entirely joking. The taxi taking us back to Granny's house hasn't that problem, but

Elizabeth, who's tripped and fallen getting into it, is crying.

She so seldom does, I'm magnanimous. 'If you dry your eyes and blow your nose, you can have first shot of Granny's skirt.'

It was part of her wedding outfit. It's a long skirt and smells of mothballs. Much as she can be a bit tricky about some things, she always makes an exciting ceremony of taking it out of its trunk, shaking it free from rustling tissue paper, then handing it over to us.

She seems to like watching when we take turns wearing it. It might be old but it's lovely and, even if it's so long we've to hike it up, it floats into a bell shape when we twirl about in it.

Elizabeth, tears now dried, fingers the flimsy material. 'It's got such a soft feel but what's the colour? It's kind of funny.'

Granny gives a romantic sigh. 'That's old gold and it's made of silk. Ah! But those were the good old days when girls had tiny waists.' She looks at us: her pale blue eyes gleam behind the spectacles. 'You two might have a bit to grow up the way but certainly not out, because it looks to me as if the skirt already fits there. You'd have been lost in the blouse, though.'

'Where's it?' I ask.

'Long gone, I'm afraid.'

'Mum's dress is lovely too,' says Elizabeth,

climbing into the skirt and stroking the sides. But on this occasion we seem to have lost our audience. Granny's apparently lost in her own world and has forgotten that we're here. It's probably what happens if you live on your own. You start speaking to God.

'Oh, Lord, I do hope that Betty's done the right thing.' Now she's muttering, but loud enough for us to hear.

Elizabeth stops mid-twirl. 'I don't think you should worry about Mum,' she says.

Granny starts, and if it had been anybody other than her, I'd have sworn she's gone a bit pink. 'I'm sorry! You're right. Of course, Eliza – it's only–' she falters. 'Would Dod be a bittie short in the grain?'

'What does that mean?' Elizabeth's voice is sufficiently cold for Granny to drop the subject and for me to think she's criticising Dod.

And there I was thinking that Granny liked him! There's no doubt that she absolutely loves his driving. Whenever she gets into our car, she holds onto her hat, leans forward and, as soon as the car starts, she shouts, 'Faster, Dod, faster!' She seemed to like being in his company as well, but after the wedding and this remark I'm not so sure. Maybe it's because, recently, Elizabeth and I heard him scold her for wanting to pinch some peats off a stack we were driving past.

'That's stealing,' he'd said.

'Och, Dod, I'm just wanting one or two.'

But Dod, putting his foot down in more ways than one, said, 'It's easy seen ye dinna ken the hard work involved in cutting them.'

Maybe Elizabeth's thinking about this conversation when we're getting ready for bed because she says, 'I think that Granny's looking a bittie sad. Well, you know how she always makes us kneel at the side of the bed to say our prayers?'

'Uh huh. Says it's awful Mum doesn't make us do it at home.'

Ignoring this, Elizabeth presses on. 'What d'you think about us singing her that song she taught us. She loves hearing it.'

'The Peat Fire Flame? Och, Elizabeth! It's no very cheery – she aye greets when she hears it. I've a better idea,' I say, then, prepared to make a sacrifice. 'After we do the Lord's Prayer, she likes us to *God Bless* our favourite people.' I pause, thinking about the mischief of keeping Granny anxiously waiting for her name to appear, which it does, but usually after Mum, Dod, Elizabeth, Rabbit and Belinda.

'Mm.'

'Well, this time, I'll put her name first.'

'That certainly would be a first,' says Elizabeth coldly. 'Sometimes you can be a right wee pig. No, let's put a tartan rug between us, pretend it's a fire and sing her that song.

She really does love it. Poor Granny. She doesn't ask us for anything and she did give us the bonny frocks.'

So we surprise Granny, warm our hands over the imaginary flame and, though I know that Mum would prefer electric, we sing about people yearning for the light hill folk apparently long for. When Granny cries, I do not say to my sister, 'I told you.' Instead, when it comes to the *God Bless* bit I keep my word and give her hard work at writing a mention, too.

22

A LITTLE HELP GOES A LONG WAY

It's Sunday, and after going to church, the next highlight's a visit to our grandfather's grave. It might be in Nairn but it seems a long way from Fern Cottage. I'm tired and am only halfway there, whilst Granny and Elizabeth are practically out of sight.

'Come on, Janie. You're making me feel like a duck trailing her young. Catch up!'

But I can't. Neither Elizabeth nor Granny consider that someone with shorter legs than them has to work twice as hard. Nor are they fussed about stepping on cracks in the

191

pavement or crossing a road dominated by apparently blind old women cycling on basket-bearing bikes. Eventually, however, I get to the last frontier before the steps leading up to the cemetery. It's called the Jubilee Footbridge and spans the River Nairn. The water's so fast flowing, deep and brown it could be home for loads of kelpies. Avoiding them means a race over the bridge and managing to catch up, just as Granny's asking, 'Do you remember your grandfather, Elizabeth?'

'Oh yes. He used to sit me on his knee and call me his little lady.' Elizabeth is matter of fact, whilst Granny, who'd been looking rather glum (again), perks up. For someone with bunions, she's remarkably light-footed and practically bounds up the steps. 'Come on, slow-coaches!' she calls down from the top.

She's got a very acute sense of smell, which might explain her thing about peat fires. The bunch of sweet peas she'd asked us to pick from her garden, and which she now holds in her hand, seem a better deal.

'Dolly Mixtures are the same colour but don't smell half as bonny,' I say.

'You're right. These are my favourite flower. I had them in my wedding bouquet,' she explains, then, pointing to a nearby water tap, says 'Fill up that green vase, will you, Janie?'

She means the metal-green fluted one

192

placed on our grandfather's gravestone. I'm curious to know what water sounds like dropped into it from a distance, but Granny stops the experiment, saying, 'Please don't start guttering about – if you splash in any more, you'll get us all wet.'

The flowers make a sweet statement, colourful against the grey of the gravestone. Granny looks hard at it, pats the top of it, nods her head as if she's been having some secret discussion, then blows her nose.

Seagulls wheel above us. Sometimes they make such a clatter of noise you'd think they were the leaders of an angry Nairn gossip group, but today there's only a few, their cries desolate in the still air.

'They sound like lost kittens,' I say.

'More like the cries of the souls of lost sailors,' Granny says, at which point my sister raises her eyebrows.

I'm about to ask if the rippling voice of the nearby river would be confusing for men of the sea, but Granny tucks her hankie up her sleeve and, taking both our hands, says, 'Time to go home, and let's walk together this time. When we get back, you could maybe read me a wee passage from the Bible, Elizabeth? I'd like that. You're fair coming on with your reading. The doctor says I've got something called glaucoma and reading small print's especially difficult for my old eyes.'

I could boast that my sister's had plenty practice with the *Red Letter* but I've a feeling neither she nor Granny would like to hear that.

Monday promises more excitement.

'There's four-leaf clovers in the grass bit under the old apple tree. Go and see if you can find any,' says Granny.

Her garden wall, like all the others in that street, backs onto the Nairn Show Field, where preparations are underway for the Annual Agricultural Show. High hessian sacking's been put up between the house gardens and the entire length of the field to block access and the view. However, if we climb Granny's apple tree, which stands knee-deep in the middle of a patch of long raggedy-looking grass, we can just glimpse a little of what's going on in the field. It mightn't be much but there's a bit more to see there than what's supposed to be flour-ishing in the growth below.

'Granny says clover'll bring good luck and, if we get any, she'll show us how to press them.' Even to myself I sound dubi-ous, but Elizabeth's more determined.

'We'll never find anything in grass this long. We'll need to cut it first, an' I bet Granny'll be pleased when we do. There's a lawn mower in the garden shed. I'm sure it'll be easy to use. Come on.'

We didn't expect the machine to be so heavy. It needed our combined strength to lug it out from behind an old chair, a broken wicker basket and some rusting pails of distemper paint. An ancient shovel gets knocked off a peg on the wall in the process.

'That could've brained me,' complains Elizabeth and gives the machine a spiteful yank.

As we eventually manage to haul it from the shed, then over the gravel-chipped, box-hedged path leading to the grass, I start to think there's something to be said for a raggedy green patch that surrounds an old apple tree. There's storybooks with pictures so like it, if it wasn't for the prospect of finding those good luck leaves, I might have argued about continuing with the plan.

Elizabeth, however, is steely-eyed; and when we finally make it onto the grass she grips the machine handle, saying, 'Jane! Don't bother sitting down. We're going to have to do this together.'

It's a slow job. The machine's blades, which originally looked so dangerous, are reluctant to turn and when, with a deal of sweat and back-breaking effort, we get a sufficient run to get the mower to move, they seem to merely flatten the grass.

'I don't know why there's a roller,' pants the head gardener. 'The blades are doing that instead of their proper job.'

As the machine is forced along, it makes an ugly rasping sound like it's echoing our disenchantment.

Normally we'd love to see the sun, but today we're hot enough without it beating down on us. My face feels as if it's on fire.

'You've got dirt on your lips,' observes Elizabeth.

I scrub at it until she says she thinks it's actually freckles. An hour passes and, apart from three bald, pale wiggly-looking cut-grass swathes, we're not much further on. The machine's voice is heard less and less, and certainly not by Granny. She's busy inside with Jessie Catto, who's her typist. She's so small she's dwarfed by a typewriter machine built on the lines of a traction engine but driven by the smoke of Jessie's fags instead of steam.

As well as books that carry a Christian message, Granny writes romantic stories: surprising, really, when she talks so fondly of our grandfather but often tells us that she thinks kissing's vulgar. We might wonder if she's saying the same to Jessie, who's getting married to Frank soon. But they're deaf to anything outside, where a squawking seagull scolds us from the top of one of the house chimneys.

'If Dod was here, he'd cut it in seconds with a scythe,' I say, looking at my hands, 'and he wouldn't get blisters either.'

'No, and I think we're cutting off the clover heads as well.' Elizabeth gives the machine a reflective kick. 'I bet it's nice down at the beach.'

There's a roaring noise in my head. I'm unsure if it's the distant sound of Nairn's sea reaching us on the warm air or my brain's being boiled. The fruiting season for the garden's strawberries and raspberries is past, and the plums growing on their tree near the house are still too sour to taste.

'I'm that tired I canna even be bothered going inside for a drink,' says Elizabeth. I'd agree if I'd the energy. We're leaving times between action and exhaustion so long now that small birds are coming down from their vantage point in the apple tree to peck at grubs we've made homeless. Someone in the show field must be hammering in a fence post nearby – signs that at least some industry's taking place somewhere close. It makes an oddly soothing sound as we throw ourselves down on one of the newly cut strips and close our eyes.

This, we are shortly to find out, is as stupid a move as is trying to cut Granny's grass.

23

SHOWIES TIME

Sunshine glints on the blade.

We've raced upstairs, slamming into the bathroom, locking the door, then, together, peeping through its window onto the garden below. Down beside the apple tree, an old man in khaki overalls leans towards the scythe he's holding. In as practised a way as Lala sharpens his razor, he starts to sweep a sharpening stone over the cutting edge. The metallic rhythmic sound reaches us through the window we check and re-check is secure.

'That must be Granny's gardener. I didna know she had one. I wonder if she knows he's such a horrid manny,' says Elizabeth, her voice trembling. 'If she heard him using all those swear words, she'd give him a week of Bible readings.'

I'd be glad of Rabbit's company, but Mum had said, 'Why don't you leave him at home with Belinda? He'd keep her company.'

I was about to argue when she'd held her finger up, before continuing, 'You know, she's probably still recovering from yon bad fall she had recently. She must've had a terrible fright. It's a wonder she didn't have her head cracked open. Precious things need to be kept safe, Janie.'

Considering the present situation, I imagine both she and Belinda would be pleased I'd heeded her warning.

'But that manny wouldna really have cut off our heads, would he?' I manage, despite chattering teeth.

Elizabeth nibbles a nail, sniffs, then says, 'Maybe not, but I'm glad we didna stay tae find out, and that this door's got a lock on it.'

I'd have stuck out my tongue if my busy teeth hadn't stopped it. It's probably best they did, because the man's seen us looking out at him and shakes his fist before getting back to sharpening his scythe.

It's early evening and, after what seems to have been a long week, Mum and Dod have come to collect us. We haven't much to put in our suitcase, but it's leather and weighs a ton. Still, we've managed to slide it down the stairs. Now, and only leaving a slight chip on the newel post, it's waiting collection.

Heaving it into the car, Dod says, 'I'm hearing you quines have been having a go at hay-making.'

'Oh, but you're an awful tease,' says Granny, who's come to supervise. It must be the tone of Dod's voice because she hears *everything* that he says. 'I think Hamish was sorry he gave the girls such a fright. It's just a pity that he's so short in the grain.'

I register disapproval in the words but fail to make a connection. Dod's never threatened us with a scythe!

Meanwhile Granny carries on, 'But he was in a bit of a hurry to get on with helping the folk at the show field. He'd only popped in to give a quick cut to my grass. He wasn't expecting to find it turned into something like a battleground. In a way, I suppose, it's my fault. I told the girls to go out and look for luck.' She smiles a little. 'And they certainly didn't expect to get Hamish! You know, I'd quite a job coaxing the two of them out of the bathroom. Who knows? They might still be behind that locked door if I hadn't said you might take them to the Showies when you came to collect them.'

Elizabeth and I exchange excited glances. We're never out late.

Nairn has acres of green links and, soured of recent garden activities, we'd been coaxing Granny to take us there. With its background of the Moray Firth and hills, enchanting in a paler blue behind it, it's got an area that forms a natural amphitheatre. It's where the Nairn Games are held. Two or three weeks beforehand, on a nearby piece of rough ground, the travelling fair people start to arrive. We'd been watching them set up their amusements, stalls and rides. They're all in such brightly decorated colours you couldn't fail to notice them, even if you've to wait until night-time before the Showies actually start.

And even supposing Granny did take us to them, then I bet Elizabeth would fall into the outside paddling pool first.

'I don't know why you bother going near it. You're always falling in. You'd be useless in a circus,' I'd said, as we inevitably trailed back to the house to dry her out. 'You should stick to paddling in the sea. You manage fine there.'

Her reply was predictable. 'I dinna want tae join any old circus an' I only go look at the paddling pool to please Granny. She says it's one of Nairn's finest features. Anyway I'm trying to get better at balancing but the wee wall surrounding it's a bit narrow. It's easy to slip off and if I didn't always fall in first, I bet you would as well.'

Now we hear Granny saying to Mum and Dod, 'I've found the paddling pool exerts a strange siren call to Elizabeth, so I'd advise avoiding it and heading straight for the Showies. It would make a nice end to everyone's holiday.'

So we're going! In our excitement, Elizabeth and I hug each other, then Granny, and, on account of the vulgarity of kissing, give her a swift goodbye peck before getting into the car.

As we drive off, I look back and see her waving both hands, and imagine her going back into that big house – full of shadows and huge bedrooms where mirrored wardrobe doors swing out unexpectedly with your reflection strangely coming towards you. I suppose she'll make for the sitting room. There, our grandfather's framed photograph sits over the enormous, highly polished radio, which is never switched on because she says she can't hear it. Then all she'll have for company is the memory of our grandfather and our visit.

As if reading my thoughts, Elizabeth says, 'Granny could have come with us. I bet she'd love a go on these.' We're parked near the Showies and she means chairs, swaying high up and suspended on flimsy-looking chains. They clink in the light sea breeze. 'I dinna fancy goin' on them,' I say. 'They could easy take off and land at Cromarty.'

'Maybe, but I bet she'd love the music,' says Elizabeth.

It's certainly a lot cheerier than the organ so earnestly played in her church by the sober, grey-suited organist. Deaf or not, Granny would certainly hear this brand of music, but even as its tinny sound shrieks above the soft crash of the waves, and we hurry towards it, the voices of the folk selling their wares rise over all, even the generators, into the gathering dusk.

'You know, girls, I think this is better than a circus,' says Mum. 'It's got all the glitter, thrills and excitement of one but without any distress cries coming from animals happier in the jungle.'

'Oh, bad luck, wee ones. Try again!' cries a neat, brown-faced woman, her eyes as bright as her dancing earrings. Her stall, like the others, is outlined in coloured lights, combining with the music to make it look alive and jolly.

She hands us three more ping-pong balls, which, when thrown, promptly leap out of the jam jars set before us.

'Roll up, roll up. It's easy to win,' she says, turning to other custom when it's obvious that both Mum and Dod are unwilling to hand over more money. We wander amongst country folk with sun-bleached eyebrows and skin as burned as the show people, and townsfolk, a little paler, and children whose faces are hidden behind huge clouds of something very pink.

'It's candy floss. Terrible for your teeth,' says Mum, who's got false ones.

'Come on! Let's have a go on the dodgems, and you can drive, Lizzie,' says Dod.

I cling onto Mum's hand in case she follows, amazed that Elizabeth's dashed to jump alongside him in something that looks like a bath with a steering wheel.

Her knuckles show white as she grips it.

She stares ahead. Nothing happens.

'There's maybe not enough petrol,' I say to Mum, which may well be what my sister's saying to Dod, but then he braces himself, the cars jolt forward and Elizabeth starts to spin the steering wheel as if her life depends on it. And maybe it does, I think, watching the other drivers trying to crash into each other.

'I hope she's not going to drive the tractor like that,' I say.

A wire's fixed to the back of each dodgem, which reaches up to the top of the carousel to make sparking connections. Apparently there's entertainment in either being blown up or caught in a massive pile-up. When, after a few minutes – and there's been a satisfactory level of screams, bangs and yells from the car occupants – a power switch must be thrown because all the cars stop. It's impossible to think that people will consider their money well spent when they stagger out of their killing machines.

'Ooh! That was great,' says my sister, wiping her hands on her blouse and looking dazed but delighted.

'I thought you pair might hiv joined us.' Dod sounds disappointed.

'I'd much prefer the waltzers,' says Mum. 'A little less dangerous. Look!' She points to a carousel, made vivid with swirling brightly coloured artworks painted on its sides. The

204

roof is striped in white and a red the same shade as that painted on the steps leading up to the ride.

Mum leads the way. 'Come on, there's one seat left.'

Parked on a surface, bumpy as the Glenferness switchbacks, is a line of chariots. Outside they're decorated in a mixture of gold and crimson swirls, whilst inside the upholstery is all in red. I've never been surrounded by such rich colours or seen a ceiling lit by so many light bulbs. This must be how Cinderella felt, I think, as we climb aboard.

'Bunch up, quines,' says Dod, sitting in the middle and stretching out his arms behind him so that he can pull us together. For a moment, there's only the sound of clinking coins as the ride attendant collects the money.

'That's right. Hold onto the wee one,' he says, then pushes down a switch. Elizabeth's opted to lean forward to clutch the shining chrome safety handle in front of us, whilst Mum and Dod suddenly do the same, one-handed, the other holding onto me. The music drowns out my protest for independence when, with a huge surge of power, our chariot takes off.

There's an almighty force powering us up and down the bumps, whilst we spin round and round in dizzying turns. Beyond the

205

enchanted circle that holds the fairground, it's dark. The sea stretches a planet away from human noise and light. I'm glad, now, to be tucked snug between the adults, but Mum's laughing so much she says she's going to lose her teeth if she hasn't got a free hand to keep them in.

'Stop!' she shrieks.

'Dinna fash yersell,' laughs the operator. 'Ye'll get them back afterwards, unless they fit me better.' Then with his shirt straining over his barrel chest, he stretches his sunburnt muscled arms across the back of our car and gives it an extra spin.

24

SCHOOL!

Back home, Belinda, who's tucked under my bedcovers, whispers so she doesn't disturb Elizabeth. 'My dear, what a good thing you didn't take us to Nairn. Thanks to all your cold compresses, my head got better after my fall but, just think, we could all have lost our heads. What a common sort of man that gardener is! You girls must have had a dreadful experience. What d'you say, Rabbit?'

But Rabbit only hums the beginning of a hymn that Granny likes to sing. It's called 'Abide with Me.' I think he's a little off key but appreciate the thought.

'That's terrible singing. I wish you'd shut up, Jane,' sighs Elizabeth. 'I'm trying to get to sleep. Are you not remembering it's school tomorrow?'

I could tell her I'm only singing to accompany Rabbit, but I'd like to keep her awake so she too can reassure me.

'What was your first day at school like?'

She takes a deep breath, then, 'Some of the pupils threw my schoolbag into the ditch. We didn't get either free milk or school meals then, so Mum had to make me sandwiches and they got wet. They tasted horrible, but other than the cocoa the teacher's sister Miss May always made for us I'd have been starving.'

I'm scandalised. 'That's terrible! If that happened to me, I'd tell Dod on them.'

'He wasn't our father then,' says Elizabeth.

'Neither he was. Goodnight,' I say, wondering: if Mum's changed her name to Bremner, will Dod turn into Dad? I could ask my sister but don't. Her answer would give her the last word.

After Dod and Mum marry, life doesn't seem much changed – except if he's not already out doing farm work, Nell will be glued to his side, watching him having breakfast.

He's there today and, as I join him, he says, 'Big day for you today, Janie.' He dips a spoon into a cup of milk, then transfers it to his plate of porridge. It makes a measured accompaniment to every mouthful. I copy him, liking the contrast of the spoon made cold by its milk dip against the hot porridge it holds.

Nell watches with the same degree of interest but she's waiting, ready to lick the floor clean should anything fall on it.

'Puss, puss!' Mum's calling.

Pansy, who's obviously brought up her family to fend for themselves, has decided on an easier life as a house cat. She's been sitting in front of the fire, waiting until she hears the sound of a saucer being put on the scullery's stone floor. On her way there, she aims a careless swipe at Nell. She, however, never changes her gaze. Her teeth begin to chatter and she starts to slaver.

'Beasts! We're never done feeding them,' says Dod, and hands Nell a bread crust. 'Och, but you're a greedy brute. See, Janie, if you're ever offering a dog food, don't tempt him, give it to him right away, then he won't snatch your fingers and maybe get a taste for them.'

Mum comes into the kitchen. 'After having your porridge the old-fashioned way, that'll be the second lesson of the day, Janie,' she says. 'Now, as soon as you're finished, and as it *is* your first day, I'll drive you to school. You can walk home, though. You'll have Kenny for company.'

She means one of the children of the farm help who's come to work at Tombain and lives in the Tomdow cottage. They only came just before the wedding so we haven't had much of a chance to get to know them, but I'm pleased. At least the little girl who everybody denies stays there (but I'm convinced does) will now have some company.

As we get into the car, Mum searches in her dungarees and, after going through most of its pockets, finds a sixpence. 'Ha! I knew there was another one.' She hands it over. 'I forgot that you'll need a play-piece too. That should buy you enough for the week. Elizabeth already has her money so, if you ask her – nicely, mind – she'll maybe get you something at the shop as well. Now that she's got her bike, she'll have the time to nip over to the shop and get you something too. Otherwise you might starve!'

She says it with such relish I assume she's joking. More serious, however, is the way that she slams the car into reverse and, looking forwards, remarks, 'Hallelujah! She's started first go. She must've known we need to catch Eliza. Thank heavens our garage hasn't a door.'

As we shoot out there's a clamour of farm-yard cries. 'Damn beasts aye getting in my way!' says my animal-loving mother, braking hard. As she searches for a better gear, I see Duck pecking the drake, bought, supposedly, to give her husbandly company. The poor bird tries to escape but Duck's determined he gets a piece of her mind as well as her beak. As he runs for cover to the henhouse, she flaps her wings to help him get her message. She's definitely having the last word.

'She's such an old rogue,' says Mum, back in control and driving away from the noise. Hunched over the steering wheel with her nose practically scraping the windscreen, she speaks light-heartedly. I can't believe she's as cheery when we get to school and she's waving goodbye. She's obviously forgotten that even if I've been looking forward to going to school, it's still a bit nerve-racking.

Seeing Elizabeth is kind of reassuring. I expect she's there to make sure I don't get the same first-day treatment as she did.

Instead, she says, 'Did Mum give you money?'

As soon as I show her my sixpence, she grabs it. 'That'll buy us loads of biscuits,' she says. 'If you'd been any later, I wouldn't have had time to get to the shop before school goes in. Quick now! I don't want to be late for Miss Milne.'

Her anxiety's a surprise because Elizabeth

likes our teacher. I'm sure I will too. Having seen both her and her sister in our church, I know that they smile in recognition to everyone in the congregation as if they mean it. They're always smartly dressed and wear face powder, which, even if it is laid on thickly, doesn't hide the paleness of their complexions. Miss Milne's as stout as Miss May is thin. She house-keeps in the adjoining 'tied' school house, which shares the school's grey exterior but not its high windows.

I will learn that the top of the rake and hoe's handles, wielded by the boys on occasional gardening duties, will be all that can be seen from inside our classroom. Chat and banter might float in if the windows are open, but Miss Milne gives them scant attention. It's possible, however, that Miss May might look out from her netted and flounced curtain windows which also give out onto the garden. She'll easily see the gardeners from there. If she does, she's unlikely to pin much hope of a bumper crop from the patch on which they are supposedly labouring.

The garden's walled on every side but the one where laurel bushes line the way to an open shelter-shed. From there, Elizabeth's now wheeling her bike. The minute she disappears, a boy advances.

'You're Lizzie's wee sister,' he says. He's wearing a grey knitted pullover under a grey jacket, with matching short trousers. His teeth show white in a sunburnt face – and in a grin that makes me uneasy. 'I bet you're no' half as hardy as her.'

I tighten my grip on my schoolbag. 'Am so!'

Another two boys join him. Beginning to look like a team, they size me up.

'What's in the bag?'

'Mind your own business.' Let down by a quavering voice, I stamp my foot, wishing I'd their rackety boots. They'd make a louder statement and, if a real war broke out, could come in handy.

'Ha, ha! Just a wee quinie but cheeky with it,' says the boy who's a fine one to speak. He makes a grab for the bag. Inside it, there's only a pencil, rubber and a bit of torn-up towel for wiping a slate clean, but I'm determined to defend it. I swing it round my head, then, aiming it at his, cry, 'I'm telling Dod on you, you insolent boy!'

Ever since Mum said the stirks had this look about them and explained its meaning, I've been dying to try the word out. This moment seems right, but whilst one of the group looks as if the word appeals to him, the other two find it hilarious.

'Ha, ha! Dod's *insolence*. That's a big word for sicca wee quinie. We'll call you *Dod's Insolence*, then! Dod's Insolence!' They make it sound like a song, attracting the interest of the other pupils until another lad, taller than

212

any of the three, ambles towards us, hands in his pockets, ball under his arm.

'Come on, boys. Pick on somebody your ain size,' he says. 'Whit aboot a quick game o' fitba?'

'Good idea, Davy, she's ower small,' they agree and troop after him to the playing field. There's a big oak tree in the middle, which spreads out sheltering arms and, along with a thrown-down jacket, makes for a handy goalpost.

Soon after, Elizabeth returns. 'I was going at such a rate I near fell off, carrying those bloomin' biscuits.' She brandishes a brown paper bag stuffed full of pink wafer-thin-looking things. They might have hampered her progress, but her timing's perfect.

A bell, repeatedly swung, rings out.

'Schoo-all,' everybody shouts, so I join in, except I think they're shouting 'Stoo-all'.

'Ha, ha! She can say "insolence" but nay "school". The words float mockingly after me as I join the group of pupils gathering to flock behind the stout, bell-wielding, clock-holding figure of Miss Milne into school.

The boys' boots clatter on the classroom's wooden floor, whilst dust particles, caught by a sunbeam, dance in the air, disturbed by a slightly open window. On one wall, there's pictures of scenes of farms and farmyards, where Duck might be interested to learn that here her relations mingle happily with

213

hens, and smiling men in spotless clothes lean on clean implement. Taking up a lot more space on another, and hung by string over a stout nail, is a map drawn on oiled cloth. It means nothing to me, and is of little interest, especially as its colours, if varied, are faded.

With the care of someone handling a precious item, Miss Milne places the clock on top of the piano, then, spreading her dress tidily about her, places her ample rear on the stool. It'll be the only time she doesn't stand in the classroom and might explain why, throughout the day, she'll lean so much either over her lectern-type desk or against the cast-iron radiator on which she winds her soft, pale plump fingers. Already her feet, poised over the piano pedals, are slightly swollen.

'Good morning, children.' She bows her head as the pupils, gathering round, respond in a sing-song way. Spreading her fingers over the keys, she looks over her shoulder and says casually, 'Before we start, I'd like you to welcome some new faces. We have Jane, Victor, Sandy and Violet.'

There's just enough time to clock that those grouped together in shy acknowledgement of their names must be the Tomdow family before Miss Milne continues, 'Now, we'll sing, "Jesus Loves Me"'.

Thanks to Granny, Rabbit and church, I

know the words and join in as lustily as the cheeky boy. He assumes a look of angelic innocence and turns up the volume. I follow. Then Elizabeth nudges and shoots me one of her darkest of looks. 'Ssh! Not so loud,' she whispers.

I sigh. It could be a long day.

25

AN EDUCATIONAL EXPERIENCE

'Alec Macgregor. Come out here!'

Miss Milne wheels round from the blackboard, lifts the lid of her desk and takes out a heavy-looking brown strap, forked at the end. Her chalky fingers grasp it whilst her soft voice grows as sharp as her well-powdered nose. There's a momentary silence broken by a droning sound coming from the road. It's a passing tractor. I wish I was on it.

There's two girls in Primary Seven: Violet and Moira.

'Moira, you'll be Jane's pupil-teacher. You'll be looking after and helping her settle in,' Miss Milne had instructed.

Moira does her very best, saying, 'First day's aye the worst. Jist keep yet heid doon.' I like her open, sunny-natured face and the

215

way she seems happy to share her desk and bench. It's even vaguely reassuring that she's quite unfazed by the sight of our belt-wielding teacher. 'Dinna you worry. Teacher usually only belts the boys,' she whispers.

It's no comfort to a small one sitting near-by. He's got large anxious eyes and three-penny-sized freckles that stand out on his white face. He begins to lick his lips and drum his fingers on his desk, gazing wide-eyed as Alec, the cheeky boy, hands in pockets, strolls to the front of the classroom.

Ignoring the 'heid doon' advice, I'd been watching, fascinated, as he industriously dipped bits of blotting paper into his desk inkwell. After fishing them out, he rolled them into pellets, then, carefully taking aim, and using his ruler as a firing device, flicked them at his pals: all the while with a straight face. His missiles met their target every time. At length, and with the teacher fully occu-pied, drawing on the blackboard, things were beginning to heat up. His pals scowled and were plainly planning to return fire when Alec had a miscalculation. One of the pellets went off course and landed at Miss Milne's feet.

It was a combination of poor aim and tim-ing. A few minutes beforehand, Elsie Mac-intosh, a girl with a lisp and red ribbons in enviably long, fat plaits, had been struggling to recognise the letter 'S'. Miss Milne was equally challenged, drawing pictures to illustrate it.

With patience stretched to the limit, she tapped the blackboard with its scattering of long-necked objects. 'Look, Elsie,' she'd said. 'You usually see them on water. What do you think they are?'

Elsie screwed up her face in deep thought, sucked a plait for a second, then, brow clearing, beamed. 'That'th eathie, Mith. It'th a loth o' bonny boathies.'

'No! Not boathies, I mean boats. They're actually swans, Elthie – I mean Elsie. Swans! And they hisssss!' She said this with feeling and banged the blackboard, which wobbled on unsteady legs and almost disappeared in a cloud of chalk dust. 'Now say after me, "S is for swans".'

'Th ith for thwans.'

Despite Elsie's best efforts, they haven't helped Miss Milne's temper (nor stopped a snigger sweeping round the classroom) until the unexpected arrival of the pellet at her feet does.

She glares. 'Stop that or I'll laugh the other side of your faces,' she snaps.

As Alec mooches towards her, she lifts the strap. It lands on his outstretched, ink-stained hand; the forks wrap round it as if determined to have the last word. His palm dips slightly, but he keeps a smirk in place until Miss Milne raises the strap again.

'Please, miss, I need the toilet.'

The small boy's voice startles her. A girl sharing his desk retreats to the edge of its bench. As he stands up, clutching himself, Miss Milne darts an exasperated look at him, then, stepping forward to have a look, frowns a little. There's a damp patch where he's been sitting.

'Oh, very well, James, and see Miss May afterwards, and you, Alec, go back to your seat and get on with your writing.'

Whilst James practically runs out of the room, Alec strolls back. His head's high, but when he sits at his desk, I see him rubbing his palms together. He might have been trying to do this quietly but it makes the sound of someone running sandpaper over wood.

It's the interval and Moira's gone to show Violet a space in the laurel bushes so large it's like a green-leafed room.

I'm sorry to see her go, especially since Elizabeth's taken on the minder role. The biscuits she said were such a bargain aren't really biscuits. Mattie must have been delighted to get rid of so many wafers, normally used to sandwich ice cream but now soft,

'Tastes horrible,' I say.

In an unusual instance of determination to share, Elizabeth says, 'Stop complaining. We got a whole bagful. If you're that fussy, you can wash them down with the milk. Come on. It's beside the boiler in the cloakroom. Mrs Haggarty puts it there.'

'Mrs Haggarty?'

'She stokes the boiler in the winter and she's the cleaner. She's super – the big ones get to sit with her at her table at dinnertime. Afterwards, they help carry the dirty dishes over to the canteen. They get a right laugh with her, she's aye so cheery.'

The milk comes in silver-topped half-pint-sized bottles, along with a box of straws in a crate. We've to keep the tops. Apparently blind dogs benefit from them; it's not clear to me why. The milk's cold and tastes different from the warm stuff that comes courtesy of Charlotte. In winter, the boiler's heat will often be needed to thaw out the bottles' contents. Meanwhile the big iron monster remains unlit and I wonder how James will dry the wet patch on his shorts. Then he appears wearing different clothes.

They fit him better and even if he hasn't a play piece he looks cheerier. 'Miss May sorted me, and I'm not hungry,' he says, screwing up his nose at our offered wafers.

I don't really want drying-out attention from Miss May but need to find a toilet. I'm sure there's one in a lean-to affair at the top of a small but very steep hill with the canteen sited at the bottom.

'I'm telling the teacher on you. Use yer ain,' snaps an affronted boy when I peep

219

round the corner of what is very obviously not the girls' toilet.

Our ones are beside the bike shelter. The school has a variety of sheds. All share the boundary wall between the school and the railway track but green doors with huge spaces, top and bottom, mark my destination. They lead into two tiny stone-floored cell-like spaces occupied by the lingering smell of long-dead fish. Whitewash on the walls helps make for a brighter place, but you wouldn't want to stay here long – especially in winter dark, when there's no light outside or any inside these bleak little places.

Thinking that the toilet paper might be handier as tracing paper, I sit down. A second after, there's a crash, clatter, rumble and a roar. The toilet chain swings and my wooden seat vibrates enough for me to think I might get splinters off it. I might have cried out, but all sound is drowned out as a passing train shrieks that it's on its way to Dunphail station.

Into the small following silence, the school bell tolls.

During the interval, Miss Milne must have wiped off the swans so vigorously there's a chalky cloud hanging above the blackboard. Starting to draw on it again, she says, 'This is something for you, Jane.'

I'm anxious until she's finished, when it's

220

a relief to recognise she's drawn a recognisable apple and a bat jammed to a ball. She taps her artwork and continues, 'That's for "A" and "B"! It's the beginning of the alphabet – the letters you'll use for writing.' She picks up a limp-looking book from her table. 'And here's your reading book. When you go home, you must cover it. It's school property. New books are too expensive for our funds. Look and see if you can find letters like I've drawn in it.'

Worried in case the book, with its well-thumbed pages, disintegrates, I lift the first one with my fingertips. When Elizabeth got her first book, I'd a good look at it and don't remember it having this one's gluey smell or worn cover. The *Red Letter* might lack coloured illustrations but I bet its stories are livelier than the gentle activities pictured here. Anyway, I've seen them already. Quite soon, and tiring of the letter-search, I watch Moira.

She's busy. 'Up light and down heavy,' were Miss Milne's instructions to the class working on their writing skills, Carefully, Moira dips a pen's nib into the inkwell sunk into the desk. She taps the surplus back, then, scarcely breathing, bends over her lined jotter.

The word *'Writing'* appears in beautiful script. Smoothly, she moves on to words below it. I don't know what they say, but

221

Miss Milne, looking over Moira's shoulder, smiles in approval.

Alec's equally occupied, but his pen makes such a scratching sound I glance over and see a lot of ink splotches all over the paper. So does Miss Milne, whose hands start to tremble.

'*Wirting*, Alec? That's "wirting" you've written ... again. How many times have I to tell you, this is an exercise in wrriting.' She stabs a finger over the offending word on the page and looks at it in disgust since it's now covered in ink. 'You always get your "R"s in the wrong place and what a mess! You're just not trying.'

'Oh but I am, Miss,' protests Alec, assuming a look of complete innocence. 'I *are* trying.'

26

AN ERROR OF JUDGEMENT

'So, how's the scholar?' Mrs Bremner asks when I deliver the milk.

'I lost my schoolbag.'

She swings round from the sink where she's been peeling tatties with a knife. A thin metal rod is all that's left of its bone handle.

'How?'

I know the Bremners don't have much, and treasure the small possessions they do own, but all that's forgotten as I spill out resentment, 'It wisna my fault. When I got hame, I was too tired tae go back and look for it. Us wee ones might get out of school early, but by the time Kenny and me walked that long road home, the bigger ones who all had bikes could've beaten us to it if they hidna been caperin.' I squirm on the sofa and include Lala in a room-sweeping glare.

'If the wind changes direction, your face'll stick,' warns Mrs Bremner. 'So whit happened tae the bag?'

'Well! The school lavvies are terrible. I only went the once, so by the time we were halfway home I wis fair burstin'.' I clutch myself in recall, then continue. 'I pit ma bag doon afore I went behind a bush, then I forgot to pick it up afterwards.'

'What did your mum say?'

'You'll mebbe no believe this, but she never even asked how I got on at school!' I haven't yet recovered from the shock, but manage to continue. 'No! The minute I got home, the first thing she said was, "Where's your bag?" I draw breath, then continue. 'When I told her where it might be, she tried to get me to walk back.' I'm outraged. 'All that way! Said she'd give me an apple if I went. She was ower busy tae tak me.'

Mrs Bremner screws the sink tap very firmly, then says in a quiet voice, 'So, then?'

'Well, she did eventually tak' me in the car.' I consider for a moment, then say, 'I didna think it could go so fast.'

Mrs Bremner, raising an eyebrow, now asks, 'Was there anything much in the bag?'

'A smelly old reading book. Teacher told me I'd to cover it, but Elizabeth said she'd do it, along with her own books. According to her, I'd use too much brown paper and wouldna do it right either.'

I shift along the sofa. These days, it's getting so uncomfortable: either my legs are growing or my kilt's shrinking.

'And did you get homework?'

'No, that was it.'

As tattie peeling resumes, I add, 'Mind you, one good thing about school's the dinners.' Sensing that in some way I've fallen out of favour, I add, 'But the custard's nay sae good as yours.'

Mrs Bremner begins to sound less frosty. 'So ye get custard at school! That's funny, we're haen some for oor tea. It's on the fire.' She nods at the long-handled black pan. It's small compared to the aluminium containers used to transport our school meals from the Logie one where they're cooked.

A jokey man delivers them the five-mile distance. Today, carrying them through to the school dining room, he noticed the classroom door was open.

Earlier on, Miss Milne said she'd eyes at the back of her head, but I'm not convinced. Whilst busy at the blackboard, she neither saw him pulling faces nor us sticking out our tongues at him. It was fun but probably not interesting enough to include in this dinner tale.

'Mind you, Mrs Bremner, and Lala,' I add, feeling I don't want to exclude him since he seems to be actually listening, 'teacher said there was enough for second helpings an' poor Sandy Burgess got a right row jist cos when it came tae the pudden, he said he only wanted the pastry bit of it.'

It had been a worrying moment. Miss Milne, ladle in hand, looked so outraged at the request, for a moment we thought she might throw the whole caboodle over Sandy's suddenly anxious face.

'You'll take this and like it,' she'd snapped and splashed on enough custard to smother the taste of the small piece of jam tart she'd so grudgingly given.

'Mebbe she thought he shouldna be sae fussy. What else did you get?'

'Mental soup. That wis for starters.'

'That wid fair help ye wi' yer sums,' she twinkles, whilst Lala drops his eyes to concentrate on filling his pipe.

'Ooh, I dinna ken aboot that,' I say, recalling being given a slate and trying to copy

225

figures from the blackboard onto it with a slate pencil that screamed if you pressed too hard on it. The slate cleaning cloth Mum had given me had come in handy, but it needed a lot of spit to get it to work better.

'So, Janie, whit wis the best thing aboot the day?'

'That's easy! Playtimes.'

I could tell them how imaginative Moira and Violet had turned their laurel-bush home into a shop, inviting everybody to come and buy. Then, remembering both Elizabeth and my disappointment that not one person wanted to exchange the crisp note of a laurel leaf for lots of Mattie's soft wafers to buy imaginary sweets, I opt for a more successful tale.

'I got to hold one end of a skipping rope. Ye ken this, some of the quines are so good that when the rope's spinning they can run in and skip, then run out without stopping the rope. They do it in time to something called "Two Little Dickie Birds". Would you like to hear what they say?'

Without waiting for an answer, I get off the sofa and, in time to jumping on the spot, chant: 'Two little dickie birds sitting on a wall, one named Peter and the other one Paul. Fly away Peter, fly away Paul. Come back Peter, come back Paul.'

Mrs Bremner shakes her head. 'You'd certainly need to be quick and good at that.

226

Peter and Paul, eh?' She casts an eye at the photographs on the mantelpiece. 'But I bet there weren't any loons skipping. What were they up to? Nothing good, I bet.'

I agree. 'Miss Milne read them a story about the bump on a toad's head. Said it was a jewel, so, as soon as it was playtime, they went looking for one. They'd a knife and said if they found one they'd cut it open to see if it wis true.'

I take a breath, imagining the horror of it, then with pride add, 'But Elizabeth told them not to be so daft.'

She laughs. 'And what did they say?'

'If conceit wis consumption, she'd be deid.'

A long silence descends. I wasn't sure what the words meant but thought, because the boys had doubled up laughing after they said them, that it was a kind of joke. Now I'm frightened to see pain manage a flicker across Lala's still face, whilst Mrs Bremner looks shocked. She's got a big angry-looking scratch on her arm, which she covers with a protective hand as if suddenly aware of it.

The clock ticks, the fire crackles and there's a smell of burning.

Mrs Bremner breaks her silence. 'Och! The custard.' Darting to save it, she mutters over her shoulder, 'Mebbe ye'd better go for your ain tea.' I get a message of hurt and dis-pleasure and, without the offer of a Butter

227

Ba, slink home.

'Consumption's another word for TB, and it's what two of the Bremner lads died of,' says Mum when she finds me in bed, sorrowfully holding Rabbit and soaking his vest with my tears. She sits beside me. 'It's only recently that there's been a cure for what was a terrible scourge. In darker days than we have now, caring for sufferers must have been dreadful and backbreaking work. Mrs Bremner was not only running the home but caring for two and all at the same time.' She pats me gently on the shoulder. 'Of course you wouldn't have known any of this or that there was only a couple of months between each death, but maybe you'll understand why, to this day, an awful shadow's been cast over the family.'

Remembering the photograph where they're missing, I say, 'Dod couldn't have been very old.'

'No, he was only ten, but old enough to know and be frightened by what was going on. It didn't help when someone told him he'd be the next one to die.' She sighs and shakes her head. 'People can say such thoughtless things. Lord knows how Mrs Bremner managed to keep the rest of the family safe. It's a terrible disease.'

She gets up and in a brisker voice says, 'But she did. She's a remarkable woman and, despite the history, all the rest of the family are hale and hearty. Now come on through for your tea. You'll be hungry, and afterwards we've a surprise for the two of you.'

Mum and Dod are heading towards the old hayloft, which is above the neep store and tractor shed. The Bremner's house is only a few yards away and I panic when I see Mrs Bremner waving her fist from her porch.

Turning and catching my expression, Mum says, 'I've spoken to her and explained that you didn't mean any harm. It's all right – just you run over and have a wee word with her.'

I'm ready with an apology, but Mrs Bremner beats me to it. 'Hold out yer hand, Jeannie,' she says, and I do, because she's smiling and opening her fist to drop something into my palm. 'I forgot tae gie ye yer Butter Ba,' she says.

'Ooh. Ta!' I cry, suddenly light-hearted. 'I'll see you the morn.'

I skip over to Mum and Dod, standing at the loft door. Elizabeth's impatiently hopping at the bottom of the wooden steps leading up to it. 'Come on, I've had to wait for you,' she says, but as soon as I reach her she races up the steps, taking two at a time.

'Are ye right, quines?' asks Dod, then, without waiting for an answer, pushes open the door. Daylight, helped by two skylight windows, floods into a small, quiet place. It's different from the barn loft, which has the busy feel of a place regularly visited either to store or get sacks of calf feed. There, the policing cats prowl; here, Bluebell and Belinda sit, propped against a stone wall on top of an old wooden chest.

'That's my kist,' says Dod, giving a mischievous smile. 'I'm thinking ma traivlin' days are ower.'

'Och, Geordie!' says Mum, going pink, changing the subject and explaining. 'It was getting a bit of a squash in the house. This place wasn't being used, so we thought you'd like it to play in.' She adds with feeling, 'More room for everybody.'

I'm surprised we hadn't missed the cardboard box of toys, the dolls or the wooden bagatelle game kind neighbours have given us on a long-term loan. School's taken us over completely and now I feel guilty not to have noticed that poor Belinda's been moved. I bet she's not even been consulted if she wanted to go. I don't know where the pictures of Highland cattle have come from, but they're not that happy. Maybe it's because they're up to their ankles in water. They look down gloomily from two gilt-edged pictures, hung on the roof's rafters by Glesga Jock. As far as I can make out from Elizabeth, Bluebell's not a great conversationalist. My poor doll! She must be lonely.

Still, it's great to have a lot more space, even if it's only got half the potential for circus training as the barn. I'm thinking of dropping those career plans anyway. The cats have refused their training programme and Dobbin's getting too small. Heights are maybe not my thing. The tightrope practice on the fence was hardly a success – and being completely winded after plummeting from a tree I'd been climbing was terrifying.

'You will breathe – eventually,' Elizabeth had said. As it seemed unlikely at the time, her reassurance had been encouraging.

'It'll be a fine place if you want the Tomdow bairns to come and play here too,' continues Mum.

Much as I love the idea, Kenny might not. On our way home, I'd asked him if he'd seen the little girl.

'No, why would we want another when we've got Violet?'

He's probably right. I think of his sister, with her calm brow and sweet smile. If I'd one like her, I wouldn't want another.

Mine must agree because she says, 'I'm not sure about the boys, but I'd love Violet to come and play. She's super at making up games. She makes playing shoppies as good as going to see Mattie.'

I can't resist: 'Sell any wafers?'

Ignoring Elizabeth's scowl, Mum says, 'Well, I hear Violet's a real help to her mother, so if she does come, it'll only be if she can be spared. Having a big family in

231

such a wee house must be hard work.'

'Oh aye, there's a fair squad o' them,' Dod agrees, then addressing us directly, 'Jist mind, we dinna want them trampling all over the place. That park especially.' Standing at the doorway, he points down to a field of ripening oats where the wind is turning them into a sea of rippling green-gold. 'It's nearly ready for cutting – it disna need flattening.' He looks up at the sky. 'Wi' a bit o' luck we'll start roading the morn. At least this year I've somebody to help.'

As if hearing his words, clouds start to gather.

27

AND THE RAIN IT RAINETH

Once past Tombain's fields, our Knockack burn joins the Dorback, so much bigger we call it a river. It starts at Lochandorb, a wild and lonely place, with its waters surrounding a ruined castle, once a stronghold of someone called the Wolf of Badenoch.

A day we were in Elgin and asked about its ruined cathedral, Mum told us, 'That was the Wolf's work.'

'That's a funny name,' said Elizabeth.

'Surely that wasn't his real one?'

'No, actually it was Alexander Stewart, but Wolf suited him better cos he was such a bad lot. Thought that the only way to settle an argument was by imprisonment and murder. He fell in then out with the Church when it wouldn't allow him to divorce his wife. Since no journey seemed to be complete without raiding and pillaging he left a trail of havoc and destruction on his way to Elgin, where, amongst other buildings, he torched and destroyed the cathedral. It was so beautiful it was known as the Lantern of the North.'

'Would that have been a long time ago?' Elizabeth asked.

'Uh huh. The fourteenth century. But on a bleak winter's day, you can imagine the Wolf's ghost still lingering round the grey waters of the loch.'

It's the source of the Dorback. Like someone quietly leaving a gathering prone to a change of mood, it eases under a wooden bridge then away from the loch. It winds in lazy curves past a shooting lodge, the Kerrow and Culfearn Farms, before reaching the Tomdow grounds. There, a flat meadow gives shelter and sweet grasses to our cattle, but further on, previous floods have undermined the foundations of sandy cliffs, leaving them at risk of further damage.

They worry Dod. His anxiety grows. It's

been raining for what seems like forever and today so many tears stream down our scullery window they block the view.

Mum, giving up on something that usually inspires her to write her bright newsy *Bulletin* articles, says, 'Morayshire so often gets what I call the Lammas Deluge, I sometimes wonder why on earth we hill folk still farm. The farmers further south might already have celebrated their harvest festival but here's us, up to the oxters in water, and with none of our fields even cut. Still,' she adds, by way of comfort, 'I suppose we should be thankful it's not quite as bad as the 1829 Moray Floods.'

'Nay yet,' says Dod, 'but I'm worried about the Dorback eating away at the Tomdow sand crags. With that river in spate, I can almost believe that story o' a farmer about these parts losing a whole park to yon floods.'

'That's right. Yon Dick Lauder bloke wrote about it in his book. He said that a poor farmer could hardly believe his eyes when he saw a whole field actually moving.' Mum shudders. 'I'm sure it won't get to that stage, bairns, but don't either of you go near that river until the weather settles.'

She needn't worry. We don't often go to the Dorback. It's kelpie country, and when we're at school the only threat of water is when we stamp our wellies to splash each other in the playground, where deep pools have collected. Alec and his pals have been putting their skills to more creative use. They've chosen a window-less school wall, which allows them a huge canvas, then, using the pool's muddy depths to soak tennis balls, they've been firing them at the wall to make a pattern of round, black shapes. It's a piece of art unfortunately lost on Miss Milne. Her response is predictable.

'Giving the belt,' she says, 'hurts me more than you boys getting it.'

I find this hard to believe.

At home as the rain continues, so does tension. Days pass. Even the Knockack's beginning to look and sound like a river, whilst ditches and ponds fill and so change in character they seep into the countryside, making it look bedraggled, brown and unhappy. With our crops starting to look as if a sea's swept over them, we're happy to take refuge in the loft.

Elizabeth says, 'Mum would have been going daft with us underfoot (where have I heard this before), so it's a good job we've got here. Mind you, I thought Violet's brothers might have wanted to come too.'

'Och, they'd probably spoil the fun.' Presuming that the little girl must have got bored of living on her own in the Tomdow house and gone, I say, 'Maybe Violet's fed up of boys all the time at home, but I love it when she comes.'

I think of the excitement she brings when

she's happy to let Elizabeth and me be the beautiful princesses whilst she doesn't mind making horrible faces and pretending to be a wicked witch.

'When I catch you, I'm gonna boil you in my big black pot,' she shouts, clunking about in the old boots we found in Dod's kist. The Highland cows gaze down at us, as she chases us round the loft, making wild noises, loud enough to drown out the sound of the rain drumming on the roof slates. Still, and maybe it's the pervading atmosphere of damp outside, but the loft's beginning to feel as if it's being affected by the weather too.

Even Belinda's clothes are starting to smell a bit fusty and her face feels clammy. I'm not sure that she likes it here, but she keeps Bluebell company.

'Rabbit and I miss you,' I tell her one day when nobody else is around, 'but when we're not here you and Bluebell can get peace to play with the toys in the play box, even have a go at the bagatelle. Anyway, we need you both to be here when we're playing schoolies, robbers and Mrs Haggarty-time.

Belinda says, 'I don't mind being a pupil and shaking all about when having a joke with Mrs Haggarty, or even bowing my head after getting a row from Elizabeth when she's playing at being the teacher, but neither Bluebell nor I like the robbers game. We hate you girls making us prisoners in Dod's kist.'

236

I don't think she's really unhappy but she's speaking in a low, but rather nice, husky voice. She's either getting a cold or she's listening to Violet so much she's beginning to sound like her.

I straighten her frock and shake her gently. 'Look,' I say, 'it might be hard being tied up and thrown in a cellar but at the end we always rescue you from it, and once we put the lid back on the kist it's a bit of magic when it turns into a coach and Violet's a super driver. She points out things of interest as we go along and, even if Elizabeth's a bit strict as a conductress, we like being passengers, don't we?'

'You talking to Belinda?' says my sister, unexpectedly appearing at my shoulder.

'Of course. You didn't think I was speaking to myself, did you? My doll's really chatty. Don't you have conversations with Bluebell?'

Elizabeth picks up Bluebell from the floor, holds her to her ear, then nods.

'So what did she say?'

'She says she would speak but with you and Belinda around she can't get her tongue in edgeways.' She surges on. 'Don't start! And see when Violet comes round? I've got an idea. You know that Bible story Miss Milne told us the other day?'

I point to my lips, which are firmly pressed together, but am curious enough to nod. Elizabeth continues, 'I think that Dod's kist would be perfect. Let's suggest we play Noah.'

Forgetting the sealed lips, I blurt out, 'The one where Alec wanted to know why Noah needed two of each animal?'

'Ha! Knew you couldn't keep your mouth shut,' she shouts in triumph. 'But, yes. I bet she knew he was just asking to annoy her. It's a wonder she didn't give him the belt.'

'Well, he'd a right smirk on his face until she said it was a stupid question from a farmer's son.'

Elizabeth's idea's great, but Violet won't be coming for a while. It's stopped raining and her mum needs help with a huge washing built up in days when nobody thought they'd ever see the sun return with a drying wind.

28

HARVEST AT LAST

Dod threw Mum out of bed!

'I dreamt I wis binding a sheaf,' he said in his defence.

'It was one thing your knee landing on my stomach, then twisting my nightie into a knot was a surprise, but shoved out of bed?

All I can say is that it's just as well there was a rug to break my fall.'

We're delighted that she's neither injured, upset nor too surprised. Dod and Violet's dad have been scything a pathway round the side of the harvest crop. It's called roading and means clearing a way for the binder to get into the field without spoiling any of the growth. The cut stuff then has to be made into sheaves and done by hand.

First, the men make ties out of the grain's long stalks. The repetitive job that's crept into Dod's dreams has been when he's been kneeling on scythed bundles to squash them into neat sheaves to secure them with the home-made ties. When Mum sailed over-board, he must have thought he'd made a sheaf and thrown it to the side of a newly cut track.

Later, she says, 'Well, now you've the roading done, it's time to hand over to Bob and his binder.'

Dod beams as she links arms with him. 'Och, but isn't it a great moment when it starts that first round? Having worked all year with our hands, heart and brains, it's proof that we really are providers of food.'

'Too true,' says Dod. 'It's the crown of oor farming year, and even if the crop's still a bit to ripen it should do that once it's cut and in stooks.'

Compared to the smooth, rhythmic sound

239

of scything, the binder makes a noisy, metallic clatter. Frightened by the sound, and routed from their hiding places by the windmill-like whirling wooden paddles feeding the crop into the advancing greedy teeth of the binder, rabbits flee whilst hares escape in zig-zag flight.

If Nell hadn't grown so fat and lazy, she might give chase, but she's lying on the sofa at home dreaming of her next meal. Anyway, Mum wasn't keen on letting her out. She explained, 'I heard, recently, that someone's dog got its paws cut off with a binder.'

Dod, well out of the way of those treacherous teeth, sits up on the binder's high metal seat, watching for any problems with the canvas that catches the cut grain, the knotters that tie it into sheaves and making sure that the blades make proper contact on the ground. The seat is even harder than the one on the tractor pulling the binder, but neither driver Bob nor Dod complain. The farm help starts on the stooking. It's not as easy as he makes it seem. 'Even if there's a drying wind, the sheaves are still gey wet. It makes oxtering them heavy,' muses Dod. 'And we've aye to be on the lookout to keep the dry corn heads on the inside of the stook.'

Still, they manage, and after two days the crop's been cut. Now the shorn field's been transformed into pale-green stubble-striped streets, with stooks that look like wigwam dwellings lining them.

In the playground at the start of another school day, Alec is holding court. 'I've got something to tell ye, I bet ye wouldna credit it.'

Tucking his thumbs into imaginary braces, he says, 'Aye, you'll mebbe nay believe it, but it's right enough. My dad told me. Of course, mine wouldn't allow such a thing, but this wee bairn's dad did.' Sure of his audience's attention, he pauses long enough for some impatient soul to shout, 'Whit did his dad dae? Och! Get on wi' it, Alec.'

Alec continues. Now, speaking as disapprovingly as a church elder, he says, 'He let him stand on the binder board. Well! He wis only on it for a minute when he fell onto the canvas.'

'But that's where the knotters are!' someone says. 'Next you'll be telling us that the bairn was made into a sheaf.'

Alec turns to give the speaker a long look. He scratches his black hair; his blue eyes sparkle. He must be helping with the harvest at home. He wears his sleeves rolled up. They show scratches on his sunburnt arms, which are worn like badges of honour and prove that he's a stook builder.

'That's jist whit happened,' says Alec.

'Whit rubbish!' says my sister in her direct way.

Alec laughs. 'Och, it's true enough. Dad

241

read it in the papers.'

Despite herself, Elizabeth has to ask, 'So what happened?'

'Everybody got a fleg, of course. Then once they opened the sheaf, they found him an...' Alec draws a long breath: his audience waits impatiently, wondering how many bits were found and how much blood spilt. If this is a true story, it's even better than the made-up *Boys of Glen Morach* we all listen to on the wireless.

'Hurry up, Alec, the bell might go any-time,' says someone, so Alec relents. 'They couldna' believe it but he wis right as rain, the stook must've protected him.' He grins. His timing's perfect. The bell clangs.

'Schoo-all,' we cry in the harmony that Miss Milne seeks and is so often denied.

As we gather round her at the piano, she says, 'We're going to start this week with a new hymn.'

On the piano, there's a sheet of music with the words, 'We Plough the Fields and Scatter.'

'It's to celebrate harvest time,' explains Miss Milne. 'There'll be a celebration in church soon and it'll be nice for you to know this tune and words so that if you go to church you can join in.'

After she reads out the first verse and we repeat it after her, she says, 'I'll play it to you so you get the tune.'

242

'I ken it. Ma granny sings it,' says Alec, assuming a look of sainthood.

'Well, there's others less blessed,' observes the teacher. 'After I've played it, you can lead the singing.'

I listen carefully. It's hard to equate the hymn words of breezes, sunshine or soft refreshing rain with any of our recent weather. Not only that but it's a devilish tune as well. I've to stand on tiptoe to hit the high notes and practically kneel down for the low ones. But it's worth the challenge of singing over Alec.

His chest is out, his back is straight and he's confident.

'All good gifts around us.' He belts it out but heading for the top note's proving to be a challenge.

'Thank the Lord, Oh thank the Lord,' I shriek.

Elizabeth nudges me. 'Wheesht!'

Back on base home ground and managing to drown out Alec, we all finish in a triumphant cacophony of sound: 'For all his love.'

Miss Milne sits back in her seat and runs her tongue under her teeth. They make a clacking sound as they get back into position. 'The corncrakes in my old home in Stoer sound better,' she says. 'And I've never thought that they were very musical. A pest, in fact. At this time of year they make such a confounded racket nobody can get a wink of sleep for them. I suppose we should count ourselves lucky we don't have them here as well as you boys and girls.' She slams down the piano lid, goes to pick up her pointer, then whacks the blackboard with it.

'Now, I'm well aware that this is a busy time on farms and I also know that many of you will be helping out on them after school, but don't bother coming to me and saying you haven't done your homework because of that. It's no excuse.'

It's just after dinnertime and Alec's girning. 'It's all very well for Fatty Milne. I bet when she finishes her day she goes off to sit on her big backside, with Miss May running after her.'

'Oh, ah ken,' says Davy Munro. 'It's no as if we can pit off the work at hame until it suits us. My dad's got the oats cut and we've got the field near stocked but the barley's a bit to go afore the grain swells up. The crop's still gey green.'

'Aye, and ye canna cut it afore it's ready. Nay point.'

The boys warm to their theme. If Miss Milne wasn't so driven on writing and spelling, she might be surprised at their wealth of harvesting knowledge.

Davy nods. 'An' then we'll hiv tae help wi' the loading, an' heaving sheafs up onto a cart's bloomin' hard work.'

'It's no much better up on the cairt,' says Alec, 'If I've once heard my dad shouting, "Keep the corners square, the load well forward and heart her up plenty," I've heard him say it a dozen times. As if I'd get it wrong!' He sounds affronted: pride's obviously at stake.

When talk moves on to stack building, which demands the same level of brawn, time, energy and architectural skills, some of us drift away. The idea of stooks that look like wigwams provide more inspiration.

'Come on an' play Cowboys and Indians,' someone suggests.

'Bags me be a Whiteface,' says a boy with freckles even bigger than mine or James's.

'An I'll be an Indian chief,' says another, throwing his hand to his mouth and making whooping sounds.

'I'll break in some horses,' says Violet. 'Come on, James, you can be a really difficult one.' She holds up a skipping rope. 'But I'll need to catch you first.'

As thin little frightened James turns into a runaway, snorting, biting, kicking stallion, the rest of us race round the playing field, avoiding being caught and scalped or becoming steeds about to be broken in. Altogether the threat of capture, losing your head or being kicked to death is a great way to make the dinner hour pass in delicious terror.

245

The distant clatter of Mrs Haggarty wash-ing the dinner dishes in the canteen stops and she waves a dishcloth at us.

'Parlez!' We shout, reading it as a flag-bearing peace sign.

It's more than can be said for the toll of Miss Milne's bell, telling us that time's up and fun's over.

29

A HARVEST THANKSGIVING

You wouldn't think that our church had been built in 1741. It doesn't look old, but the graveyard surrounding it on three sides does. It's got some stones so ancient the let-tering on their flat table-like tops is outlined in green moss. The same shade of emerald growth thrives at the base of equally time-worn but upright stones weathered into the colour of lizard-wear.

Less simple, and with lettering written on it in a way that Miss Milne would love, is Kopuri Tom's stone. It's directly opposite the church door entrance and stands out because of its oddly light colour.

We're waiting beside it until Mum and Dod finish the not particularly harmonious business of parking our car.

'There'll be a big congregation today,' Dod had said. 'I'll jist park the car beside the coo' shed. It's a pity the Glebe's farm buildings are so near the church. They dinna leave cars wi an awful lot of room.'

'As long as *we* leave room for the cow to get in, but mind that wall, Dod, and, bairns, you'd best get out now and wait for us outside the church.' As Dod revved the engine, Mum closed her eyes.

'It looks as if someone's painted the stone and it's beginning to flake,' Elizabeth says, then points to the top of the stone. 'That's a bit like the design on the back of Mum's bonny silver mirror. I asked her about it one day and she said it's something they call art nouveau.' Her finger follows the wavy line of something carved underneath. It looks like a small branch with stars instead of leaves. 'See that? The stem forms the first letter of In Memory.'

'I canna read capital letters yet, so what do these ones say?' I mean the words underneath Tom's name.

'He died in 1877 at Relugas House. Remember yon big house at the top of the village? And it says he was a faithful servant and attached.' She frowns. 'I wonder what that means. Anyway, he came from somewhere called Rotumah. It's in the South Pacific. I

247

bet that's forever away. We'll need to look at the map when we're back in school.'

'It must be terrible dying so far away from home,' I say, my hand over my heart and looking skyward for any sign of Tom.

'Ach, Jane!' she says, turning on her heel and ramming her beret over her ears. 'Come on. Here's Mum and Dod.'

Headwear must be a sign of good, humble and church-going souls, but I don't really understand why the men on entering the church take off their hats and we don't. I wish we did. Mine feels like a band of steel clamped round my forehead. It's one of the reasons I'm glad we don't often have to come to church. We already get plenty Bible stuff from Granny. Today, however, thanks to Miss Milne's musical endeavours, I'm looking forward, at least, to singing about ploughing fields at today's Harvest Thanks-giving.

Mum's quite enthusiastic about it too. 'It's a special one in all farmers' calendars,' she says. 'And we should thank God we've managed to get it in before Christmas.'

Elizabeth grins. 'And of course, Mum, you get a chance for a blether with pals as well.'

'That too.'

Our church may be the same Church of Scotland as Granny's one, but this one's built on smaller, simpler lines. It's got such a comfortable feel that if anyone was alone in

248

this place and heard something creak, I bet they wouldn't be scared. The natural light let in by tall if narrow windows shows up the burnt-orange colour of the pine-made pews and pulpit. There's huge silver-coloured pipes above an organ which was donated by one of Dunphail's benefactors. It's played by the minister's wife, but meanwhile it's silent. The sound of the nearby Divie river, with its eternal song as it rushes past the cemetery to join the Dorback, then River Findhorn, makes a sweet alternative.

Only the occasional visiting grandee sits upstairs. Apparently, anybody else using it's considered to have fancy ideas. I'm curious to find out what it's like to look down on the minister and the folk below. Seeing hats from a different angle could be fun, but I suppose that Andy Milne wouldn't let me past the first stair-step. He's the church beadle and, as well as checking who goes upstairs, he looks after the minister, the entrance and the collection plate. He's also Mary's dad and she worries a lot about him because his chest can be even wheezier than the church organ.

We sit at the back. From it, I can look up and out the window onto a yew tree, its branches so dense no witch could possibly get in to ride on any of them. When Andy comes in, it's more interesting. He wears a grey suit and walks slowly and reverentially whilst carrying a huge Bible. Despite its weight, his damaged lungs and the winding stairs up to the pulpit, he makes it with great dignity. There he places the Bible on the lectern. His descent is slow. Then he returns, and with the same measured tread carries a glass of water. Once it's put alongside the Bible, and Andy's back at floor level, the minister appears. After he's in the pulpit, he sits down and Andy closes a small gate after him. Perhaps he's frightened he might escape.

The minister's a big man in a black flowing robe. Maybe it's because he looks a bit like a friendly spectacled crow that I think he hasn't his beadle's presence: today, especially. There's usually plenty room for him in the enclosed pulpit space, but he's squashed in between golden sheaves flanking him on either side of the seat.

He tugs at the gown folds like someone seeking tidiness, then he stands up, rests his hands on the sides of the lectern and looks down at us. I hold my breath, wondering if a careless sweep of the gown could send the glass of water, so near to the Bible, flying. It's enough to give him my complete attention.

Raising dark beetling eyebrows and looking through his black-rimmed spectacles, he starts. 'Welcome, everybody, and may I say how gladdened I am to see such a wonderful harvest of God's food and so many gathered here to give thanks for it.'

The congregation's unusual size must be as pleasing as having a church transformed by the mixed smells and colours of harvested fare, home bakes and assorted jars of jams. They're prominently displayed on trestle tables and make for a rich show in a normally plain setting.

Miss Milne's dressed in a smart but funereal black suit, whilst Miss May could be going to a wedding in frilly pink. They're sitting on the opposite side from us and a few pews in front. I wonder if, having sent us all home with so many of their home-grown apples and pears, were any left for this festival. There's certainly enough here to fill the baskets and bowls not already teeming with raspberries, gooseberries and blackcurrants.

After the minister announces the first hymn, there's a short lull. Mum manages to fit in a wee blether about parish affairs to her neighbour, and Dod finds out the latest way to get rid of a mole infestation whilst the minister's wife gets ready. With the care and attention of a motorist coaxing an engine to start, she pulls buttons, presses switches and moves her feet over the organ pedals in such a way you might think she was about to drive off. She straightens up, gives her husband a nod, then, looking straight ahead, spreads her fingers. With a great blast, the music peals out.

'We plough the fields and scatter,' we sing, and, naturally, as I fill my lungs for the next line, my sister jabs me hard.

All that practice at school and now I've been shut up! I persevere, but eventually, when things begin to verge on violence, I give up. Bored, I snatch a glimpse of a plaque on the wall behind us. I've heard Mum and Dod discussing it.

'It's been pit on squint,' Dod observed. 'If I wis looking steady at it, I'd get cross-eyed.'

'True. And even if it's a nice enough thing to commemorate a minister who served our parish for thirty-seven years of the last century, I can't think why anybody would have thought to spoil the bonny white marble with yon two pink columns of granite flanking it. I'm sorry but, to me, they regrettably resemble fatty sausage meat,' said Mum.

The thought of food's made me hungry. Despite my sister, I manage to join in the final chorus,

'Then thank the Lord, O thank the Lord, for all his love.'

As we sit down, I eye the food around us, whilst there's a discreet rustle of paper bags. Pandrop time! I wish Dod hadn't kept his in his pocket. The ones he slips us are covered in fluff.

I'm sure that the sight of the entire congregation suddenly hiding their mouths to slide in their pandrops doesn't fool the minister.

252

Either that or he must think that there's been a sudden all-embracing outbreak of gum-boils, with the occasional relocation to the other cheek. Toffee is out. The pandrop is something to be sucked and savoured. Any other way of eating it would be a mark of disrespect.

The minister leans forward, scans us, then says, 'Now, boys and girls. Today is a special one and I've a little story to tell you.'

In case it's not that little, I suck through the fluff very slowly. Elizabeth and I are wearing our heavy coats, which are as un-comfortable to sit on as the Bremner's horsehair sofa. My beret's advancing over my eyebrows and getting tighter by the minute. I shove it back up, squirm, sigh, fiddle with the coat buttons and slide down the pew in a bid to see how far I can get before my foot reaches the pew in front.

There's a strong smell of mothballs from the black overcoats of men sitting beside womenfolk, splendid in two-piece costumes and fine hats. Disappointingly, the glass of water's still in place and the minister isn't half as good a storyteller as Granny.

'Did you know that Bethlehem means house of breads?' he says, pausing for a moment. I hope he's not looking for anyone to reply. In my experience, getting it wrong's as bad as not having an answer.

Eyes down. Shoes suddenly a fascinating

sight. Breath held. Pandrop sucking on hold. Silence grows. Phew! He's moved on, but my garters are telling me they're too tight so loudly, I lose the drift of the story. Some trouble with no bread, a nice girl called Ruth helping an older lady called Naomi and asking somebody called Boaz for help.

My ears prick up at the one familiar name. Mary's brother's called Boswell – but it's Bose for short.

'Ruth impressed him so much by her kindness, he offered to marry her,' continues the minister. 'So, with the corn safely gathered in, there was a great feast to celebrate both that and Ruth and Boaz's wedding.' He snatches a glance at his watch. 'Remember, children, we must always be grateful and celebrate whatever food we have that's on our table. Amen.'

'Well, quines, what did you take from the minister's story about Ruth and Boaz?' asks Mum on our way home.

Elizabeth frowns, pulls off her beret and nibbles a nail, 'A hard life's one thing, but having a famine as well ... now that must be awful.'

'Poor Ruth! Imagine not even being able to have a jammy piece,' I say. 'Still, Boaz was a nice man. D'you think he was called after Mary's brother?'

30

A BIRD AND A BIKE

I didn't think it at the time, but yesterday morning seems like a lifetime of happiness away.

'I'm in terrible trouble,' I whisper to Rabbit. 'Any minute now, the police are going to call.'

There's a rattle on the bedroom door.

'That's maybe them now.'

'Ssh!' he croons, 'Pretend you're dead.'

I dive under the bedclothes, which Mum immediately lifts. She raises her eyebrows and frowns. 'What are you doing under there? Your sister's been up for ages. Did you not hear me calling?'

'I'm far too ill to go to school.'

She shakes her head and snaps, 'You look as fine to me as the morning you said you couldn't put a foot out of bed. I was that worried I got the doctor to come out all the way from Forres to see you. The minute he arrived, I never saw such a rapid recovery. I was fair affronted at such a waste of his time. So!' There's no milk of human kindness in her voice. 'You don't fool me, Janie. Up!'

These days I walk to school on my own. The road stretches long, wearying and dreary without Kenny's gentle company. He's gone with his family to another farm. We're unsure why: an argument between Dod and their dad perhaps. We don't ask. Questions seem to make everybody shirty at the best of times, but especially just now, with byre improvements making life on the farm busier than usual.

'I'll be glad when the work's over,' said Mum. 'The chaps putting in the damp course work really hard, but it's fair putting the beasts off their stot. Charlotte in particular's upset at being milked away from her usual stance.'

Our loft hasn't changed but play there has. We miss Violet.

'I don't know why you two can't just get on,' sighs Mum. 'You never seem happier than when you're fighting.'

We look at each other in astonishment. 'We're not fighting,' we tell her. 'We just have the occasional wee argument.'

'There's times,' says our loving mother, 'that I'm delighted you can argue to your hearts' content when you're away from here and at school.'

Clearly there's no other option than to get up and go there but remembering yesterday and my original brainwave, I've a sick feeling.

'I'm going to ask the mannies working on the byre if one o' them will give me a lift in their lorry to school,' I'd said to Elizabeth. 'If any of them say they will, would you like to come too?' I was rather hoping she'd say yes, but all she did was sniff and call me a softie.

'It's all very well for you, Elizabeth, but you've a bike!'

'Yes, but I walked before then and I never complained. You're always moaning.'

I didn't hold this conversation against her. When a kindly lorry driver took me to school and we sailed past her, I gave her a very nice smile and a wave.

'I think she's waving back at you but with her fist,' laughed the lorry driver, checking on his mirror.

In the playground, the morning started well enough with the surprise appearance of Davy Munro's jackdaw. It too had cadged a lift – but on his owner's bike. Now it was flying round the playground.

'It's nay just the bike,' said Davy. 'He canna pass a Fergie but he wants a hurl on it.' With affection, he watched the bird, which looked up from doing a worm check for a second, then carried on foraging. 'He's affa good at catching leather-jackets. He's a real pest controller.'

'Like Miss Milne,' said one wag. 'I wonder what she'll say when she sees him.'

Davy laughed and pointed in the general direction of his home. 'Och, Jake's nay need for schoolin' an' he kens far he bides. He'll mak his ain way back.' He clapped his hands. The bird, bright-eyed, looked up in an enquiring way.

'Off home, Jakey!'

As the bird soared into the air, Miss Milne appeared with the bell.

Following her into school, James licked his lips and pulled his stockings up to his thin knees. 'Ah wish ah wis that bird an' could fly away. Teacher doesn't look in a very good mood,' he said.

'Och, James, just keep you head down an' your sums right. Anyway, she's all right with you,' comforted Elizabeth. 'An' you know you're always saying you want to be a bus driver when you grow up?' Encouraged by James's attempt to smile, she continued, 'Well, I'm sure that's the next best thing to flying. Stick in with your lessons and before you know it you'll be hurling along the highways. Think! You'll be full throttle driving a bus jam-packed with passengers. Now, that's something to look forward to, isn't it?'

Not to be outdone by my sister's kindness, I put in, 'And I could be your bus conductress.'

James sniffed. 'I wouldna want you. I'd rather have Lizzie.'

Once the morning was underway and we

were all, she hoped, usefully employed, Miss Milne took up her usual stance against the radiator. Occasionally she'd drag her eyes away from the room to sneak a glance out of the window, but then something riveted her.

'Good gracious!'

She was so gripped, she didn't notice us all getting up and standing on our toes to see out too.

There's a lately harvested field across from the school. Once we were in the classroom, ploughing work must have started. A few straight brown furrows showed good progress, however something must have happened to make the plough veer off-course; the driver seemed agitated by something small and black.

'Hey, look!' cried someone. 'That bird's dive-bombing the tractor mannie.'

'Uh, that's Jake! Did I no' tell ye he canna resist Fergies? He's only trying to cadge a lift, but he'll no' like the mannie's flapping arms,' muttered Davy.

'David, you need to go and sort out that bird,' said Miss Milne, who has excellent hearing. 'And see that you apologise to the tractor man. The poor soul must have had an awful fright.' She clapped her hands. 'Right, class. Back to work. That's enough excitement for the day.'

But it wasn't. Just as Davy went to sort out Jake, Mrs Haggarty arrived. The door was open and she spoke from it. She usually looks and sounds so cheerful; it was a shock to see her worried face.

'Excuse me, Miss Milne. I've just spoken to Miss May and she's suggested I have a word with you and the bairns.' She leant on the door lintel. 'I'm fair worried. You see, my bike's gone. I can't think where it could be and I'm wondering if anybody here's seen it.'

Miss Milne looked shocked. 'That's terrible. And it's your only way of getting about, too.' With a welcoming gesture, she continued, 'Don't stand there. Please come in!'

Anybody coming to the door always gets our undivided attention and usually gives us a welcome respite from our work. Then, if the caller's invited into the classroom, we've all to stand up as a mark of courtesy. But it's a bit different with Mrs Haggarty. Considering her more part of our school family than a visitor, only half of us got to our feet.

'Och, sit down, it's only me!' she said,

Miss Milne took over. 'Did any of you see anybody on the road?'

There was a lot of chat followed by a general shaking of heads. If Mrs Haggarty had a problem, it was as much ours as hers, but hard as we tried nobody had an answer.

Miss Milne was keen to help. 'Did you see anything or anybody acting strangely, Elizabeth?' she asked. 'You come the longest way on the main road.'

'No, Miss.'

I was cross. First of all, James didn't want me to be his conductress, then Miss Milne only asked Elizabeth if she'd seen anything out of the ordinary. She obviously didn't appreciate that we each took the road at different times.

I pointed this out to my sister at playtime.

'Well, *did* you see anything?' she asked.

Before I'd time to think about any repercussions, I blurted out, 'Yes. Actually I did. I saw a funny mannie.'

Then I produced what I considered to be a killer line, one that served her right for not coming with me. 'You can see loads more from a lorry, and if you'd been in it you'd have seen him as well.'

31

A STORY WORTH THE TELLING

You'd think it was an emergency! Before I could stop her, Elizabeth had raced off to hammer on Miss Milne's house door.

Miss Milne jerked it open. 'What?'

My sister all but screamed, 'Jane's seen somebody!'

The teacher dropped her irritated look. All attention now, she said, 'We must tell Mrs Haggarty. What did he look like?'

The entire school clustered round. The idea of an audience, usually appealing, did not apply. Rooted to the spot, I longed instead to run away and hide in the laurel bushes. Afterwards, it would have been easier to say that Elizabeth hadn't been listening properly or been dreaming, or we'd had no such conversation. More creatively, I could have said that it was just a joke.

Unfortunately, it's not obvious that Miss Milne's got a sense of humour. The odd smile has been glimpsed, but if she laughed out loud the whole school might collapse with shock.

There was nothing for it. I plunged in deeper. Looking into the distance as if to get a better recall, I said, 'He'd red hair and a beard.' Actually the more I thought about it, the more real it seemed. 'And an old coat. It didna hae a belt.'

'Have not hae,' Miss Milne automatically corrected. She looked at Elizabeth. 'Didn't you say you never saw anybody coming to school?'

'*She* got a lift.' Elizabeth jerked her head in my direction. 'One of the men working at our farm just now took the time to take her in his lorry.' She added in such a way that you'd have thought it was a crime, 'It was really kind of him, especially as he's so busy.'

'So he'll maybe be able to tell us if he saw him on his way back,' said Miss Milne. 'Maybe I should phone your mother and she could ask him.'

Horrified, I said, 'She's likely out. She's very busy too, you know.'

'Well, we'll maybe just call the police and leave the investigation up to them. Now, once you've all finished your milk, we'll go back into the classroom and get on with the work.'

Miss Milne's determination was a worry. Other than making the acquaintance of Mr Plod in the Noddy storybooks, I'd never met a policeman but presumed the Forres one was unlikely to be as kindly. It's a small consolation, but it's a long cycle-haul from Forres to Dunphail. With a bit of luck, maybe his bike would get pinched as well.

Sadly, that hope died at dinnertime, when Mrs Haggarty said, 'I've told the bobbies and they'll want a word with you, Jane. But they can't come until tomorrow.'

Now, it's that tomorrow. There could have been a chance to say something last night. When we were having our tea, Dod said in a not entirely joking way, 'Missing a bike, eh? Never mind that! For a while I thought we'd lost a lorry driver.'

'From your description, it could be a tink,

but they don't pinch things. Mebbe take a loan, though,' said Mum. After that the subject was dropped, though I did worry about Elizabeth bringing it up when we were in bed. However, she was far too taken up fretting about a spelling test.

'*Difficulty*, now. That's the one I've difficulty with,' she says. At another time I might have thought it was a joke. Instead, I snap, 'It's easy. Look! It needs two "F"s to get it to rhyme right. Don't you remember Miss Milne tapping her pointer on the floor in time to saying it?'

Silence falls after I spell out the word in a sing-song way. Lying sleepless through the night, I reckon my sister's problem's been solved, but it's thanks to her that I've got a far bigger one.

In the morning, on leaving the house, Mum's parting shot doesn't help.

'It's a pity the lorry driver's away today. He could have been a help. Still, if the bobby does come to the school, all you'll have to do is tell him the truth.'

I could, but think that's a risky business. I glance back at Tombain, maybe for a last glimpse, when Elizabeth passes. She rings her bell with the importance of someone who can ride a bike. 'You'll need to hurry up or you'll be late, and that'll put teacher in a bad mood,' she says.

I'd be quickening my step past Tomdow

264

cottage anyway. Its cottage windows stare blankly back as I pass them, wondering if the little girl's returned and is watching. This particular morning I haven't the courage or time to look somewhere that now holds a deserted air.

Dod's words come back, as I carry on down the road. 'Once the byre's done, the Tomdow house must be next for improvement. And we should ask the laird if we can get an extra bit built on, too. It's really far too wee for a family.'

Mum agrees. 'And let's see if we can get rid of that old wall mirror advertising Guinness. After that, it might start to look like a house and not like the old disreputable inn that it once was.'

The ash tree beside Tomdow's steading is beginning to lose its leaves and, come springtime, it'll be the last to grow new ones. I'll miss seeing the funny-looking letters that the bare branches make against a winter sky and wonder what it's like to wake up in prison. At least I won't have to walk to school.

Our fields finish where the Knockack is spanned by a road bridge. It links two dangerous S-bends. In the future, they'll bring sorrow to the family of a scooter driver unprepared not only for them but the treacherous camber of the road as well. Right now, there's no traffic using it and, as I cross the bridge, I hear only the sound of the Knockack. It accompanies me until I climb the slight hill and walk past old Mrs Munro's cottage at the roadside.

She's out minding her vegetable patch and calls, 'Aye, aye, Janie. I see you're no' in any hurry to get to school the day. I'm no' even hearing yer blethers.'

Without Kenny, I've had to invent company and it's no fun unless you share a conversation, even if it's with somebody in your head. But, to tell you the truth, I'm a bit embarrassed that she's heard me. I've to wait until she's safely out of earshot before I call up my Funny Manny.

'You've landed me in a right load of trouble,' I tell him.

He doesn't reply, but by the time we reach the Glebe I know that he's no idea where the bike is. Anyway, he'd never dream of pinching anything. As for his appearance, it's no wonder that he hasn't had time to smarten himself up. He's a part-time kelpie catcher and he's also looking for his long-lost daughter.

'I'm sure there's one at Tomdow,' I tell him. 'Try there.'

In my mind's eye, there's such a touching reunion that, going up the last stretch, which we call the schoolie brae, I almost feel better.

'Schoo-alll!' the pupils call and I run to catch up with them filing in, the manny's image as fresh in my eye as his words of gratitude are in my ears.

Elizabeth grabs me and whispers, 'Mrs Haggarty's got her bike. She didn't know her husband had taken it.'

I should be glad, but when I think of that poor little girl waiting to be claimed, and the manny's story, I'm almost disappointed.

32

THE RIGHT ADDRESS

Mum lifts the wooden cover off the deep sink where she's been steeping clothes. Over time, the lid itself has soaked up water, making it heavy with slimy edges. She totters under the weight of it as she tries to put it aside, but it slips from her grasp, to slide over the stone floor.

'Damn! Ach, just you stay there, you sorrer,' she says. It sounds like a handy word for playground use. I store it away whilst righting the offending lid.

'Thanks, Janie.' Mum sighs, then bends over the sink's soggy collection. 'Oh, for a washing machine!'

We seldom wear bright colours, but our dull navy-blue knickers and white school blouses meanwhile entwining in a shapeless mass will be soon transformed. Once they're hung on the wire clothesline strung between two larch trees, that eternal Tombain wind will breathe enough life to balloon them into funny-looking flags flapping Scotland's colours.

But the image may not amuse Mum today. As she scrubs red soap over a blouse collar, then rubs it over the corrugated surface of a wash board, she muses, 'After the byre improvements, I never saw such happy cows! I wonder if Maudie had been in those new bonny quarters would she have kicked your sister?' Holding up the blouse, our devoted mother glares at it, then dumps it back into the water. 'Honestly! I don't know how you manage to get this so grubby.'

I don't like the way this conversation's going. 'You were saying about the byre?' I try.

Her voice softens. 'Aye. Of course a damp-proof course wouldn't mean anything to a cow, and we certainly didn't think our ones would notice the new cement floor laid over it. But without cobbles underfoot, they fair skipped into the byre. Once they were there, they took to their new ultra-hygienic quarters right away. Even the cement feeding-boxes, replacing the straw and hay haiks, got their full approval.'

She goes on. I get the feeling that she's

speaking about herself. 'You know this, Janie? They reminded me of hard-working women who've spent years running shockingly inconvenient houses. Now they're delighted to have their attics, basements and big Belfast sinks transformed into a modern labour-saving unit.'

Any minute now, and especially in the absence of a washing machine, I reckon she's going to move into the byre.

Our laird has agreed with Mum and Dod that the Tomdow cottage needs modernising and I wonder if, once the work's finished, we might fetch up living in it. I'm not sure if that'd be a good idea. It's very close to the road and hasn't any trees. I now know that our larch witches are harmless, but if the little girl comes back I'm not sure that she is.

'Mum says you've to stop going on about that little girl,' Elizabeth told me. 'She said that when you get something into your head, nothing short of a bullet will shift it.'

I'm appalled. 'I don't believe you!'

'Well, now you know what *that's* like. Anyway, it's all in your bloomin' imagination. Remember all the hours you've wasted, tapping on Granny's walls looking for a secret passage?' She gets into her stride. 'And of course, there's this business of looking everywhere for a piano. You even think that Granny might have one, she just hasn't got round to telling you where it is.'

Ignoring her, I think about the piano tuner coming to the school. He got all sorts of funny noises when he was working on it, but after he finished he played something so wonderful it drew beautiful and exciting pictures in my head. I'd love to learn how to do that. The dream of having a horse hasn't completely gone, but a piano doesn't need hay. Maybe I could get that instead.

Rubble from Tomdow's been dumped in a careless heap at the road edge. Tonight, on my way home from school, I'll look for the Guinness mirror: see if it lands here as well.

The sound of the workmen, hammering and shouting, floats through the open door. I wish Victor was coming out of it instead. He always knew what was going on at school and would tell me if there was anything new happening.

'How d'you know all this?' I asked him once.

'I listen.'

He'd said it in such a dreamy way, it was difficult to take offence or consider it might apply.

The school day starts in the usual way, but we don't spend as much time singing round the piano.

Miss Milne explains. 'Remember, it's Music and Movement today, so, boys, go and push back the desks so there's plenty room and we're in time for the programme.'

If Victor had been there, he'd have heard her add, and then may have told me, to expect a visit from the school nurse and doctor. They'll call after the interval. Unfortunately, I've either drifted off at this point or gone to the cloakroom to change into sandshoes. They're better wear for a radio school music activity that teaches song and dance.

A few minutes before it starts, Miss Milne will stretch up to the wide windowsill where the big wireless sits. As she twiddles with its two controlling knobs, odd noises emanate from it, to all but her amusement. Alec holds his nose and makes a hand signal, indicating a chain being pulled.

'I'll laugh the other side of your face,' she says unsurprisingly.

The wireless is as big as Granny's one but not as fancy – certainly not as polished and is beginning to get sun-bleached.

'What can you expect when you've something too heavy to be moved from somewhere that the sun gets it. It's a monster of a thing,' Mrs Haggarty declares, 'but there's nowhere else for it to go.' She flaps a duster at the machine in disgust. 'Tch! Newfangled ideas!'

'Good morning, boys and girls.' A lady with a voice unlikely to be heard in the playing fields of Dunphail greets us, as she must do the nation's tuned-in primary schools. 'Let's warm up and start today with a nice new song. I want you to imagine that you're donkeys. Nice trots now, as we go along.'

'That should be easy for some of us,' Alec whispers, and as the music starts he starts to galumph about in a way reminiscent of a Clydesdale horse.

Miss Milne ignores this and takes her usual spot. If I wasn't so busy looking for my bridle, I'd swear there was a glimpse of her looking amused. Meantime, the lady warbles.

Were you ever in Tibet?
Donkey riding, donkey riding
Were you ever in Tibet
Riding on a donkey?

There's cracks and whistles from the wireless, the wooden floor bounces under the weight of creative expression, garters are shoved to the ankles and faces grow red with endeavour as we trot and canter round the floor. The pong of heating sandshoes adds rubber to the smell of our over-heating bodies. Getting into the swing of things, and with a bit of shoving and pushing, we're all heading for a full-blown display of hee-hawing donkey savagery when the wireless lady must have heard us.

Her voice comes over. 'Now, boys and girls, I hope we're singing too.' She says it in a tone calm enough to control every participating pupil throughout Britain, whilst Miss Milne moves away from the radiator and begins to clear the table beside her desk. As she puts away the usual clutter of paper and jotters, she includes the small box of Unusual Objects. This could be exciting. Speaking personally, I've found that after the first few weeks on display, the porcupine quill and ostrich egg have lost their rarity appeal. Now slowed down to jogging on the spot, I start to look forward. Maybe after playtime the box will come back full of other, more exciting things.

Space cleared, Miss Milne looks at it with a satisfied expression. She checks the clock. 'Playtime in a few minutes,' she says.

A new family's come to the district and there's a child from it in every class but mine. They stick together in such a strong clan even Alec and his pals don't bother with their induction programme of tease and mockery. I don't know where the family stays but think they may live near the Dunphail garage.

There's a cluster of houses close to it and about half a mile from the train station on the Forres side, but we only pass that way by car and that's not very often. It's a part of our parish that I don't know much about, except that quite a few workers for the Dunphail

273

estate live there. Anyway, our playtimes are so full of action there's never the time or interest to ask anybody anything about where they live. Meanwhile, the new family merges seamlessly into a game of rounders and shares everyone's disappointment when Miss Milne appears.

'She's nay got her bell!' There's a buzz of surprise, especially after our teacher says in a mild voice, 'Playtime's over, children.'

'That's jist cos she's that two wifies wi' her,' says Alec, 'I'm surprised that yon ane wi' the white coat can move in it.'

'It'll be the starch,' says Moira. 'And that'll be the district nurse in the blue frock. Miss Milne said they'd be coming.'

It's disappointing to see that the table's empty of Unusual Objects and, after the ladies spread paperwork out on it, it still looks pretty boring. As they take their seats behind the desk, they seem so business-like and serious, they begin to look a bit frightening. Seeing Elizabeth biting her nails doesn't help.

'We'd like you to come up to us, singly please.' Even if the lady in the white coat speaks with a low voice, it carries command.

'Right! We'll start with Primary Seven,' says Miss Milne, and points to the newest pupil.

I watch closely and listen hard. The lady in

the white coat seems to be asking some kind of question. It's hard to hear what because she speaks so softly. Whilst the new pupils answer clearly, the others lower their voices, but always she nods, then writes something down on a form whilst the nurse looking on takes notes.

I strain my ears, but the only audible response comes from the new pupils. As if it's a badge of honour and she's hard of hearing, they shout, 'Dunphail Home Farm.'

I've never heard of it but at least, unlike Miss Milne's geography lessons, which involve whacking the wall map with her pointer and saying unpronounceable names, this one sounds local.

At length, Miss Milne says, 'Right, Jane. You're last.'

I approach the desk. My heart might be thumping but there's been plenty time to rehearse the answer. Actually, I'm so prepared I don't bother waiting for any question. Just as White-coat's pen is poised over the page and before she's opened her mouth or even looked up, I say as loudly as the new pupils, 'Dunphail Home Farm.'

33

A TALE OF ANOTHER TIME

'Are you sure?' The eyes behind the rimless spectacles look kind, but puzzled.

I hold firm. Who needs a question when they've got an answer, and have I not heard that six times? I nod my head vigorously.

'Oh well, then.' After somewhat reluctantly writing Home Farm on the form, she says, 'Now, could you go with Nurse next door, please? As you're on your feet already, she'll start with you first.'

Elizabeth, sitting at her desk in the front row, looks as if she's trying to say something, but I'm already following the nurse out into the dining room. The weighing machine, with its high measuring gauge, has been pulled out from its usual place behind two wooden boxes full of library books. They're occasionally delivered by a lady who wears a two-piece tweed suit and flat shoes. She's got a thin face and beaky nose.

'I bet she got that, having her nose stuck in ain o' her books.'

When I asked Elizabeth could this be true,

she said it would've been Alec's idea of a joke.

The machine's height lever is pulled down so quickly I'm in danger of being flattened. Then I'm weighed.

'Uh huh,' says the nurse non-committedly and records the details on a form, where I can see my name and Home Farm written under it. 'Hands please,' she continues, and demonstrates, holding hers out then turning them up and back again. I look closely at them. They're very clean.

'I see ye dinna bite yer nails,' I offer.

She smiles. 'No, I haven't got a nervous disposition.'

Goodness! Wait till I tell Elizabeth. Wishing there'd been a chance to lick them cleaner before inspection, I show my hands.

'Um,' says the nurse, 'I noticed none of you washed them after your playtime. And you've got sinks! So, be sure to wash them after as soon as we're finished. Now, let's have a look at your hair.'

'Mum makes us wash it every Sunday night,' I complain.

'And quite right too,' says the nurse, her eyes sharp as she examines my head. I'm aware that her searching fingers are lifting strands of my hair but they're so light they hardly touch. 'That's fine,' she finally allows. 'Now, d'you see that chart on the far wall?'

She means a white board with rows of

black squiggles. It's so distant it's hard enough to see, never mind anything written on it. Holding up a plain postcard, the nurse says, 'I'm going to put this over one eye at a time and I'd like you to read out what you can see.'

I'm quite pleased to be able to make out the first two lines but, hard as I try, can't progress. It's useless squinting under the card to get my other eye into action because the nurse notices. She presses the card more closely, then, just as I'm about to protest, she swaps it over.

'Let's see how you get on with your other eye.'

The letters are only marginally clearer, but by now my eyes are protesting. They feel as if somebody's stoking a fire behind my eyeballs. Eventually I give up trying to read anything. The silence is interrupted only by my heavy breathing.

'Come on, Jane, just you take your time.' The nurse says it in such a kindly way that to show cooperation I round off the session by throwing in any old letters.

'Um,' she says, clearly unimpressed. 'Looks like you need specs. We'll send your mother a letter. Ah! Here's Doctor.'

White coat appears and explains that she wants to see my throat.

'Say "Ah",' she says, flattening my tongue with a wooden spatula.

278

'Aw.'

'No! Ah!' she perseveres.

So do I, and on behalf of every other Dunphail pupil. 'It's jist the way we aw say it, Awww!'

She nods in a resigned way. 'Right. Thanks for the elocution lesson. Now, Nurse here tells me that your eyesight's not very good. What I wonder is, have you had measles?' She poises a pen above my form.

'Yes, and yon pink stuff cried Calamine Lotion disna work,' I tell her, although I don't mention the frightening sight of the larch witches getting ever closer until Mum shut the window-blind.

I'm about to launch into the horrors of having chicken pox, which has an even worse itch, when she marks the paper, gives a faint dismissive smile. 'That's fine. You can go now.'

Just as I head out the door, the nurse says, 'Don't worry if anybody asks if you've been crying. They're only red because you've been straining them.'

When I get back to the classroom, little James takes one look at me and starts to lick his lips and drum his fingers on the desk.

'Your turn now, James,' says Miss Milne.

If he hadn't been so snooty about taking me on as his bus conductress, I could have told him about eye-strain, but he's soon back and practically skipping.

'Easy and the doctor says I'm right good at saying, "Ah",' he boasts but pipes down when it appears that his pin-up girl's sight's not good either.

Miss Milne's been told about it. To our disgust, she immediately springs in to action. 'Right, Elizabeth, I suppose, like me, you wouldn't have known that there was a problem because you're so near the blackboard, but, you, Jane,' she eyes me speculatively, 'you don't pay that much attention to it anyway. The best thing for you is to come and share a desk with your sister.'

Hearing her sigh, she adds, 'Well, at least until you're both seen by the optician. And as for you, Jane, I think you're fine without Moira's help now. Anyway, she's got her own work to do. Before she goes to Forres Academy next year, she'll have to sit the Control exam.'

I don't know why but at the mention of the word the older pupils groan and Miss Milne reacts as she does until she snaps out, 'You can moan as much as you like but every eleven-year-old has to sit it before they leave for secondary education.' Her eyes blaze. 'And if you don't do well in it, you'll be put into a low class and rue it for the rest of your lives.'

Alec's hand shoots up and, before she can stop him, he says, 'Please, Miss, my sister didn't get into the top class but she gets cooking and typing and she says the boys get woodwork and they're all really useful skills.'

'With a head like yours, Alec,' Miss Milne says dryly, 'you'd want to be careful.' She looks pleased with this remark. Ignoring a sotto voce mentioning Jesus's carpentry skills, she turns her attention back to me. 'You seem to be managing your reading and sums all right, and now that you're near me I can keep an eye on you and you'll have to pay attention.' Then she unfairly adds, 'I know you waste a lot of time dreaming.'

It's been an especially long day and the wretched donkey song which hasn't much a tune to it, has stabled itself in my brain and it's all I can hear as, giving up on singing, marching and galloping, I trudge home. Tombain might now be visible, but it's still a half-mile away. Nearer is Mrs Munro, who's waiting at the roadside.

'I wis looking to hear ye singing,' she says, 'but you'd stopped. Maybe your throat's gone dry.' She looks at me closely. 'You look awful warm. What about coming in for a piece and a drink o' water?'

Even if her voice is old and croaky, her step is light and nimble, especially after swapping her tackety-boots for gym shoes.

'Come awa in,' she says, leading the way.

Her house is much the same as Lala and

Mrs Bremner's, except that the kitchen, facing the entrance, is a separate, if tiny, room. Instead of a tap, and standing on the stone floor, there's an enamel pail. It's covered with muslin and when she takes it off I see water, light brown in colour. The kitchen dresser is tall, thin and made of metal. It's painted the same shade of blue as the rim of the white mug which my hostess lifts out from one of the cupboard compartments. With a quick movement, she scoops water from the pail.

Handing over the brimming mug, she says, 'Straight fae the burn! Now, you go ben to the living room whilst I mak' you a piece.'

Despite the sun streaming through the little window beside the oil-covered table, peats glow in the pipe-clayed fireplace. They throw out such a heat I take the furthermost chair at the table. The mug feels cold on my lips and the water slides down, soothing my parched throat with the same effect as an icicle. She's right about it being burn water. I recognise its peaty, soft flavour.

'My! But you were thirsty.' Mrs Munro, carrying a buttered slice of bread in her hand, puts it on the table, 'You'll soon be ready to give me a song, but have this first.'

She takes a chair, wiping her hands on her cross-over pinafore. 'So, what did you learn at the school the day?'

I tell her about the nurse and doctor.

'We didna hiv sic fowk in my young day an if ye needed a doctor, ye'd tae pay for it. Mind you, Janie, I wisna long in school.' She taps her chest. 'But I wis learned tae work very young. I hid tae. You see my father died when my youngest brother was three weeks old.'

'That must've been terrible. You'd hae been like ma mither.'

Mrs Munro holds up four fingers. 'Aye, only my ain had twice as many bairns.'

'Four! What did she do?'

'Well, she'd have hid tae pit us in the poor hoose whilst she'd tae look for work. Her first job wis spreading mole heaps wi' a shovel. She couldna afford shoes, so she worked bare-fitted.'

You can stop complaining right now. I send the message to my feet, although I kind of envy Mrs Munro her tackety-boots. It would be fun getting sparks off them going along the road. It might make it seem shorter.

'Mind you, things did get better after a whiley,' continued Mrs Munro. 'There wis a hairst and the men that worked the place were awful decent and so that ma mither had no broken time, for ye see she'd no get paid for that, they used tae tak her tae the barn for tae mak' straw ropes.'

The old lady gets up, rubs her back, puts another peat on the fire, then continues,

'The way they made straw ropes was a thing called a thaw crook. It had a great long iron spike and was fastened roon the waist wi' rope. The men paid oot the straw as if they were putting wool on a spindle and then ma mither twisted and twisted till she made a rope.

'They were grand and strong. They had to be, for they were used tae tie doon the stacks.'

The storyteller finishes in triumph: 'Nae Glesga Jock in those days!'

Her tale, care and hardy spirit keep me company so that I reach Tomdow before knowing it. Now that the ash tree has lost all its leaves, it's easy to fancy that its bare and tortured-shaped branches are like a page out of a witch's spellbook. It's much harder to imagine barefoot women working in the fields. How tough that must have been and almost as difficult to believe as the old Tomdow cottage offering riotous behaviour within its stone walls.

Now, there's more of them piled up outside alongside a heap of broken wooden lathes and the cladding that used to cover them. The house has been left an empty shell with the Guinness sign, like a mockery of its past, lying on its side, cracked and skewed against the gable wall.

A gust of wind, disturbing the builder's

rubble, blows grit into my eyes.

'Maybe what you saw was a thirsty ghost or maybe it was just your reflection.'

I remember Dod's words as, eyes stinging, I try to wipe years of grime off the mirror, then haul it round so that it stands vertically.

We don't have any long mirrors in Tombain, so I'm not used to seeing a whole figure. The solemn person peering back is a surprise. Even if there's a late sun, which catches the house gable end, warming it momentarily, the mirror, with its lettering, seems to stay as dark as the contents of the Guinness glass in the advertisement.

As I wave, I turn my head, frightened in case there's no returning signal, then make for home.

It's a surprise to be met at the bottom of our road by both Elizabeth and Mum. 'We've been worried about you!' says Mum. 'Where on earth have you been?'

I'm unsure where the conversation might lead and toy with the idea of telling them that Mrs Munro dragged me into her house and forced water and bread down my reluctant throat. But I can't really, so I turn to Elizabeth and say, 'You must've passed when I was at Mrs Munro's.' I aim for a martyred tone. 'She was sorry for me because I looked so wearied and she took me in, fed and watered me.'

'Well, that was very kind of her. I hope you remembered to thank her,' says Mum in a half-cross kind of way. 'And now I don't suppose you'll any have room left for your tea.' She exchanges a look with Elizabeth and they share that annoying amused grown-up smile before she adds, 'But it's good you're back. Your sister and I were beginning to think you might have moved to a different address.'

34

CHANGING TIMES

'He's getting so helpless, Mam's no going to manage him much longer.'

There's a debate going on in the kitchen, which lightens the boredom of washing dishes in the scullery. As I'm on my own, it's easier to keep crockery sounds to a minimum whilst listening hard.

Meg, one of Dod's sisters, is in full flight. There's a big Bremner family who regularly visit and are all concerned about Lala. However, Meg hasn't quite the same family commitments, so she's come to stay a while, see how her parents are managing and if she can help. Unfortunately, she's finding that her mother's strongly put independence makes that difficult.

Venting her frustration to Mum and Dod, Meg says, 'Of course, she's no getting any younger herself, as well you know. And then when we got the doctor to visit and he eventually came, he examined Father right enough ... and he did seem a bit worried.' Meg's voice rises. 'But then he asked Mam how she was. Well! She banged her chest and said, "Hear that, Doctor? Sound as a bell."' Meg continues exasperatedly, 'Then, the minute he left, what d'you think she said?'

Dod's wearied; 'I can jist imagine' is lost to something resembling a salvo, as Meg snaps, 'She'd the neck to say, "The doctor didna even look at me!"'

I knew the tattie pit hasn't been visited by Lala for a while, but I supposed it was because it's empty and must be waiting for our new crop to be picked. Then I think about Nell. Now Lala hardly bothers to put his hand down to either stroke or annoy her, and seems so locked into his own world that Mrs Bremner's started to feed and shave him. Much as she's handy with an axe, she's not so smart with the cut-throat razor. As well as that, his black suit's getting peppered with little burnt holes. Someday soon he's going to have to stop smoking that pipe.

'If she's not there, he could set fire to himself,' Meg goes on. 'So she's got that to

287

worry about as well. It's no wonder she's exhausted, but will she let on?'

'Parkinson's is a terrible disease and bad enough,' Mum says in a heartfelt way, 'but if we're not careful, we'll have two invalids.'

Dod's equally anxious. 'I ken that. I wis helping Mither ower a fence the ither day, an' she wis as light as a feather. There's nothing o' her. We'll have tae dae something.'

I make the mistake of rattling the cups. The voices drop and there's nothing more to be heard. Afterwards, I tell Elizabeth about the conversation but all she says is, 'Nobody ever tells us anything important. It's no wonder we try to lug in. It's a pity the telephone's so expensive to use. At least when Mum and Dod are talking on it, they can't stop us from listening.'

'We can't do that with Mrs Bremner,' I chuckle. 'If it rings when Mum and Dod are out and she's looking after us, as soon as she picks it up, she puts it down again.'

On a weekend a couple of weeks later, Elizabeth and I, feeling like outsiders, watch from our kitchen window. There's a big collection of the Bremner family milling around the old house. They've come to help Lala and Mrs Bremner move to an old folk's home in Nairn. All but Mrs Bremner, unfamiliar in a black coat, look grim. Surprisingly, she practically skips into a waiting car. Lala, as grey as the day's sky, supported by two helpers, is taken out of the house to join her.

Preparing to leave and make sure that they arrive at their new home safely, Dod says to Mum, 'We ken Balblair wis once the poor hoose but it's got beds and folk that'll care for the old boy. It's the best we can dae but dinna ony o' ye bother comin' oot tae say cheerio. It'll mebbe cause an upset. Ye'll see them once they're settled in.'

Although he might not have meant it as such, he's right about the *once*. After our first visit to this home, Elizabeth and I won't make another one.

Still, when we do go, we're met by Mrs Bremner, who looks well. She's wearing the flower-sprigged overall she has for best and greets us cheerfully at the front door of a place built on the same stark lines as our school, but much bigger.

'Lala's in the mannies' wing,' she says. 'I'm nay sure if he likes it there but they keep him bonny and clean and they're never done polishing the floor.' She adds in a pleased way, 'I like to feel useful so I gie them a hand.' She stretches one out, twiddling less swollen fingers, and gives a little smile. 'See? Nay hacks on them either.'

Dod shows her the sore scores in his own hands. 'Mebbe I should move in here wi' you.'

'You widna be as handy,' she says. 'Jist

stick tae visiting Lala. He'll be pleased to see ye but I'll not come wi' ye. I'm helping them here tae pit oot the wifies' tea in their ward.'

We follow her directions and find a big room lined against each wall with single iron beds, all occupied. There's one in the middle and that's where, as if stranded, Lala lies. When we go to him, only his eyes move and even they've lost their colour. We've no idea if he's pleased to see us, but the bare surroundings are hardly welcoming. It's so hushed here, the sound of people breathing seems loud.

I stroke the area of starched white sheet covering the top of the light green counterpane spread over his bed. There's a strong smell of floor polish. I say, 'Nay pipe smoking here, Lala. I s'pose the nurses will be keeping an eye on you tae mak sure ye dinna sneak a fly puff.' He blinks. Elizabeth keeps quiet but puts out a hand to cover Lala's long fingers. They don't move.

'Better run on, quines,' says Dod after a few uncomfortable minutes. 'I'll catch up with you.'

35

A CAT CALLED SMILER

Dod had said, 'Well, quines, I'm afraid that Lala didna last very long.' He cleared his throat, there was a moment's silence, then he went on, 'But now the Old Lady's settled in the Anderson Home in Elgin and that suits her better.'

Mum agreed. 'An' she's even got a bit of colour in her face. She's nearer her own folk too and she aye likes to be busy, so it's as well that the staff let her help.' She gives a little laugh. 'As a matter of fact she considers herself more one of them than a resident.'

I sit on the horsehair-filled sofa in the old house, remembering the conversation. It was the nearest thing we got to an acknowledgement that Lala had died, so by this time, I imagine, he'll have caught up with his two dead sons. I hope so, and that he's able to talk now and enjoy a blether with them. Just in case they're wondering about Mrs Bremner, I whisper a little message.

'Now, dinna you be worrying aboot her. She's doing fine. She's away from Nairn an' off to the Anderson Institute in Elgin. Dod didna think she'd like living in the middle of the town. But she does. Says it's fine and handy for buying Butter Bas and she's never stayed in a bonnier or bigger hoose other than the Balblair one, an' as ye ken it was all right there but oot o' the way.'

Of course, there's no response from Lala. The funny thing is that even it's still got their furniture; without either him or Mrs Bremner the house feels emptier and a lot less welcoming than our loft. The ornate clock that Mrs Bremner so faithfully wound has stopped and the teeth have gone. So have the family photographs. I won't see them again until many, many years later when Evelyn, one of Dod's nieces, will send them to me. Those long-ago faces look out and roll back time: memory jogs. Meanwhile, here, the smell of old tobacco smoke lingers, whilst sound only comes from the wind funnelling down the cold chimney. The hens have gone.

Dod relocated them with ours to the Tomdow steading. He's heard about the deep-litter system. It means keeping hens inside in a warm house with lots of artificial light. It tricks them into thinking that it's springtime, so they lay lots of eggs and just now there's a good market for them. We still don't have electricity but make do with bottled-gas lighting, which seems to work. Now, after teatime, either Elizabeth or I will collect the eggs after renewing the water in their drinking fountains and dishing out fishy-smelling pellets.

'They're so much easier and cleaner than hens' mash,' says Mum. 'But the trouble is the cats like them, too. So once you're finished, quines, make sure you put the lid back on the pellet bin.'

All in all, it's a nice job. Passing the Tomdow cottage doesn't worry me any longer. Having bad eyesight's explained quite a lot (if not why my new spectacles should be framed in a disgusting flesh-coloured pink) but if it's dry I cut through the field to the steading where it feels warm and welcoming and the hens seem happier in their new surroundings. Maybe Mrs Bremner's ones are relieved not to have an axe-threat hanging over them, whilst the others don't now have Duck hassling them.

She's getting old, her head's more tousled than usual and she doesn't wander about as much. Mum says she's got rheumatics in her right leg and her feet are probably cold, if a lot cleaner. These days, she sometimes condescends to keep Drake company for a while in the stick shed.

I've heard and seen her in full cry beside him. His head's tucked under his wing, so he's plainly not listening, but Mum says, 'I bet she's telling him about the good old days when she'd head for wild debauches in the muddy meadows and afterwards she'd reel home beneath the wondering moon. She'd wake everybody up with loud ha-ha's.' Mum laughs, too. 'By comparison, Drake must think he'd led a blameless life.'

And they say I've an imagination!

'What's a debauch?' asks Elizabeth.

'I'll go,' I say one night that it's Elizabeth turn of duty but she's fretting about her homework.

'Have you not any, Janie?' asks Mum.

'Mrs Munro helps with my reading,' I tell her, thinking that the children's section of her *People's Friend's* may be a pale imitation of Mrs Bremner's *Red Letter* but it's a lot better than the school's smelly First Reader. I've read it loads of times and only once found it interesting.

'Well, you'll certainly learn plenty about hard work from her. And she doesn't mind you calling in on your way back from school?'

'No. She says her bread would get stale if I didna eat it an' she likes a wee news.'

Adjoining the Tomdow steading is a small storage room. It's where Pansy's offspring stay. As soon as they hear the click on the steading door latch, they spit hostility but go no further than hiding behind the pellet bin. Even if its lid's still on, the smell of fish comes through. It must be awful for them not being able to get the lid off. I bet if Pansy was here, she'd have figured how to do it ages ago.

Now, lifting it off, I hear the sound of small swears. 'Sheesht, you ungrateful animals. Here!' I scatter a handful of pellets in their direction. 'You should be catching rats instead. Now, shoo, you lazy lot!'

It's not nice being this horrible to the cats, but, try as I might, they refuse all attempts at friendship. I suppose that Pansy's told them to trust nobody. The hens are far more rewarding. All right, they're being brought food and water, but at least they run towards you like a welcoming party, and it's a bonus that those nesting in the old stone straw-filled feeding trough don't mind anybody foraging under them. It's great to be able to do it without fear, and of course wearing specs helps.

They might be the subject of ridicule at school and uncomfortable to wear, with their legs clamped round my ears in a vice-like grip, but faced close to a hen they're a barrier between their beaks and my eyes. I look into the beautiful red-orange ones of Mrs Bremner's Rhode-Island Reds. Along with their crimson combs and rust-coloured feathers, I'd think they were beauties were it not for their scaly yellow legs and toes that end in ugly talons.

'Bonny eggies,' I tell them, by way of encouragement and an intending departure. Replacing the bin lid, and sensing everything's OK, I'm about to lift the door latch to leave when there's a small pitiful mewing sound. I cast about. In the small space of the storage room, the gas light robs colour, casts harsh shadows and hisses as much as the cats slinking well out of reach but keeping a watchful eye.

There doesn't seem to be anything different. A car passes on the road outside. There's seldom traffic at this time of night and I wonder who it could be. Then the noise comes again. I'd have sworn it was a kitten crying if all the cats hadn't such plump figures. Maybe they've swapped pellets to become hunters and it's a half-dead mouse trying to escape. Damn!

'Miaow.'

When a black-and-white kitten peeps round the pellet bin, it's a shock, but immediately I hunker down, then, slowly putting out a hand, try a soft wheedling, 'Puss, puss!'

A small kitten advances, walking as delicately and carefully as if on a tight rope. With its tail up, it looks more anxious than scared and surely incapable of putting out claws. It's enchanting how it comes right up, allowing its head to be stroked. It looks as if it wants to be lifted.

'There's nothing of you,' I whisper, at which point it breaks into a rapturous purr. It seems to like being held in my arms, perhaps it's on account of the other cats. Looking balefully down from their straw throne, their message is clear: *that one doesn't belong.*

'I'm going to take you home with me,' I say, stroking the newcomer. 'And we'll call you Smiler. Anything as wee as you and able to purr as cheerful and loud, needs a name like that.'

Smiler mews and holds on tight.

Mum's feeding Pansy in the scullery when I get back. Having seen her take regular swipes at Nell whenever she tried to join her at the fireside, I'm pretty sure another animal's going to get an equally hostile reaction, so I take this one into the kitchen.

'See what I've got!'

Book in hand, Elizabeth's sharing the sofa with Nell, who opens one eye when Mum comes through. I pop the kitten on Elizabeth's lap. 'Meet Smiler.'

Taking one look, Mum snaps, 'The barn! Now!'

'Och, Mum,' says Elizabeth, putting down the book and cradling Smiler, 'We canna do that. Look at it. It's far too wee and it's most awful cute.'

As if understanding the words, Smiler mews. Now fully awake, Nell freezes.

'It's a poor abandoned orphan,' I cry, 'if we put it in the barn, the cats will bad use it – it's not theirs or the Tomdow ones either.'

There's a pause. Having my sister onside's a bonus, but we'll need a clincher, so I continue. 'And it's only used to humans. Elizabeth, give Smiler to Mum to hold, but be canny, both of you. It's so thin, you could break its ribs.'

Smiler easily adapts to the transfer and cranks up the purrs. Mum, obviously finding it hard to resist the ball of fur, strokes its head. When she lifts its tail, Smiler gives a small reproachful look from eyes that are an emerald-green fringed with gold. Mum smiles. 'So you're a tabby, then, and quines…' she says, casting her eyes heavenwards, 'I suppose you're right. Even if she's got a splotchy-looking face, she is cute but too thin. Maybe once she's been fed for a week or two, she can join the other barn cats.'

Skilfully changing the subject, Elizabeth wonders, 'Where d'you think she came from?'

'Probably an RAF family. If they were posted away from Kinloss, they might not have been able to take her. That must have been hard for them. Maybe they thought that dumping her somewhere warm with a light would mean somebody would see and take care of her. She's obviously used to folk, but look at her, she is starving! Go, you, and get her some milk, Janie. We'll need to feed her here. Pansy'll have a fit if she sees competition.'

'At this time of night, she'll be wanting out. I think she's a bit like Duck about night-time adventures. Mebbe she'll be looking for a debauch,' Elizabeth offers. She pats Nell's head. 'Not like you, you old fatty.'

But Nell's oblivious to anything but the sight of Smiler hoovering up the contents of the saucer. When it's been licked clean, the collie, looking disappointed, gets up, checks for any food crumbs she might have been sitting on, jumps down for a final saucer-check, then climbs back onto the sofa again. She resumes her study of Smiler, who, having tidied her bib and tucker, returns her gaze and gives a soft call.

'Look! She's speaking to Nell,' I cry. 'She's the same colour. Maybe she thinks she's her mother.'

'I doubt that very much,' says Elizabeth, 'but she'll be awful lonely without one. What about her coming to bed with me, Mum?'

I kind of hope that Mum will let her because she hasn't got a Rabbit for company. But it's Smiler who settles the matter.

When she lands on the sofa and cosies in between Nell and my sister, Mum says, 'You wouldn't think that something so little could be so fly, but, Smiler, I wouldn't get too close to that tail. The smell's bad enough from where I am.'

Ignoring our ribald laughter, Nell doesn't move. No matter the size of cat, she must be figuring that they're all best left alone. She stares straight ahead, whilst Smiler looks as if she's sitting pretty.

36

PANSY'S HAD ENOUGH

Soon after Smiler's arrival, Nell gets brave. Not only does the new arrival share her rations but having her around also makes the collie protective towards her little companion and able to snap at Pansy's claws. When the pair are not out and about, they're taking up space either on the sofa or by the fireside.

If Pansy, livid at having been so usurped, wasn't swearing under her breath when we were present, she was trying to scratch her rivals when we weren't. Eventually, giving us all up as a bad job, she's decided to sweep grandly out. Now she's gone to live with our neighbours at Culfearn.

'Honestly, she's quite disgusting. The Culfearn folk said she made a great fuss of them, carried on as if she were a faithful animal who lived only for her masters,' Mum related, and went on, 'When we went to check if they were all right about having her, she made quite sure we saw her sitting patiently at their door, yearning to acknowledge their care for an unloved waif. As for us, well … she cut us dead.'

'I bet she doesn't get Smiler's fancy diet,' says Dod.

Mum's quick. 'Pansy'll never starve. She's a great hunter so that pleases her new owners, but I'm pretty sure she'll soon bend them to her will. They'll be buying her the best of liver in no time. Anyway, Smiler's got such a minute appetite you wouldn't grudge her a bittie nice mince, would you? She needs building up.'

'Like Nell?' Dod glowers at the dog as he speaks to her. 'If you could pick tatties, then you'd be some use, but you wait. The wintering sheep will be here any time now. Then you'll hiv tae work an' you're bound to lose some o' that beef you've pit on. Otherwise we may hae tae pit ye in the meat ring.'

I might have thought he was serious if I hadn't heard his discussion with Mum.

'Nowadays the demand's more for beef than milk,' he'd said. 'Seemingly, there's a nice Aberdeen Angus bull for sale in Nairnshire. He's got a good history of producing bull calves and they've got a better build for carrying beef.' So that eliminates Nell.

'Black with broad noses and behinds?'

'Aye.'

There's silence. I think that Mum might not want to see the back of Frankie. But, really, she's the only one. I might miss Pansy, but not him and once his malign presence has been swapped for Black Douglas, I think she appreciates the difference.

This bull may share Frankie's penetratingly shrill voice but not the smoking red eyes. His ones are benevolent. He's got a small waddling figure and doesn't need a ring in his nose. Mum even goes as far as to say she thinks a daisy in his shiny plush coat would be more his style.

'The Nairnshire farm's no' half as exposed as Tombain,' says Dod. 'It's probably made him a bit of a softie. We should pit him doon by the Tomdow howes for a start.'

He means the sheltered valley that the Dorback runs through.

'That's a good idea, but we'll need to make sure he's on the meadow bit nearer to Culfearn. We don't want him near the crags. They're so sandy, if there was a spate they could easy collapse on him, and his harem as well.' Mum says it in an absent-minded sort of way. She's got that pre-occupied 'Monday morning' look and even if I'm overjoyed that it's the tattie holidays, there's no chance I'll get to hang about the house playing with Smiler.

'Janie, will you leave the cattie alone! She keeps me company,' says Mum. 'I like the way she sits on the arm of the sofa, chats encouragement and helps me with my word count.'

'Nell'll be jealous,' I try.

'She'll be outside wi' me being useful,'

302

says Dod, looking at Mum as she sets her typewriter on the table. 'We need tae check that the wintering sheep are settling on the hill. There'll be more food for them there than from where they came, but they need to get to know the lie of the land. I don't know why folk say they're stupid. Sheep are pretty cute at figuring out both food and danger spots.'

I'm about to mention kelpies and kettle-holes, but Mum's already set out a pencil and jotter.

I get the message. Still, I offer, 'I could go to Culfearn and do tattie-picking with Eliza-beth. I heard you say everybody's short of pickers.'

'Mebbe next year, but if you really want to be helpful, go and wash the dishes. Then go and play outside or in the loft.' She might as well have slammed the door.

Down beside the Knockack, the cry of geese comes first. It's a sound like a squeaking barrow. When they come nearer, they're so high, they're almost invisible. It's doubtful if I could see them anyway: I'm not wearing my specs. They limit acrobat work. Dangling upside down from the birch branches, I listen to those atmospheric calls. They punctuate the burn's murmuring voice and mix with the distant bleat of the win-tering sheep carried on a soft wind. For this time of year, it's an extraordinarily lovely day.

Spiders are doing a bit of trapeze work between the gorse and juniper bushes. I'm torn between admiration for those delicately woven lures and pity for the insects caught on them. Mind you, I'd be delighted if they trapped more midges.

'It's autumn. You shouldna be here,' I say as they swarm around my head. It's useless swatting them from this position – ruins balance, too. As I land on my feet, leaves fall in a golden shower. On the ground, they lie scattered and already almost fragile-looking. Indifferent to anything but the taste of blood, the midges persist. Bracken leaves are a useful deterrent, so I grab a stem. It doesn't come away easily but eventually I manage to twist it off. The leaves are turning to a colour not unlike our Rhode Island hens' feathers and when I start to whirl them about me they make for an elegant, if not very efficient, switch. With the midges continuing their assault, they're a good excuse for returning home. Surely a conscientious mother wouldn't begrudge a request for midge powder.

But she's still at her writing. I can hear the typewriter, so I sneak in by the rarely used front door. I think she may have heard me because I'm hardly in when the typing stops and she bawls, 'Go away out o' here, *now!*'

She must have hearing like a bat, I think, and go out again, slamming the door to express my feelings, immediately realising that this may have been a mistake. She's right after me.

'Janie, was that not you knocking at the back door?' she asks. But she's not looking for an answer. I follow the direction of her horrified gaze and see a headsquare-topped woman dressed in a suit. She's going down our road at a walk bordering on a trot.

'Damn! I think that's the laird's wife,' Mum says.

37

SPINNING A YARN

Elizabeth stretches in bed, moans about how lifting tatties gives her a sore back, then says, 'So, what did Mum do?'

'She ran after the wifie, full of apologies, and took her back to the house. Insisted she have a cup of tea.' I'm still amazed by this example of our mother's turnabout, let alone display of hospitality, but then allow, 'Her typewriter was still on the table, so I suppose that the laird's wife would have seen it and maybe realised it wasn't the best of times to call.'

'And what kind of wifie is she?'

'She seemed fine enough. Speaks different fae us but she liked Smiler.'

'Well, that says a lot, and she didna take the huff when Mum shouted at her?'

I'm a bit sour thinking about grown-ups who think it's all right to yell at little children. 'No, they'd a bit of a laugh,' I say, scratching a midge bite. It's dark, so I can't see if it's bleeding, but it's unlikely there'll be any sympathy coming from my sister. She's too busy groaning about having to go tattie-picking in the morning.

As a diversion I ask if she's seen Pansy.

'No, but I'll tell you who I did see. Black Douglas! The tattie field that we're working on's next to Tomdow's grounds. We're high up, of course, so if we want to see him we've to look down, whereas it'd be difficult to miss the Culfearn bull. If he wasn't in the field opposite us, we'd certainly hear him. I think he must be picking up on the racket the Kerrow one makes. He's new. Bought at the Perth sales or so, one of the tattie-pickers said.'

'Perth!'

'Aye, a fancy, expensive job and he must know it. Ready to rule the roost and not only at the Kerrow. He must be wanting the Culfearn bull to get the message.' Elizabeth tuts. 'Both seem to think it's a competition and whoever bawls the loudest's the winner.' She pauses for a moment, before going on,

'Douglas must've thought he needed to join in.'

Thinking about fat, easy-going Douglas with his big behind, short legs and ladies enjoying a pleasant spot in his meadow beside the river, I think of the winding path leading from it to the top. 'He must've been keen. It's a fair old climb.'

'Uh huh, and I don't think he'll bother doing it again. Och! He started off well enough and he certainly can scream, we all heard him coming, but by the time he arrived at the top, he'd run out of puff. All that he could do then was to lean on the fence separating him from us and puff like an old mannie. You should have heard some of the tattie-pickers in the squad teasing him.' Elizabeth sniffs. 'They wouldn't have done that if it'd been Frankie.'

'Bloomin' cowards,' I say. 'Who's in the squad anyway?'

'There's the farm workers from roundabout. I'm the youngest and the only quine, but there is a wifie there and she wouldn't torment a fly. She's Mrs Coutts. Comes from the Dava. I bet you know her husband. Works on the railway, goes to church every Sunday.'

She means the tall, angular, straight-backed man who cycles there. I know this because I catch him on the binoculars, amazed that he manages the long Tomdow hill climb without ever having to get off his bike. Clad in Sun-

307

day best, complete with shiny cycle clips, he maintains a steady, dignified course. Unlike Black Douglas, I don't think Mr Coutts would ever get out of breath.

It sounds as if his wife is equally strong, as Elizabeth continues, 'She's just wee but she's a great worker. She gives me a hand if I haven't finished my stint before the tattie digger makes its next round. She told the mannie driving the tractor pulling it, that sculls were heavy enough to carry without tatties in them and to give me a pail, like she's got, and to stop going so fast.'

'And did he?'

'No, I think it made him go faster.'

'That's terrible!'

There's a smile in Elizabeth's voice. 'Aye, but he soon changed his tune after the other tattie-howkers shouted he was a helluva hasher and threw tatties at him.' She turns in bed without groaning and muses, 'And I suppose that kind of cheered us all up a bit. I bet that driver's no idea how hard work picking tatties is, and it did get a bittie easier when he went slower. Still, by the end of today I'd hardly enough puff left to bike home.'

Spurred on by the dismal thought of the long trail to school, I take a chance. 'Why don't you take the shortcut through the woods? I bet that's quicker.'

'Dinna be daft. It'd puncture the tyres.'

'No, I meant going on foot.'

308

I don't say I am planning a sneak practice on her bike, nor do I need to because she says that Dod's going to give her a lift. He wants to speak to the tattie squad. See if they can come to us after they're finished at Culfearn.

'So, are you part of the squad?'

'Aye.'

Despite myself, I'm impressed enough to say, 'Dod'll no pay you.'

'He will sot. You're just jealous.'

'Quiet, bairns. It's half-past nine!' calls Mum, which is timely and not unusual.

Next morning when Dod comes back from Culfearn and he says he needs a hand, wages aren't discussed. But if I'd heard of danger money, then the present activity might qualify.

'Haud onto that fence post,' Dod instructs. He's got something he calls a 'mell' and it's the size of a hammer that a huge giant would use.

We're out on the moor to fence off an area, which, thanks to the Lammas Deluge, has deepened a bog enough to make it dangerous: even for smart sheep. Gingerly holding the post and worrying about what Dod's about to do with the mell, I think back. At least it was fun and exciting up to this point. Sitting amongst the fencing clobber in the tractor-drawn trailer, I'd looked back at the farm.

Had smoke come out of the old house's chimney, the view of Tombain would have been as it always was. Still constant and edging one side, was the sheltering fir plantation, and the larch trees too, their pointed tops leaning towards the house, as if watching over it, whilst the farm buildings huddled close by. In the distance, Morvern and Embo were distinct and blue as harebells. The weather had kept. There might have been frost in the night, but now the sun ruled the sky and all the fields still, but for the one next to the moor. On it, short grass rippled in green waves. Yet, and this too was unusual for our high Highland croft, there wasn't a breath of wind.

I could've shouted to Dod but driving along the rough track leading to the moor needed all his concentration and once we'd arrived at the boggy bit the trailer had to be unloaded. By the time that was done, I was out of breath and only able to watch as Dod picked up a huge metal pointed pole.

'Ye might have to wait a wee while,' he said. 'I'll need to make some holes in the ground wi' the punch first.' With all his power, he drove the pole into the ground, cursing at the muffled thump-sound of a stone being hit.

As he readied for another go, a grouse flew out of a nearby tussock of heather. With a cry that began like a hoarse giggle, it went into clumsy flight. 'Go back, go back!' came its call as it went in the opposite direction of the field where I was now heading. Still, the day stayed calm. Still, the short grass rippled. Still, last night's frost lingered in the field's hollows, despite a hard, bright sun. It glanced on what I thought was wet grass. Then, out of nowhere, something brushed against my face: light as a cobweb's thread.

I looked closer. It wasn't the grass that was moving. Instead, caught on it and making it seem so, were millions upon millions of single threads spun by millions upon millions of tiny spiders. The sun glanced on them as they swung from their tethered green posts, like minute empty washing lines blowing on a drying day. But it would only take a whisper of wind to free those tiny spinners on their gossamer-like threads. Then, using them as parachutes, they'd be able to float away as had the one that drifted across my face. A long time later, I'll learn that they're called balloon spiders.

Meanwhile, entranced, I gazed down on a tiny world of huge industry, where everything above it remained quite, quite still. And easy for Dod's voice to carry. 'Right, Janie!'

'Haud tight,' he repeats and now I'm back and in the present and watching him grip the mell with both hands. Now he stands on tiptoe. Now, with a wide swing, he brings it up. Now, my eyes follow its course. Now, for

311

a split second it shows black against the blue sky. Now, it comes crashing down with all the power and weight of a cannon ball.

And now they'll all be sorry because now I'm quite, quite sure I must be dead.

38

A HELPING HAND

'Ye'll need tae haud the fence posts tighter if ye dinna wint them tae dirl,' Dod advises.

I look at my hands. They throb and tremble from the impact of the mell landing hard on top of the post round which my grasp was so unsure. Whilst Dod's aim was perfect, I think back to the neep hasher. At least I could stand back from it. I'm about to tell Dod this when he walks to the next hole and drops in a pole.

'Ach, your hands'll soon feel better. Jist mind whit I telt ye an' *grrrip* hard. Come on, we need tae get this fencing finished afore it's dark!'

Unlike Shadow, who's a Cheviot, our new sheep are called Blackfaces and are specially able to cope with all the tough conditions Scotland can deliver. Our flock has been ranging the hill, keeping their distance from us, but eventually one comes to investigate. Others follow, then form a line of shaggy, grubby coats. Under them, balanced on trim ballet dancers' toes, are legs splodged with the same black that covers their faces. They've all got horns, but they don't look dangerous. Maybe it's because they're shaped like bicycle brakes.

Amused by their interest, I say, 'Hey, Dod! They're as nosy as Shadow, but I dinna think they look half as snooty.'

'No. That's the trouble wi' a long nose, ye can only look doon it. As well as that, when she wis wi' us, we'd nay other sheep. Mebbe she thocht she wis a human.' He nods at the Blackfaces. 'But this lot's got the usual herd instinct. Makes them worth the watching. See how they followed the first sheep? If one got into that bog, the others might follow.' He looks at the Knock and raises his head, as if looking beyond. 'It happened at Lochandorb.'

I'm aghast. 'How?'

'The loch wis frozen over and the shepherd thought he'd take a shortcut across it. It wis a bitterly cold night an' he wanted to hurry them to shelter and for himself as well. Only there's springs under the loch and they can thaw out bitties. When the leading sheep went over one, it fell in and the others just followed. The shepherd could dae nothing aboot it. He wis near drowned himself.'

'What a terrible thing to happen!' My cry is something of a bleat but makes the sheep scatter.

'It was that, Janie.' Dod pats my shoulder, clears his throat, then taps one of the posts. 'But this should keep the brutes safe.' He stands back to admire the fenced enclosure. 'We did a grand job, but we'll need tae get home. It'll soon be time tae get Lizzie back.'

It's a much happier Elizabeth who bursts in the door. Throwing down a pile of Mickey Mouse comics on the kitchen table, she says, 'I got these from one of the tattie-squad folk. He said his brother and sister are finished with them.' She gives a little hop. 'As well as that, they're having a wee Halloween party tonight and we've been invited. Dod says he'll take us, but we'll need to go dressed up. I'm going to go as Willie Winkie. That should be easy an' I could say his poem for my Halloween piece.'

Mum looks up from cleaning a basketful of eggs. Her brow creases. 'Janie, I don't suppose you'd like to be a Willie Winkie as well?'

Hearing Elizabeth's sigh, she hurries on, 'But mebbe you could jist do a wee poem.'

The cheerful faces of Minnie and Mickey beam out from the shiny paper. I know there's colour, fun and adventure inside it because Elizabeth sometimes buys one from Mattie. I've always to wait ages until she

314

finishes reading it. Now that she's got a whole pile, I bet she'll still do the same with these. I haven't got a wee poem – well, I have, but the minute I stand up to recite anything, I always forget. Not only that but I'd been looking forward to sitting, cosy, at the fire with Smiler.

Overwhelmed between a day of hard work when I could so easily have been brained and the rewarding prospect of having the comics all to myself, I burst out, 'I dinna wint tac go.'

Dod, arriving in time to hear this, says nothing but looks so disappointed I feel guilty. Having had no intention of helping, I now say, 'But, Elizabeth, I can look out dressing-up stuff for you.'

'I'm fine. Dod's goin' to give me a shirt an' he says there's yon green metal candlestick that Lala and Mrs Bremner had. I'll get a shot of it.'

'So, where's the party, Dod?' Mum asks.

'At the Lamonds'. One of their loons was at the tattie howkin. He said a few of the Dava bairns aye go roon to their hoose. An' the quines would be welcome.'

Mum looks at me, questioningly. When I shake my head, she hands me her cloth. 'Right! If that's the case, you can take over cleaning these eggs and don't use Vim on them. It breaks the shells' natural seal.'

Nell had been rolling in something very dead and she'd brought the memory of it into the kitchen. 'You're an orra smelling brute!' Mum had cried and taken her outside to throw a bucket of water over her. Now Nell's back, damp, in the huff, in the kitchen and only marginally less offensive, whilst Mum, Smiler and I are in the sitting room.

I love this room and can't believe we're actually in it. It's usually kept for Saturday nights, when we keep up with the fortunes of the MacFlannel family on the wireless. Afterwards, we roll back the room's small square of carpet and, whilst Mum's the audience, Elizabeth and I dance on the black painted wooden floor to the music that Dod plays on the melodeon. Sometimes we sing bothy ballads. Maybe Dod'll entertain the Lamonds with a few of them tonight.

It's such a cold night I couldn't bear to think of the dolls freezing in the loft. Now they're tucked in on either side of the deep chair I haven't had to fight with Elizabeth to stake my claim. Thinking the dolls will be bound to enjoy the comics, I hold up one of them so that they can see the pictures. Mum, with some muttering, has lit the fire. It burns with a blue flame licking round a log's silver coat which, if it hadn't already released a sweet perfume, would tell us we're burning birch.

The fireplace has grey tiles topped with a highly polished mantelpiece made of dark wood. A small glazed vase the colour of a summer midnight stands at one end of it, whilst on the other a figurine of a naked lady balances on a small block of green marble. I wish I'd her long hair, but following the school nurse's visit, there's been a nit alert, so it seems unlikely. Flames cast shadows over the book-lined walls, the tilley hisses and Smiler, in raptures, is sitting on Mum's knee. She's so engrossed in her newspaper that the only sound she makes is the rustle as she turns a page.

I hold up a comic, sniff and try to concentrate on the adventures of Pluto but see nothing funny about him. Surely no dog's ears could possibly stick up as straight as his, no matter how big a fright he'd got. With the back of my hand, I dash away a hot tear rolling down my cheek, taste its salt and sniff again. The fire spits and crackles.

'You haven't got another cold, have you?' Mum sounds a bit fed up.

'No,' I try not to sniff again.

Mum puts down her paper and gives me a long look, 'You're surely not crying?'

Her concern is too much. It opens the floodgates.

'I gotta an affa row fae Dod,' I bawl.

'Because you didn't want to go guising?'

'No, no!'

'What then?'

'I felt bad that I wisna goin...' I stop for another gusher.

Mum's exasperated as she says, 'But you were very clear when you said that you wanted to stay here.'

'Mmm. I did. But I think Dod wis affa disappointed so I ran after them to say that I hoped they'd have a nice time.' I blow my nose then go on, 'And I near missed them – they were already in the car and that meant I had tae shout. I've heard them cryin'oot something at school and afterwards everybody has a great laugh. I wisna sure what it meant but thought it must be something cheery, so I yelled it out.' My lip trembles and I dash away more tears.

Whilst Smiler opens her mouth in soundless sympathy, Mum says, 'If you greet any more, you'll be waterlogged, but go on.'

'Well, the minute I did, Dod stopped the car an' when he came oot he was in a right rage.'

'So what *did* you say?'

'I *only* said, 'Good riddance tae bad rubbish!'

39

A NEW ARRIVAL

'I ken how tae ride a bike!'

'How?' Elizabeth, back from her last day at Culfearn, stops in her tracks.

Knowing I'm having to brazen this out, I say, 'On your bike, of course. You werena using it, an' I learnt it all by myself.' I rush on, unable to stop pride and excitement swelling my chest. 'I jist used an upside-down pail to get onto the saddle and to gie me a bit o' balance. After that, I knew I'd to pedal like hell.' I take a deep breath. 'An' that's what I did. I just took off! Of course, I fell off a few times, but I'm sure I've got the hang o' steering and braking now.'

'You shouldn't swear, the brakes aren't very fancy and you should'a asked me first. Anyway, you needna bother thinking you can have my bike just cos I'm not around.'

'I dinna want it. Mum says she's going to get me a second-hand one. There's a great bike shop in Forres. They sell them dirt cheap.'

I'm expecting my sister to protest, but she doesn't. It's a surprise when she shrugs.

Later on, I expect she'll start gloating all over again about the wonderful time she had at the Lamonds' Halloween party and the friendships she's made with the tattie squad. Right now, however, she's looking remarkably cheerful.

'Mum got mine there an' it's been fine, but actually,' she slows down to savour her news, 'I'm goin to buy a new one an' it'll have gears, a big saddlebag, a bell an' brakes that really work. See? And look whit I got.' She pulls some notes from her pocket and flourishes them. 'That's ma wages! So after you pay me for my old bike, you can use it as much as ye like.'

Autumn's giving way to signs of winter. It's the end of the tattie holidays. The leaves that made the gean trees overlooking the garden look as if they were on fire have all gone. Without them, the trees seem cold and forlorn. We no longer climb up them to spy on Lala at the tattie pit. Something like a giant molehill has taken its place.

'Thank God we got the crop picked and covered so quick,' says Dod. 'An' we were lucky to get that squad Lizzie was in. Getting fowk tae pick tatties is getting tae be a nightmare. It was good o' Mrs Munro tae come an' gies a hand, but she's over seventy!' Dod shakes his head in wonder. 'An' even if her an' Mrs Coutts worked as hard as anybody else, she's no so young either. We'll mebbe hiv tae think o' something different for next year. I've been reading in the *Farmers Weekly* about something called silage. Sounds a better option and no so weather dependent, but at least we'll have oor pit full o' plenty tatties for stock-feed once the winter sets in.'

'Wheest! Don't tell the cows that,' Mum advises. 'If Charlotte hears that she might be kept tight o' a tasty bite until the snow comes, she'll go on strike. She's strong-minded is Charlotte and, as for that new coo, Morag, that we bought from yon croft in Sutherland, she's maybe heard already. Did she not chase you into the steading and bawl at you to give her some hay and a tattie to go with it?'

'Ach weel, she needed tae settle in,' Dod allows. 'She'd come a long way.'

'Maybe, but she must already know that you're a big softie,' scoffs Mum. 'I saw you pinching tatties for her from our own supply.'

'It'll all be strange for her, and coming from where she does she'll only understand Gaelic,' Dod says. 'Anyhow, actions speak louder than words.'

On our first day back at school, I realise this is true after I shout, 'Wait for me, Elizabeth!'

She says nothing, but I get the message. Already, she's clicked her gears, rang her bell and now she's off on her brand new Raleigh bike. Like her, I'd wave goodbye to Mum but am still not confident enough to take my hand off the bike's handlebars. Instead, I concentrate on catching up.

She's halfway along our road when she slows down. Good! She must be waiting before we get to the main road. It'll give me a chance to show how fast her old bike can go! Head down, I pedal like mad, then, taking the lead, remember the brakes warning too late, as is the cry, 'Mind the gate!'

It's one that Dod's made. It was stretched between us and the main road before I crashed into it. Actually, it's really like a fence, so I have to be grateful that, on impact, it disintegrated into a tangle of wires.

'Honestly, ye should watch where you're going. Did ye not see the cows out of the fields and grazing aboot the place?' says Elizabeth, helping me up. 'Dod aye puts up this gate to stop them going onto the main road.'

The home-made barrier might look insubstantial, with its light poles supporting three lines of wire, but their barbs make it effective. It's amazing that the only damage is a grazed knee. Whilst I dust dirt off it with a hanky, then bend down to lick it properly clean, Elizabeth sorts out the jumbled wires.

Replacing the barrier, she says, 'Come on. We're going to be late. We're lucky ye didna snap any o' the wires and the bike seems OK too.' Before she gets on her own one, she hands over a hanky. 'Here. Take this one. It's cleaner. Tie it over your knee.' She deals out a long measuring look, then declares that I'm fine and once more sets off.

I follow, but this time am not inclined to keep up with her. The whir of my bike tyres as we swoop down the Tomdow brae is company enough. Not even the wind that blows cold on my face holds me back. This is the nearest thing to flying imaginable. Up the small brae towards Mrs Munro's house we go. Smoke's coming from her chimney but she's not around to see or hear me shout to a pheasant, 'Hey you! You'd be better on a bike!' The bird, startled from feeding in a stubble field, ignores the cry and, as if clock-work powered, runs, head outstretched, on and on. Flying seems outwith its reach. I've the same problem going up the schoolie brae.

Maybe it's because school's at the end of it, but on getting there I find there's more excitement than usual. A new girl's arrived. She's got her back against the tree in the playground and Alec and his pals are teasing her. 'Mina! That's a funny name. Are ye sure it's not Jemima?'

She's big, plain and looks scared. She doesn't respond. Maybe she doesn't understand them or their humour. Instead, she casts about, as if trapped. It wouldn't have helped that, drawn to the spectacle, the rest of us crowd round to watch. She opens her mouth, but only manages a strangled cry. She shoves lank, mousy hair away from her brow and shakes her head.

She is, after all, a big girl, but had either Davy or Moira not been finishing off the last of their tattie-picking at home, I suspect they'd have stopped us from joining in a chant, and repeating over and over again, 'Mina Mina – rhymes wi' Jemima!'

Suddenly, and with a loud roar, she rushes at us, hurling her schoolbag round her head, helicopter-fashion. It's much as I did on my first day when I was teased, but suppose I lacked Mina's sheet-white face, with its terrifying grimace, and the trace of spittle gathered at the side of her gaping mouth. Nobody fled then, but this must be the one time everybody beats the toll of the school bell. As one, leaving the girl behind, we pelt into the classroom. Minutes after, Miss Milne comes out of her house to investigate the phenomenon, somehow managing to herd in the new girl.

'She's got a knife!' The whisper comes from nowhere and whips round the classroom as the newcomer takes in her surroundings. Fear and hostility charge the air. She shakes her head, then pulls back as if to escape. Miss Milne holds onto her. There's uproar. Arms about each other, they sway together as if in some crazy dance. The girl's breath came in anguished grunts. Her stockings slide down. She's as big as Miss Milne, but, as momentarily it looks like she might be pushed to the floor, the teacher uses her weight to better effect. Somehow, she manages to pin down the girl's frantic hands and, for a second, stills her. Then, with a wild cry Mina breaks free. Passing the piano, she hurls her schoolbag at the clock. It lands in the open doorway through which she's fled.

Not only is it amazing that she's been able to resist the girl's undoubted strength, but, knife or not, we reckon Miss Milne has the courage to chase after her. The sound of footsteps running over the stone floor of the cloakroom dies as the outside door slams. Elizabeth and I, holding hands, sob along with most of the other pupils, whilst James licks his lips and drums his fingers.

'Good riddance tae bad rubbish,' someone eventually tries, but nobody laughs. In the frightened atmosphere of our classroom, Alec and his pals, heads down, mutter amongst themselves. Then one of them offers, 'Ach! We wis only teasing. We aye dae that tae newcomers. It's jist a bit o' fun. It's easy seen she canna take a joke and her a big girl!'

'Aye, an' she might be wanting tae get her ain back. She's mebbe waiting in a ditch for us.' Alec sounds rattled. It makes me gladder than ever that I'm able to ride a bike. I'm still getting out earlier than the older pupils, but today Elizabeth says, 'If you wait for me, we can go home together.'

I don't jeer at her. There's been too much of that today already.

It's not long before Miss Milne comes back. She's on her own. Her brow's untroubled as she reinstates the clock, which despite a cracked face is still working. 'Right. Get on with your lessons,' she says as if nothing's happened, and for once we do as we're told.

We'll never see or hear about that disturbed girl again. Maybe it's because we all feel a little guilty but telling our parents about her might cause further trouble. Thinking our part in it, best forgotten, we don't discuss her. She only came to school for one day and that apparently was enough.

40

LOCAL DRAMA

The local hall gives a better sort of drama than what poor Mina offered. Country dancing, rurals, badminton and the drama society succeed each other every night of the week except Fridays, when everyone whists, dances or holds variety concerts to raise funds for their interests. There's talk of getting new curtains, but not everybody feels a need for them. But the dramatic society does, and it's their turn tonight.

They're putting on a play. It'll make a change from the usual display of local talent, gifted or otherwise for music, dance and humour. Because it's so busy on the farm we can't always manage to be there, but this time it's different.

I'm almost sick with excitement and so's Elizabeth. She says, 'I cannna believe we're going. I heard Mum say so and that she wouldn't miss it for all the world and Dod said neither would he, only he hopes that the piano's been tuned.'

From the outside, our wooden-built hall looks a bit like a huge boat at anchor, but the creaking floorboards inside give the impression of it being in motion. The station's a short walk away. It's handy for Bert, who not only works for the railway but is also the hall keeper. Setting out the rows of seats must have been hard work, but on the night of the concert he's delighted to see every one being taken.

'Grand body heat! There'll be nay need for paraffin heaters the night,' he says. 'But once the show starts I'll need tae tell the wifies in the kitchen tae turn doon the tea urn. It makes the place affa steamy.' In an act of courage, he adds, 'And to stop their blethering.'

We've come early so we get seats near the front and a good view of the stage. The ancient mustardy-coloured curtain stretched over it look as if they were put up at the same time as the hall was built but haven't worn so well.

'I can see why they're needing new curtains,' says Mum, as a buzz of activity comes from behind them, along with the intermittent sound of someone hammering.

'Uh huh, an' that'll be Alec Jack doing the final touches.' Dod stretches his legs in front of him and folds his arms. 'He didna get in tae make the set until the afternoon. Ah jist hope it disna collapse.'

Tension rises as curtains-up time approaches. The noise behind them subsides into whispers. Some wag in the audience observes a little girl, bored with inactivity, running back and fore to the toilet, and says, 'That's an affa watery wee quinie.' We muffle giggles. The same person who waves at Bert to put out the lights now pulls a heavy cord to open the curtains. Behind them, the piano strikes up.

'Nay tuned,' tuts Dod.

Unaware that the curtains have done no more than twitch, the pianist gets into her stride. Mum's laughing. I wish she wasn't so loud. The curtain-puller tugs again. Still nothing happens. Mum's giggle's so infectious, Dod's grin gets bigger.

'We're nay ready,' shouts the stage manager. Somebody must have told the pianist there's a hitch because the music stops. The audience stops breathing then round each curtain side a pair of hands appear. To the sound of material tearing, a little dust and rapturous applause, the curtains are finally opened and the play begins.

I'm not sure what it's about, but it's not boring.

Alec's joinery skills are obvious in the sitting-room setting. It's got a door on either side. It's even got a window with curtains.

All eyes train on the blue-and-white gingham, as someone says in a whisper loud enough to overcome a stage one, 'Ooh, they're right bonny. I think he's mebbe taken

329

them fae his ain kitchen. Wonder if he asked the wife if he could.'

'He must've. They look starched to me. Alec wid niver have got them to look sae fancy,' someone else answers, not bothering to keep his voice down.

Audience participation, now established, is prepared to be helpful. Having watched the first person coming on stage through one of the doors but failing to make a dramatic exit through the one opposite, the watery wee quinie's also ready.

'Mind! The ither door disna work,' she shouts, as soon as the next character comes on stage.

The player's inclined to argue. He glances over in her direction, then, cutting his lines, strides over to the door. 'Dis so. Look!'

As he twists, shoves, then eventually puts his shoulder to it, the scenery wobbles.

'Canny!' cries Alec off-stage.

'Right enough,' the player sighs, giving up. He nods to the wee quinie, then carries on with the script.

'Telt ye,' she says with some satisfaction, after which somebody promotes the value of a clout in the lug for impudent and spoilt children.

I'm busy keeping my eyes peeled for the actors who forget to duck as they flash past the window on track for the working door. However, the wee wifie Smith's so small she got past it without being seen. It comes as a surprise when she appears onstage. And to herself as well.

'Ooh I'm nay supposed tae be here, but at least I came through the right door,' she says, interrupting players already mid-stage and mid-dialogue. She throws a hand over her mouth.

'Och, it's aye fine tae see ye any road,' shouts somebody from the audience.

She giggles, then, waving a small hand, skips off the stage, giving a thumbs-up as she makes it through the working door.

At length and despite Bert's best efforts, sounds of chat and clattering china from the kitchen tell us that no matter how entertaining the play, there's no way that tea's going to be held back. Interval time is decreed. The piano strikes up whilst, to tumultuous applause, the curtains are unceremoniously hauled back into position.

There's a lot of chat about the state of them over tea, cakes and sandwiches.

'It's all very well for the other groups to say they don't use them, but they will if they're running a concert for their own funds,' says Mum. 'Honestly, you can get so much more done if you consult and cooperate with each other.'

'Are you staying for the dance afterwards?' someone asks.

We know that Dod loves dancing, but

Mum, who insists that she can only do the Charleston, says right away, 'No. As soon as the anthem's over, we'll be heading for home.'

41

LET IT SNOW!

'I wish you'd leave your sledges in the bike shed,' says Mrs Haggarty. 'I've just tripped over one as I was coming in.'

She must've been up early to light the school stove. The cloakroom radiator it heats is warm enough for mittens and hats flung over it to steam and give off a homely smell.

'Jings! You'd think somebody had been making Sheep's Head Broth,' she says with a mischievous glint.

She's been making a path between the school and the canteen and now is heading towards the stove carrying something small on her shovel.

I peer at it.

'Can ye nay see withoot yeR specs, Specky?' Alec mocks.

The truth is, I hate my specs. They're still too tight round the ears and make my eyes feel as if they're being pulled out on stalks.

332

With either rain or snow blurring the lenses, they're pretty useless outside too. I think Elizabeth's the same. She doesn't need them for the blackboard because she's so near it, but I'm back sitting beside Moira and can't see it without them. It's seldom very interesting and certainly it's never been as fascinating as what was on Mrs Haggarty's shovel.

'Course I can see. It's a moosie,' I say.

Ignoring Alec, Mrs Haggarty turns to Davy, who's just come in. As he hangs his balaclava on a coat peg, she says, 'I heard you cleaning your feet before you came in. You're a good loon. Now, could you open the stove door, please? Mind, it'll be hot. Use your foot.'

'Nay bother.' Davy presses his foot on a latch as big as one you'd get on a barn. The door swings open. He steps back from the heat whilst orangey-red flames leap out. They might look like hungry imps but, undeterred, Mrs Haggarty advances.

'Dinna!' I cry.

But it's too late. The cleaner has swung the shovel towards the flames, decanted it, then kicks the door shut.

'The bloomin' thing was dead, Jane!' She sounds exasperated.

'It might jist hae been frozen!'

'Well, it won't be that now,' the cleaner replies with a heartless laugh. 'Now, some of us need to go and do some more work.'

Mrs Haggarty's hard heart's been as much a surprise to me as the start to our day, when Elizabeth jumped out of bed to look out of the window.

'I thought we'd slept in. It's so light! Dod did say that he smelt snow last night, but I thought he was joking.'

I was hopeful. 'Is there a lot?'

'Not enough to keep us from going to school. Come and look for yourself. It's funny,' she paused for a moment. 'It seems awful quiet. I canna even hear Duck, but I suppose we'd better get up.'

By now, she was blowing on her hands to warm them, then climbing into her clothes. Reluctantly, I followed. Through the night, there'd been enough snow to cover the outside world in a white blanket and the larch trees in powder. By the look of the menacing sky, we could expect more, whilst there was a curious stillness on the land below as if it was waiting for something to happen well beyond human control.

It wasn't like that in the kitchen. As soon as we appeared, Mum swung into action. 'You're up early! Good! I'll need to go and check that all the home animals are all right.' She tightened her coat belt. 'I'll leave you to get on with your porridge. After that you'll need to wrap up warm, wear your wellies and take a spare pair of stockings.

According to the wireless, the weather forecast's not great. Dod and Nell have gone to take the sheep off the hill.'

I felt aggrieved and still sleepy. 'Never mind the sheep, *we* might get stuck in a drift and perish.'

Mum was unfazed. 'It's unlikely. Anyway, Dod says that the road's fine and clear at the moment and you'll be all right on the bikes, and if the weather does get worse he'll come and collect you.'

'I canna eat all this. It's too thick,' grumped Elizabeth, putting down her spoon.

Mum's reply was exasperated. 'There's Charlotte's good cream to go with it and you'll need something to stick to your ribs this morning.'

'It's OK. I'll get something at the shoppie. Come on, Jane.'

Unless I tried to follow in the tyre marks left by Elizabeth's bike, it wasn't difficult biking in snow, but when we reached, then passed, the school she stopped for a moment, truly annoyed.

'Ye dinna need tae come too. Ach! I wish ye'd stop copying me all the time.'

'But I want a piece, too,' I cried. 'And nay pink wafers either. Anyway, you said I'd to come with you.'

'No, I didn't. Well, it's not what I meant!' She got back on her bike and raced off, and by the time I'd reached the post office she was already inside. Even if she had been with me, I didn't imagine she'd see the lady in black. Every time we've passed the shop I've looked out for her, but never saw her again. And now there she was. Standing at Mattie's house door and looking real enough. I'd have tried waving, but she'd disappeared before there was a chance. Maybe wearing specs outside's not such a bad idea, I thought, going into the post office, where Mattie had stopped organising the post and the posties to attend to her customer.

'Ah! Here's Janie, too, uh huh, uh huh.' She smiled. 'My, but you're hardy girls and growing too! I thought the Tomdow brae would maybe be blocked and Postie wouldn't manage to get up it.'

'Och, the road was fine, but I think Mum's getting anxious in case there's more snow and she can't get her article posted tomorrow,' Elizabeth declared, stamping her feet and leaving a big puddle of water on the stone floor. She looked round the shop, then earnestly asked, 'Miss Robertson, have you anything that would stick to my ribs?'

Mattie dimpled. 'Uh huh. I've got the very dab. What would you think about these?' She pointed to a plate of pastry slices oozing with dried fruit. 'Fly cemeteries,' she said. 'Fresh from Deas the baker this morning. That should do the trick.' She lifted a brown paper bag. 'Two?'

Making a point of independent-thinking, I asked for a snowball and my own bag.

'Certainly, certainly.' Mattie cheerily popped the coconut-covered cookie into a separate one. 'You'd get plenty of them outside today but don't eat any but this one.'

Getting back on our bikes, I spotted the lady in black, amazed when Elizabeth waved to her.

'I dinna ken why you're waving,' I said. 'There's naebody there.'

'There is so. That's Mrs MacGillvray, Mattie's auntie. She comes and helps her whileys.'

In a bid to even the ghost-sighting score, and despite the fact that this one was waving back, I said, 'Well, I canna see her. I think ye must be seeing things.'

But she was already off and calling over her shoulder, 'We'll be late.'

But we aren't, which is a pity because we might have been spared the mouse's cremation. However, it's thanks to Mrs Haggarty's labours over the stove to which the poor mouse has made its sad contribution that there's a pleasant warmth from the radiators in the classroom.

As we make our usual gathering round the piano, Miss Milne says, 'There's lots of lovely hymns for this time of year, so we'll start practising some for the Christmas party.'

The very mention of *party* makes a buzz of excitement. She continues, 'We'll be having it in the hall, but it's nice to have some decorations here as well, so after the singing you're going to cut crêpe and gummed paper and make streamers with them.'

'Please, Miss, how will you hang them up?' Alec asks.

Miss Milne thinks for a moment, then regards him somewhat doubtfully. 'If I thought you'd be responsible, you could. Miss May has a ladder.'

'James could hold it,' says Alec, and looks almost as pleased as James when she agrees.

'It's snowing,' says someone. Despite Miss Milne's call to order, we race over to the windows. They're too high for me to see out of, but, looking upwards, it seems as if someone's emptying a huge bolster of feathers from above. The flakes fall as if they're in a hurry and will do it forever.

42

SLEDGES, TRAYS AND SLIDES

Lining one side of the schoolie brae is a beech-leafed hedge. Its dead leaves will stay until spring. In the chill wind, they made a crisp whisper alongside the hiss of the sledge runners tracking down the road. A snowplough had cleared it after dinnertime. Since then, there's been no more snow, but the morning's waiting-feel's come back. December days are short enough, but it's getting dark earlier than usual.

Snow on the telephone wires makes clear white lines against a blackening sky, yet, meeting Dod with the tractor and trailer at the bottom of the brae, is a surprise.

'You look ready for Siberia,' says Elizabeth, looking at his milking cap thatched in Charlotte's cast hair, the old army greatcoat tied with binder twine and worn over his boiler suit. Gaiters, cut from old wellies, cover his boots.

'Aye weel, according to the weather forecast, there's a storm on the way. Your mam wis worried about you, said you might get stuck in a drift. Mind,' he winks at Elizabeth,

'Janie was a bit feart, but you both look as if you're a long way from perishing.' Taking a bike and hoisting it onto the trailer, he says, 'But I thought I might hae met *you* on the road earlier, Janie.'

It's not the time to say that time flies when you're trying to perfect a hunkered position going down a fast slide at school. Instead I say, 'I thought I'd better wait for Elizabeth in case *she* got stuck in a drift.'

Dod heaves aboard the other bike. 'It's a mercy I'm here then. Noo, whit wid that string be doing on the back of both your bikes?'

Even if he says it with a twinkle, Elizabeth and I chorus, 'No idea.'

We're not really, really scared of getting one of Dod's rows, but, it seems Alec and a pal are. Neither my sister nor I want to get the boys into trouble, nevertheless we were impressed by their reaction.

'That's Dod Bemmer comin' roon the corner on his tractor!' Alec had sounded horrified. Both boys had been pulling us on their sledges with our bikes. Now they leapt off, and in one swift movement with the knife that Alec uses for everything, from cleaning his nails to carving on any bit of wood, he'd sliced the connecting string.

'We're off! We dinna want him catchin' us,' he said and, with that, they fled.

Floating through the empty air came the

sounds of their curses.

'They've been left wi' such short string to pull their sledges, they'll be barking their ankles,' whispers Elizabeth. 'Mind! Dinna say anything aboot them tae Dod.'

We might hardly have recovered from being decanted into the snow, but the lie about the string came smoothly. One dark look from my sister makes sure of that. I'd have loved to have told Dod how hurtling down the schoolie brae on bike-pulled sledges had been as exciting as sliding on a tin tray down the hill beside the canteen.

Mrs Haggarty lent some of them to us at dinnertime. 'Here! If you've no sledges yourselves, use these. Just don't break your necks.' She added, 'Otherwise I might have to sling you in the boiler, ha ha!'

After a few tray-travelled runs, the piste already created by the sledges gained a fine gloss. Then it came alive with the sound in equal measure of terror and delight as we shot down the slope. At the bottom, a few feet across from it, there's a wall. Those who didn't want to risk crashing into it at the speed of sound concentrated on making a slide nearby. Soon, it too had such a glassy surface that the safest way to avoid falling was just to sit down on it.

'Ye'll wear a hole in your breeks. Look! This is how ye dae it,' boasted Alec. With his rackety boots sounding like someone taking a stick over corrugated iron, he shot downhill, somehow maintaining his crouched-down position until the end, when he jumped onto his feet. 'See,' he shouted. 'It's easy-peasy.'

'Wi' a bit o' practice I bet I'll dae it better,' had been my foolish remark, and one, as I'm sitting on a wet cold bum on the trailer, I'd time to regret. Home has never appeared so warm or so welcome.

Dod thinks the same. 'It's started tae drift and by the look o' it the road'll be blocked by the morn,' he tells Mum. 'It wis beginning tae fill in when we were coming up the Tomdow hill. Thank God we've managed to get all the beasts in about the place.'

'Uh huh, it'll be easier to get them fed, but I'm praying this weather doesn't last and that the road gets cleared quick. I've seen us having to wait days for it to be opened.' Mum looks anxious but smiles when I say, 'Maybe we winna get to school the morn.'

'Mebbe not. That might please you.'

I'm not so sure. Today was fun. Not only were there snowball fights, sliding and sledging, but in the classroom we did circle games and whilst we were making the streamers Miss Milne read us out something she called a ballad.

'It's a simple story told in simple verse,' she'd said, but I thought that, easy as it was to listen to, getting a tale about a king sitting

342

drinking blood red wine and to reel it along in rhyme was pretty clever.

'Mum, I widna like tae miss the party,' I say.

'Well, we'll have to wait and see. It's in the lap of the gods.'

It's a wholly unsatisfactory and confusing answer.

The stone hot water bottles that Mum's put in our beds give off a fierce if limited heat. They're heavy. Risking scalded feet, I kick mine to the bottom of the bed and cuddle Belinda and Rabbit in case they're not warm enough.

'Hey, Elizabeth, I think you shid tak Bluebell intae bed wi' ye. The poor thing'll be starving. She might be sitting bonny on the top of the chest of drawers, but I bet she's starving.'

There's no reply. She's probably tired after helping Dod check all the animals are still safely sheltered; even so, it's amazing that she's able to sleep through a storm that threatens to break into the house. The window rattles as if protesting at the wind forcing in its icy draught and hailstones hit it like someone throwing gravel. There's a surge of sighs coming from the larch trees, with the occasional snap then thump as a branch falls. Snow's beginning to fur up the window.

I bury my head under the blankets and try

a wee song with Rabbit.

My sister turns in bed and mutters something rude.

43

TELLING TALES

It must be later on in the morning than we thought and we're wakened by Mum, who's carrying two cups. 'It's cocoa,' she says, handing them over. 'And just you stay where you are. The road's blocked. No school or postie today and, as well as that, the phone's not working. Dod's going to take me in the tractor to the kiosk at the hall so's I can dictate through my article to the *Bulletin* folk and,' she clicks her teeth, 'I don't suppose they'll have as much as a flake of snow in Glasgow. Still, I suppose we should be glad that last night's storm's passed.'

On her way out she adds, 'We've been so busy checking the beasts this morning, I haven't had time to see if Duck or Drake's all right. When you do rise, see if you can find them, and if you could feed the hens that'd be another great help. Our own road's blocked, so we'll have to cut through the field. Be sure and follow our tracks to Tomdow, otherwise you'll be up to your necks in snow.'

'Have you plenty change for the phone?' Elizabeth asks.

'Aye, I've been down the side of every chair in the house, and I'm sure Mattie'll have plenty as well.'

'Uh huh, uh huh.'

'Don't be cheeky about your elders, Jane.'

Mum must've been in a hurry because she never mentioned the Snow Queen's visit. She's come after the storm and covered our fields in glittering white. Helped by a hard sun in a faultless sky, the drips that she's frozen into crystals shine from every larch branch. Her cold breath on our windows has left ferns growing on the glass. In the far distance, the firth shows icy blue against mountains covered in snow that softens the lines of everything and muffles the Knock-ack.

Lost to the magic of this wonderland is Duck.

'Come and see this,' says Elizabeth, beckoning at the door of the recently vacated hen-house.

Inside, in a nest box, Duck and Drake are cuddled up. Duck regards us with a cold eye whilst Drake keeps his head tucked under his wing.

'Wait till we tell the hens,' laughs my sister.

They, unlike the happy couple, are full of

345

activity and oblivious to anything but the appearance of fish pellets.

'Let's check up on the steading beasts,' Elizabeth suggests on our return.

It's almost as busy and noisy as a town. Black Douglas is in Frankie's old pen and conversing amiably through a separating gate with his harem. Chaffinches take the chance of foraging amongst the straw feed before flying back up to the rafters to continue with their casual gossip, whilst in the absence of Maudie, long since gone to market, Charlotte uses head girl status to chide Morag for banging on about her rights and to be glad that at last the tattie pit's been opened.

If it wasn't for the thought of missing the party, I'd be happy to stay in this enclosed world forever.

As if reading my thoughts, although not quite in agreement, Elizabeth says, 'Ooh! I'm already missing school. I hope the road clears.' She crosses her fingers, and although that's never worked for me it seems to for her, because soon after, normality returns and, as a triumphant festive ending to the term, we're actually all set fair for the Christmas party.

'I must say the new teddy Santa left in your stocking's very polite and it's good that Elizabeth's new panda can keep Bluebell company on the dresser,' says Belinda, 'but d'you think your school party was better than today? It's been Christmas Day after all.'

On account of the excitement from which Mum's so keen to spare herself, I've been packed off to bed early.

I think back. 'Well, I got to wear white socks then and the leather soles on my red shoes were perfect for sliding on the hall floor. There weren't any chairs on it, so there was loads of room for games. Races too and, Belinda, I can't believe it, nobody stopped us!'

'Not even your mother?'

'No. She was too busy gassing to the other wifies sitting round the hall.'

I warm to my theme. 'And then there were birlies.'

'Birlies?'

'Yes, you take a partner's hand and go round and round. It's super. You get really dizzy.'

'I could do that with Bluebell.'

'You could, but you'd need more than two for "The Farmer's in his Den" and "The Grand Old Duke of York".'

'Are they good fun?'

'Not really,' I say, thinking about Miss Milne looking down anxiously from the stage, where she was thumping on the piano. 'Moira and Davy told us not to push or shove.' Remembering looking down on the tinsel, the tree and Santa competing with us

347

when we were singing 'Away in a Manger' I add, 'But it was nice when we were all up on stage and I could sing as loud as I liked.'

Rabbit's already snoring and Belinda's beginning to sound sleepy. Still, she says, 'As Elizabeth's not here, you won't disturb her, so tell me a story. I like the ones about you growing up in Tombain.'

And so I begin.

The publishers hope that this book has given you enjoyable reading. Large Print Books are especially designed to be as easy to see and hold as possible. If you wish a complete list of our books please ask at your local library or write directly to:

Magna Large Print Books
Magna House, Long Preston,
Skipton, North Yorkshire.
BD23 4ND

This Large Print Book, for people
who cannot read normal print,
is published under the auspices of

THE ULVERSCROFT FOUNDATION